DATA VISUALIZATION WITH FLASH BUILDER

DESIGNING RIA AND AIR APPLICATIONS WITH REMOTE DATA SOURCES

CESARE ROCCHI

Routledge
Taylor & Francis Group

LONDON AND NEW YORK

First published 2011
by Focal Press

Published 2017 by Routledge
2 Park Square, Milton Park, Abingdon, Oxon OX14 4RN
711 Third Avenue, New York, NY 10017, USA

First issued in hardback 2017

Routledge is an imprint of the Taylor & Francis Group, an informa business

Notices

Knowledge and best practice in this field are constantly changing. As new research and experience broaden our understanding, changes in research methods, professional practices, or medical treatment may become necessary.

Practitioners and researchers must always rely on their own experience and knowledge in evaluating and using any information, methods, compounds, or experiments described herein. In using such information or methods they should be mindful of their own safety and the safety of others, including parties for whom they have a professional responsibility.

To the fullest extent of the law, neither the Publisher nor the authors, contributors, or editors, assume any liability for any injury and/or damage to persons or property as a matter of products liability, negligence or otherwise, or from any use or operation of any methods, products, instructions, or ideas contained in the material herein.

Library of Congress Cataloging-in-Publication Data
Rocchi, Cesare.
 Data visualization with Flash builder : designing RIA and AIR applications with remote data sources / Cesare Rocchi.
   p. cm.
 ISBN 978-0-240-81503-9 (pbk.)
 1. User interfaces (Computer systems) 2. Information visualization. 3. Cloud computing. 4. Flash (Computer file)
I. Title.
 QA76.9.U83R63 2011
 004.67'8--dc22
                  2010047932

British Library Cataloguing-in-Publication Data
A catalogue record for this book is available from the British Library.

ISBN 13: 978-1-138-42635-1 (hbk)
ISBN 13: 978-0-240-81503-9 (pbk)

Dedication

Even when there is only one author on the cover, a book is the fruit of a choral work. The content in the following pages would have never been possible without the help of the folks at Focal Press. First I want to thank Matthew David: besides being a great writer he is also a great editor. My biggest thanks goes to Paul Temme, who offered me the possibility to write this book. I want to thank Anais Wheeler: your "check in" messages helped me to deliver on time. Laura Aberle has been a great manager throughout the review process. Thanks to Carlin Reagan for organizing the schedule to match all the deadlines.

Finally, I want to thank Giorgia and my family for supporting me.

CONTENTS

Section 1

Section 4

Section 5

Companion website: www.datavisualizationflashbuilder.com

SECTION

1

YOUR FIRST INFORMATION-RICH APPLICATION

In this section you will learn to build a Flex application. You will discover that Macromedia Flex Markup Language (MXML) is a great markup language to quickly create a working application. The application will load data from RSS and will display information accordingly. To get to this result, we need some theory about the Flex framework and to get acquainted with the Flash Builder IDE. Are you ready?

The Flex Framework

It all began when somebody at Adobe woke up and said: "Sometimes I feel I am resolving similar problems each time I work on a new project." After some mumbling, a friend replied: "Why don't we put in the same place a set of solutions to the repetitive problems you solve each time?" At that moment Flex was born. Flex is not a "place"—it is a framework. Although there is some dispute on the definition of the word *framework*, I like mine: Something that helps to connect different components of a project; it can encompass libraries, patterns, and a scripting language. Flex is all of this: it embeds a library of components (visual and nonvisual) and a scripting language (ActionScript 3), and implements a set of patterns to adopt in different situations. There are a few reasons for this:

- It is easier to develop.
- It favors the team to work consistently.
- It aggregates objects/components into something useful.
- It reduces repetitive tasks.
- It favors the creation of reusable code.
- It decouples dependencies between components.

In this section I will give you a brief introduction of the Flex framework. Although you will create applications with Flash Builder most of the time, it is nonetheless important to know what is under the hood.

Overview

Flex has born-to-build interactive applications that run on browsers (via plug-ins), desktop (via Adobe AIR), and mobile applications, thanks to the recent addition of the new Flash player on smart phones and mobile devices. Although it is a general-purpose framework it is best suited for data-driven applications, which gather data from remote web services and display interactive visuals.

To be precise, the Flex compiler transforms MXML code into ActionScript code and then runs the compilation. Later, we will see how to save and check the generated code from the compiler.

There are two languages to create Flex applications: MXML and ActionScript 3. MXML is an eXtensible Markup Language (XML)-based language, used to define the layout of the user interface and its behaviors, whereas ActionScript 3 is the core scripting language, mainly adopted to define the logic. To create an application we create a set of files that are fed into the Flex compiler, which generates an SWF file that is visualizable in every browser with the Flash player installed (Figure 1.1).

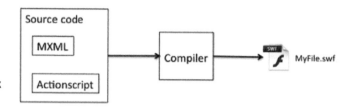

Figure 1.1 Flow to create a Flex application.

MXML is similar in concept to HyperText Markup Language (HTML)—there are tags and properties. Tags can be embedded in other tags according to a semantics defined in a Document Type Definition (DTD). This is an advantage, especially for designers, because tag-based languages look more friendly and are easy to work with. For example, if you come from web development, it should be easy to grasp the following piece of code.

```
<Canvas backgroundColor="#ffffff">
  <Button label="Click me"/>
</Canvas>
```

You should find out pretty soon that there is a canvas with a white background containing a button of which the label is "Click me."

Besides two languages, the Flex framework also includes a set of graphical components like buttons, labels, and menu/text controls, plus a set of smart containers to organize the layout of the application. You can experience the set of components by visiting *http://examples.adobe.com/flex3/componentexplorer/explorer. html*. The development kit also includes a debugger to assist you in bug hunting.

Installing the Flex SDK

The Flex SDK can be downloaded from *http://opensource. adobe.com/wiki/display/flexsdk/Download+Flex+4*. You can choose from an already compiled version or download the source code and compile it on your own. In any case, you should end up with a folder structured like Figure 1.2.

Let's have a look at the main folders. The Bin folder contains executables. For example, to compile a Flex application you just need to type the following:

```
${flexsdkfolder}/bin/mxmlc MyFile.mxml
```

This generates an SWF file that you can visualize in the standalone Flash player or embed in an HTML page. The Frameworks folder (and especially its subfolder Lib, short for Libraries) includes all the files needed to create, run, and debug Flex and Adobe AIR applications. There you can find libraries for text, utilities, JavaScript bridges, etc. The Samples folder contains commented source code of examples built by Adobe.

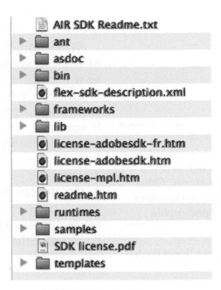

Figure 1.2 Structure of the Flex SDK folder.

Flash Builder

To ease the development of applications, Adobe has created Flash Builder. It is an Eclipse-based plug-in that includes many features to speed up development, debugging, and profiling. It features:
- Code completion
- Syntax highlight
- Design view (styling skinning)
- Interactive debugger and stepper
- Refactoring
- Profiler
- Remote data wizard
- Wizards to configure local backends
- Introspection of data services

Downloading and Installing Flash Builder

You can obtain a free version of Flash Builder for evaluation from *http://www.adobe.com/go/try_flashbuilder*.

Since Flash Builder is based on Eclipse there are two installers available: standalone and plug-in. The standalone version includes everything you need to run Flash Builder since it embeds a basic version of Eclipse. If you have already installed Eclipse (e.g., you use it to develop Java applications) you can download the plug-in version. In both cases, you will end up with what you need to work with Flash Builder. The installation process is automated so we can go straight to the illustration of the IDE.

Overview of Flash Builder

When you open Flash Builder it should look like Figure 1.3. At the top we have a set of buttons that we illustrate in the next section. If you are not an Eclipse user it is important to familiarize yourself with the notions of *perspective*. A perspective is a particular configuration of windows and panels. If you have a background in Flash it is pretty similar to the concept of workspace in Flash Pro CS5. Flash Builder, unless modified, opens in the Flash perspective, usually adopted to develop.

On the left there is the package explorer. This panel allows you to browse the structure of your project, add/change libraries, include/delete assets, add new files, etc. This tree reflects the structure of the folder that contains our project.

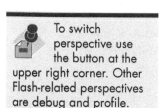

To switch perspective use the button at the upper right corner. Other Flash-related perspectives are debug and profile.

Figure 1.3 Overview of Flash Builder.

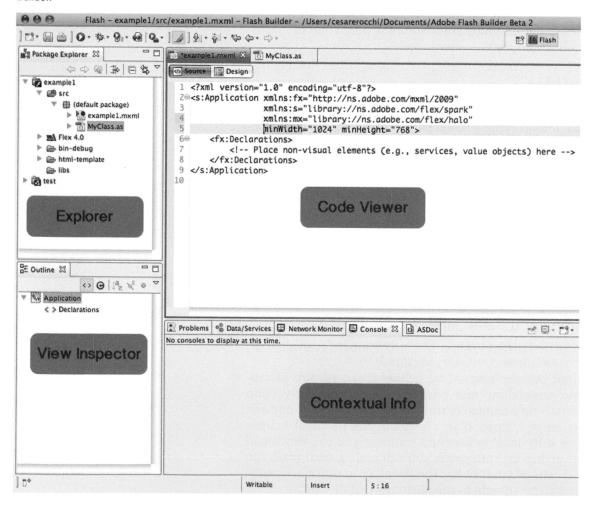

Below is the Outline panel, the role of which is to show the hierarchical structure of the application. We will describe it more deeply in the "Using the Design View" section. The code viewer window takes much of the space available because it contains a tabbed view of the source code files to edit. At the bottom there is a tabbed view with contextual information, which changes according to the state of the application. For example, it shows problems during the compilation, errors in the console, network traffic, etc.

We now have enough information to create our first project from scratch.

Creating an Empty Application

From the File menu we select "New Flex Project." This opens up a wizard window that allows us to define our first project. At the top we have to provide a name. The second important choice is the application type (see Figure 1.4). Here we choose Web.

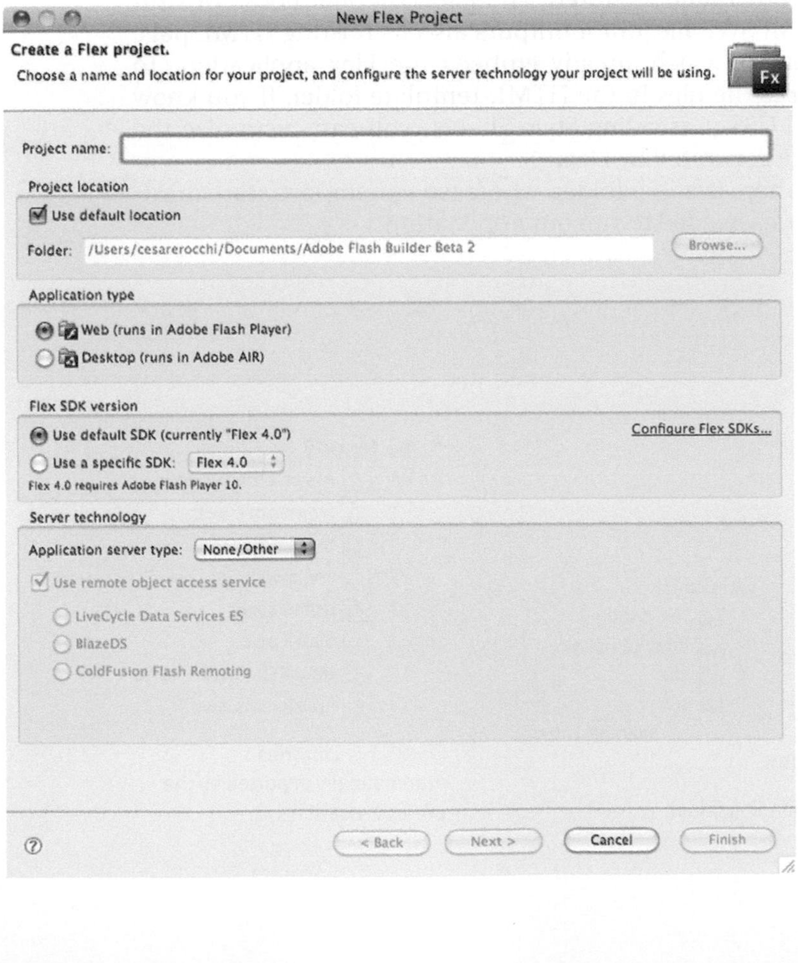

Figure 1.4 Wizard to create a Flex application.

A package is a way to organize source code. In Flex, apart from the default package above, each package corresponds to a path on the disk. Usually packages are structured like inverse URLs, for example, com. studiomagnolia. components. In the project folder (either in src or Lib) there will be a folder with the following path: com/ studiomagnolia/ components.

 We are a company and we would like to customize the template for all the projects created by our employees. Can we? Sure, just modify the files in {$flex_directory}/ sdks/{$flex_version}/ templates/swfobject. Flex imports that directory to create the HTML-template folder.

Then we can specify the SDK to be used in the project. This is a choice we can also modify later. If we want to take advantage of the new features introduced in the last release of Flex, we choose Flex 4. Now we move to the next step. Here we keep the default value for the output folder and click Finish. As you can see from Figure 1.5, the Flash Builder has already created a bunch of folders for us.

This is a pretty standard organization of folders, well known by Flex developers. The src folder contains MXML and ActionScript source files. It is important to note that the src folder does not *exactly* reflect the organization of the folders of your project. In fact, if you check out your workspace, there is no folder named Default Package.

You might also notice that Flex 4 is not present in the project folder. This item in the project is used to specify the library path. If you open the node, it will show the list of libraries (automatically linked) that are needed to run the Flex application (Figure 1.6).

The folder Bin-debug is where the compiled application, the built-in debug mode, is stored. The Flex compiler does not simply create an SWF file, but it outputs also its hosting HTML page already set up, which already embeds the Flex application. To do so, it uses the files in the HTML-template folder. If you know HTML and CSS (Cascading Style Sheets) you can customize the HTML page generated by Flex.

Finally there is a Lib folder, where we can import/store third-party libraries needed to run our application.

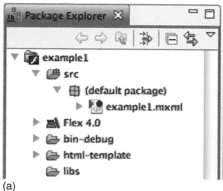

(a)

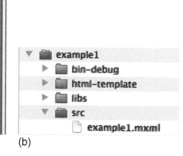

(b)

Figure 1.5 (a) Project explorer and (b) its corresponding folder.

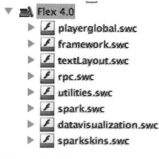

Figure 1.6 Libraries automatically imported by the project wizard.

How to Run/Debug

We can visualize our Flex application in two modes: run and debug (Figure 1.7). Run just compiles the source code, generates accessory files, and runs the default browser opening the corresponding HTML page.

Debug does the same job as run, but the resulting application is compiled in debug mode. In this mode you can interact at runtime with the application, check the value of variables, step through the source code, and hunt possible bugs.

Figure 1.7 Run and Debug buttons.

Using the Design View

When you open an MXML source file you will notice that there are two options in the upper left corner: source and design (Figure 1.8). The source view allows you to see the MXML code and the design view shows its visual counterpart.

```
example1.mxml
Source   Design
1  <?xml version="1.0" encoding="utf-8"?>
2  <s:Application xmlns:fx="http://ns.adobe.com/mxml/2009"
3                 xmlns:s="library://ns.adobe.com/flex/spark"
4                 xmlns:mx="library://ns.adobe.com/flex/halo"
5                 minWidth="1024" minHeight="768">
6     <fx:Declarations>
7        <!-- Place non-visual elements (e.g., services, value objects) here -->
8     </fx:Declarations>
9  </s:Application>
10
```

Figure 1.8 Source and design views.

At the moment the application is empty because we just have one element (line 2), which is the stage of our Flex application. Let's populate it with a button. We move to the design view and we drag a button component from the list on the bottom right to the design view. A visual component is placed on the stage (Figure 1.9).

If we double-click it we can change it's label. If we switch back to the source view we can check the corresponding generated code (line 9). See Figure 1.10.

As you can see, creating the visuals of a Flex application is a matter of drag and drop. Components can be placed and modified in a WYSIWYG (what you see is what you get) way. The corresponding code looks clean and ready to be further modified by a developer.

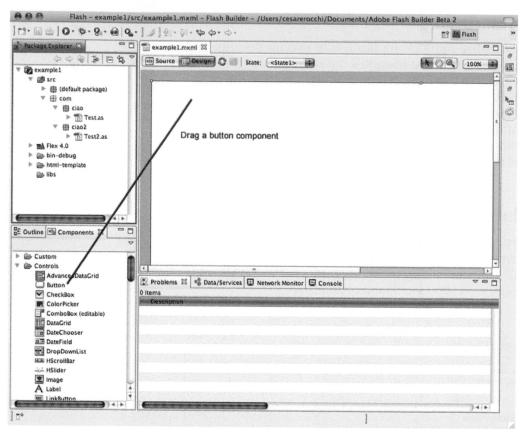

Figure 1.9 Dragging a button into the design view populates the application.

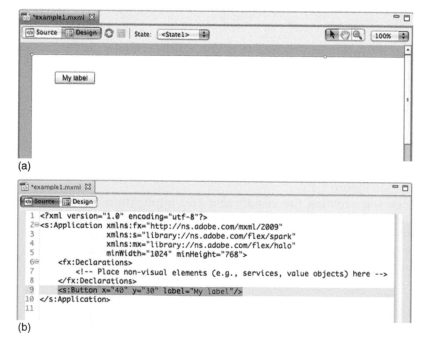

Figure 1.10 (a) The design view and (b) its code counterpart.

The Application Tag

We said MXML is an XML-based language. One of the rules of XML languages is to have a root tag, which is a tag that wraps every other tag. That is used by the interpreter to start rendering the application. If you are familiar with HTML you know that the root tag of each page is `<html></html>`. In Flex, the root tag is `<Application></Application>`, prepended by a namespace.

Namespace

A namespace does not pertain just to MXML but to every XML-based language. XML elements can have the same name but different sources. To overcome this situation the notion of namespace has been introduced. A namespace is a set of names identified by a unique URI (uniform resource identifier), which represents the source of the names. For example, the Flex 4 SDK includes two different component libraries, the old Flex 3 and the new one. Since some of the components have the same tag name (e.g., `Button`), for the Flex compiler it is impossible to detect which is the button to use. By using a different namespace you can easily specify which component to use: `mx` for the old library and `s` for the new one.

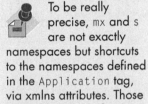

To be really precise, mx and s are not exactly namespaces but shortcuts to the namespaces defined in the `Application` tag, via xmlns attributes. Those shortcuts point to their URIs: *library://ns.adobe.com/flex/spark* and *library://ns.adobe.com/flex/halo*.

```
<mx:Button />
<s:Button />
```

Visual Components

In this section we will take a look at the visual components already available in the Flex library. As noted in the introduction to this section, the Flex framework embeds a library of visual components to create user interfaces. There are two classes of visual components: controls and containers.

Controls

Controls are interactive visual components like buttons, checkboxes, and data grids. They are enabled to react to user-initiated interactions like clicks, drag and drop, and keyboard activity. Each component is customizable in appearance (style and skin) and behavior (logic). There is a Classic button and many variations such as the Toggle button and the button bar (laid out as a tabbed bar). There are also commonly used controls to enter data: checkboxes, dropdown lists, and the Radio, Date Picker, Text Input, and Text Area buttons, and so on. Advanced controls include the Color Picker, Tree, Data Grid, etc.

Containers

Containers are components built to layout controls like Panel, HGroup, and VGroup. This type of component is very useful to visually organize the graphical interface. A container is an area that can host components or other containers. For example, if you need a horizontal layout of controls you just wrap them in an HGroup. Let's suppose we want to build a form for a search engine with the layout shown in Figure 1.11.

The code will look something like this:

```
<s:HGroup>
    <s:TextInput .../>
    <s:Button .../>
</s:HGroup>
```

If the "crazy" manager changes the requirements and wants it vertically arranged, we just change the wrapper and we are done:

```
<s:VGroup>
    <s:TextInput .../>
    <s:Button .../>
</s:VGroup>
```

Padding and Alignment

One crucial property of containers is padding. Much like HTML DIVS rendering, a Flex container has a padding property that allows defining its internal border—that is, the distance between the border and the content hosted in the container. Figure 1.12 shows different examples of padding with corresponding code. Children components are placed within the blue area.

Figure 1.11 A simple search form.

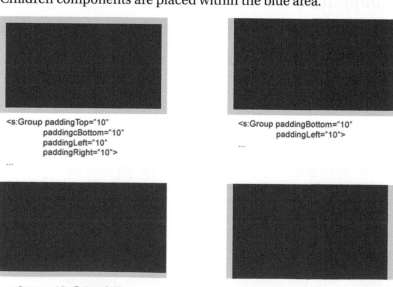

```
<s:Group paddingTop="10"
         paddingcBottom="10"
         paddingLeft="10"
         paddingRight="10">
    ...
```

```
<s:Group paddingBottom="10"
         paddingLeft="10">
    ...
```

```
<s:Group paddingBottom="10">
    ...
```

```
<s:Group paddingLeft="10"
         paddingRight="10">
    ...
```

Figure 1.12 Different examples of padding.

This behavior applies to all layout containers:

- Group
- VGroup
- HGroup
- Panel
- TitleWindow
- TileGroup

Another important feature of containers is axis alignment. Content hosted by a container can be arranged vertically and horizontally. For example, let's say we want three buttons vertically aligned, as in Figure 1.13. We achieve this result with the following code:

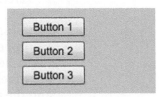

Figure 1.13 Vertically arranged buttons.

```
<s:VGroup
        width="240"
        paddingTop="10" paddingRight="10"
        paddingBottom="10" paddingLeft="10">

    <s:Button label="Button 1" />
    <s:Button label="Button 2" />
    <s:Button label="Button 3" />

</s:VGroup>
```

Now we want them to be horizontally centered. We just need to provide a new value for such a property:

```
<s:VGroup
        width="240"
        horizontalAlign="center"
        ... >
```

You probably think I am wrong because I wrote "provide a new value," and in the first example we did not specify a value for the `horizontalAlign` property. In some sense you are right, because it is not specified in the source code, but Flex adds it for you. Some of the properties of Flex components are initialized to their default values if you do not provide one. So, if sometimes you feel that Flex does something "magic," that is (partly) achieved by default values. In this particular case, the default value for `horizontalAlign` is left. The same behavior applies to the `verticalAlign` property, which sticks content to the top, middle, or bottom.

Sizing Components

The appearance of graphical components, either containers or not, can be arranged and personalized by setting their properties. The first group of properties you might want to change are the geometrical properties: position and size. There are many ways to specify these properties, each based on a different paradigm:

- *No values.* The first way is to not provide any value. As we have seen in the case of groups, Flex provides default values for the properties you do not specify.
- *Explicit values.* You provide a static value of a property (e.g., width="200").
- *Percent-based values.* You provide a relative value of a property (e.g., width="50%").
- *Constraint-based values.* You provide a constraint value of a property (e.g., align="left").

To develop complex applications, where many components are widely used, it is important to know each of these approaches and the combinations of them. For example, explicit values work only in containers that do not implement automatic layout. In the following code, the x property of the first button is overridden by the layout of the vertical group, so do not expect the x to be 200.

```
<s:VGroup>

    <s:Button label="Button1" x="200"/>
    <s:Button label="Button2"/>

</s:VGroup>
```

The same holds for the following code.

```
<s:Group>

    <s:layout>
        <s:VerticalLayout/>
    </s:layout>

    <s:Button label="1" y="300"/>
    <s:Button label="2"/>

</s:Group>
```

If we omit the specification of layout, then we are free to arrange positions as we like.

```
<s:Group>

    <s:Button label="1" y="300"/>
    <s:Button label="2"/>

</s:Group>
```

In this case, the button is positioned at 300 pixels from the top border. This is due to the fact that the default behavior of Group is BasicLayout, so the code above is equivalent to the following.

```
<s:Group>

    <s:layout>
        <s:BasicLayout/>
    </s:layout>
```

```
    <s:Button label="1" y="300"/>
    <s:Button label="2"/>

</s:Group>
```

The same holds for HorizontalLayout. Sizing by means of percent-based values is pretty intuitive—you just specify which percentage of the parent container has to be "reserved" to your component. For example, if we have two groups, horizontally aligned, each taking half of the stage, we can use the following code.

```
<s:Application ...>

    <s:layout>
        <s:HorizontalLayout/>
    </s:layout>

    <!-- Left group -->
    <s:Group width="50%">

        <s:layout>
            <s:VerticalLayout/>
        </s:layout>

        <mx:Image source="1.png"/>
        <s:Button label="button1"/>

    </s:Group>

    <!-- Right group -->
    <s:Group>

        <s:layout>
            <s:VerticalLayout/>
        </s:layout>

        <mx:Image source="2.png"/>
        <s:Button label="button2"/>

    </s:Group>

</s:Application>
```

In this example we have set up an application with a horizontal layout. Then we have built two groups of which the content is arranged vertically. In each of the groups we have specified a width of 50%. See Figure 1.14.

Figure 1.14 Percent-based layout of groups. The area of groups is highlighted in gray.

This ratio between the two groups is kept also when the parent container is resized, unless some more specific constraint (e.g., minWidth) has been specified.

You are invited to discover for yourself the following layout.

```
<s:layout>
    <s:TileLayout/>
</s:layout>
```

Including Scripting

You might remember from the introduction that MXML code is "transformed" into ActionScript code and then compiled into an SWF file. In fact, Flex *is* an ActionScript library that has been devised to simplify user interface (UI) development. Each MXML tag corresponds to an ActionScript class or property. Before compilation, Flex performs the "transformation," where each tag is translated into its corresponding ActionScript class. The design of Flex allows the designer to "inject" ActionScript code into Flex. Such a code is merged with the one automatically generated during the transformation phase.

ActionScript code in an MXML file has to be wrapped by the following tag:

```
<fx:Script>
    <![CDATA[
        // AS code here ...
    ]]>
</fx:Script>
```

As an alternative, a source code file can be imported by specifying it as an attribute:

```
<fx:Script source="code.as"/>
```

The "transformer" copies the ActionScript code included in the MXML file. Do you want to have a look at the generated code? We just need to tell it to the compiler by passing an argument: `--keep-generated-ActionScript`. Here is how to do that. Right-click on the project and select "Properties." This opens up a modal window. From the list on the left, select "Flex Compiler." Almost in the middle there is a field: "Additional compiler arguments." You might notice there is already one argument, to specify the locale of the application. We append our new argument and click "Apply." See Figure 1.15.

Now we can run or debug our project. If we check in the `Bin-debug` folder there is a new folder named Generated that contains the ActionScript code. See Figure 1.16.

The code is recreated every time you compile the application. If you want to save a particular version of the generated code, make a copy of the folder.

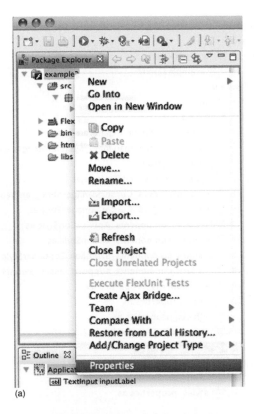

(a)

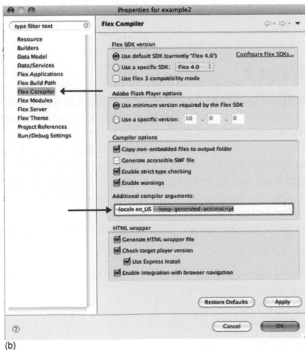

(b)

Figure 1.15 How to save generated code.

Figure 1.16 As files generated by the compiler.

ActionScript 3

ActionScript 3 is an object-oriented language based on the ECMA 262 specification (visit *http://www.ecma-international.org/publications/standards/ecma-262.htm* for more information). It is pretty similar to JavaScript, so if you have a background in Web frontend programming it should be easy to grasp it. Here we will provide a quick introduction to the language. For a more detailed description you can have a look at Colin Moock's excellent book, *Essential ActionScript 3.0.*

Variables in ActionScript are defined by the following syntax:

```
var variableName : Type = actual value;
```

For example, if we want to create a variable myNumber of type Number with value 12 we write:

```
var myNumber : Number = 12;
```

Constants have the same syntax:

```
const MYCONSTANT : Number = 12;
```

Fundamental types include:
* Number
* int
* Uint
* String
* Boolean (true of false)
* null
* void
  Some examples need no explanation:

```
var name : String = "Cesare";
var age : Number = 30;
var iAmRich : Boolean = false;
```

Besides fundamental types ActionScript has a set of complex types, which include:
* Object
* Vector
* Array
* MovieClip
* Date
* ByteArray
* XML
* XMLList
* Function
  Let's see some of these in code:

```
var anonymousPerson : Object = {};
var me : Object = {name: "Cesare", age : 30};
```

Object is the most generic class in ActionScript. It is the root of all other classes. To create a new instance of Object you can use the { } notation. It is allowed to pass parameters in key-value form, like in the second line. An alternative syntax is based on the new operator.

```
var me : Object = new Object();
me.name = "Cesare"; // dot notation
me["age"] = 30; // associative array notation
```

In this case you are not allowed to pass parameters at construction time (when you create it). So you create an empty Object and you set its properties via the dot notation (second line) or `trace()` is a special function in Flash/Flex that allows us to print statements in the console. It is useful for some quick debugging. Remember that `trace()` statements appear in the console only when you debug, *not* when you run.

the associative array notation. The same holds when reading the properties of an object.

```
trace(me.name);
trace(me["age"]);
```

Arrays

Arrays are a handy way to manipulate collections of data. In ActionScript 3 arrays can be created in two ways:

```
var ciphers : Array = [0,1,2,3];
var ciphers : Array = new Array(1, 2, 3);
```

You can also create an empty array and populate it afterwards.

```
var ciphers : Array = [];
ciphers[0] = 0;
```

In this case, we use an index-based notation to store a value in the first position of the array. The index-based notation works also when you want to read data in an array.

```
trace(ciphers[0]); // outputs 0
```

Though the second might look more familiar to object-oriented developers, it is known to be faster at runtime, so I encourage you to use it.

Arrays in ActionScript 3 are sparse—that is, you can have an element at position 0, one at index 4, and nothing in between. Values at positions 1, 2, and 3 are undefined, like in the following example.

```
var ciphers : Array = [];
ciphers[0] = 0;
ciphers[4] = 4;
var len:int = ciphers.length;
for (var i:int = 0; i < len; i++) {
    trace("element at index " + i + " is " +ciphers[i]);
}
//Output is
element at index 0 is 0
element at index 1 is undefined
element at index 2 is undefined
element at index 3 is undefined
element at index 4 is 4
```

The for each loop is a bit smarter, in that it shows only elements that are not equal to undefined.

```
for each (var o in ciphers) {
    trace("o = " +o);
}
// Outputs
o = 0
o = 4
```

This might look a bit weird, since the length of the array is 5, but this is a consequence of sparse array design.

So far we have seen examples of homogeneous data stored in an array, but in ActionScript 3 we are allowed to store various data types in the same array: strings, numbers, and even objects or other arrays. For example, let's say we want to model a business card by means of an array. We agree with the development team on the following convention:

```
0   Name
1   Surname
2   Phone number
3   Email Address
```

Then we could build my card by means of the following code:

```
var myCard : Array = [];
myCard[0] = "Cesare";
myCard[1] = "Rocchi";
myCard[2] = 555123456;
myCard[3] = "c@cesarerocchi.com";
```

Whenever we need to read a data we simply access the corresponding index:

```
trace("My surname is " + myCard[1]);
```

In this case, we are just printing out a value, which is transformed into a string by the trace() statement. If we needed to manipulate a data it is a good practice to explicitly cast the returned value to the corresponding data type.

```
var phone:Number = myCard[2] as Number;
```

This way we have access to all the methods of the Number class and the compiler will not complain about type inconsistencies.

The array includes also convenience methods to add or remove elements. Methods widely used are push() and pop(). The first adds an element at the end, whereas the second removes the last element of an array. The first method is useful because it manages positions automatically, so you don't need to know in advance the length of the array in order to add one more element. The same holds for the second.

Classes

In addition to using built-in classes in ActionScript 3 and the Flex framework, you can create your own classes. The notion of class pertains to object-oriented programming. A class is something that enables you to perform the following operations:

- Creating instances
- Reading/writing values

An alternative method is to get the type by means of the function getQualifiedClassName (myCard[1]), which returns the corresponding type. In any case, the casting is needed if you want to call methods of a given class.

Beware! The push() and pop() methods do modify the array, so it is not the same array as before the call. These are known to be called *destructive* operations. For example, if you just want to read the last element access it by the index not via pop().

To deepen your knowledge about this matter you can read the excellent book by Yard et al., *Object-Oriented ActionScript 3.0*.

- Call methods (to perform actions)
- React to events

Although it is a very important topic, we will not discuss why and when you need to create a new class, since it pertains to the design of a project. Here we will just provide technical details on the way you define your custom classes.

To create the most essential class you need to define a package and a name. As you remember we have said that the package is a way to organize code and each package corresponds to a path on the disk. So, for example, the following source code file has to be stored in the path `com.studiomagnolia.model`:

```
package com.studiomagnolia.model {
    public class Person {
        public function Person () {}
    }
}
```

Another requirement, inherited from Java design, is that the file name of this source code has to match the name of the class, so there will be a file named "Person.as," otherwise the compiler will complain. You might notice a function on the third line. That is the *constructor*, a special method called when you create an instance of the class. The class is declared *public* so it is accessible anywhere—that is, every other piece of code can work with this class (after importing it). The alternative to public is *internal*—that is, the class is visible only within the same package.

Properties

A class with just a name is pretty useless because we can just create instances of it. Let's add some property to store data.

```
package com.studiomagnolia.model {
    public var name:String;
    public class Person() {}
}
```

 A warning is not something crucial for the compilation process. In fact, an application with warnings compiles and runs. Sometimes a warning can be a source of misbehavior at runtime, so it is advised to address any before the final release.

A property in a class is defined by means of `var`. Each property has an access specifier (public), a name, and a data type. The accessibility of a property is a bit more complex than the one of the class. A property can be:
- *Private*—only the class can access it
- *Protected*—only the class and subclasses can access it
- *Internal*—only classes in the same package can access it
- *Public*—everybody can access it

If you do not provide a specifier the default value is internal and the compiler will show a warning, like in Figure 1.17.

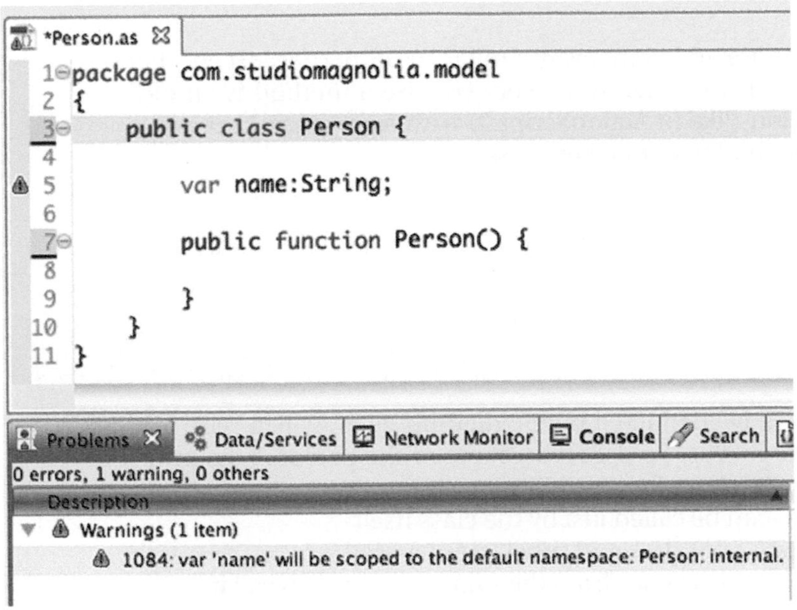

```
*Person.as ✕
 1⊖package com.studiomagnolia.model
 2 {
 3⊖    public class Person {
 4
⚠ 5        var name:String;
 6
 7⊖        public function Person() {
 8
 9        }
10    }
11 }
```

```
⚙ Problems ✕  °⚙ Data/Services  🖽 Network Monitor  🖵 Console  🔍 Search  ⟨⟩
0 errors, 1 warning, 0 others
Description
▼ ⚠ Warnings (1 item)
      ⚠ 1084: var 'name' will be scoped to the default namespace: Person: internal.
```

Figure 1.17 Warning by the compiler.

Now we can use our class in a project. To create an instance we use the same syntax illustrated for the array and then we can access (read/write) the property name.

```
import com.studiomagnolia.model.Person;
var p:Person = new Person();
p.name = "Cesare";
trace(p.name);
```

We should remember to import the class before using it. We will see that the Flash Builder will help us in this task. Notice that if we defined the property as private the compiler would throw an error, like in Figure 1.18.

If you have a background in scripting languages like JavaScript or Event ActionScript 1 or 2, it might seem tedious to specify accessors for every property (and method as we will see below), but this prevents unexpected errors at runtime.

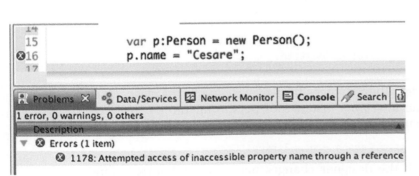

```
14
15        var p:Person = new Person();
⊗16        p.name = "Cesare";
17
```

```
⚙ Problems ✕  °⚙ Data/Services  🖽 Network Monitor  🖵 Console  🔍 Search  ⟨⟩
1 error, 0 warnings, 0 others
Description
▼ ⊗ Errors (1 item)
      ⊗ 1178: Attempted access of inaccessible property name through a reference
```

Figure 1.18 Accessibility error by the compiler.

Methods

Methods are added in a way similar to properties, except that the keyword is *function*. To be very concise a method is an old-style function (like in ActionScript 2) with a specifier. Let's add a greeting method to our Person class.

```
package com.studiomagnolia.model {
    public var name:String;
    public class Person() {}
    public function greet():String {
        return "Hello" + name;
    }
}
```

Here we have defined a public method greet, which returns a string made by "Hello" plus the name of the person. Like properties, methods have four visibility specifiers:

Have a method that does not return any value? Just declare its return type as void.

- *Private*—can be called just by the class itself
- *Protected*—only class and subclasses can call it
- *Internal*—only classes from the same package can call it
- *Public*—everybody can call it

As with properties, the default value is internal.

Constructor

As we said above the constructor is a special method called when an instance of a class is created. By rule, the constructor has to be public and there is no need to specify a return type. At instantiation time we are allowed to pass parameters, which populate the instance. For example, let's say that by design a person with no name can't exist. One way to implement this requirement is to pass the name as a parameter in the constructor. So we refactor our class like in the following code.

```
package com.studiomagnolia.model {
    private var name:String;
    public class Person(name:String) {
        this.name = name;
    }
// greet method omitted.
}
```

This definition changes the way we can use the class. We cannot create an *empty* instance of person anymore—we have to specify a name at instantiation time, as in this code.

```
var p:Person = new Person("Cesare");
```

What if the designer changes her mind and says: "Name is optional, it might or might not be specified"? We can exploit another feature of constructors (and methods in general): default arguments for parameters.

```
public class Person(name:String="") {
    this.name = name;
}
```

In this case, we are either allowed to create an unnamed person or a named one, so both the statements below are valid.

```
var unknown:Person = new Person();
var me:Person = new Person("Cesare");
```

The same can be applied to methods. Let's say we have a different greeting according to the language being used. We can redefine the method as follows.

```
public function greet(lang:String="en"):String {
    var myGreet:String;
    if (lang == "en") {
        myGreet = "Hello " + name;
    }
    else if (lang == "it") {
        myGreet = "Ciao " + name;
    }
    return myGreet;
}
```

In this case, if we do not provide any value the default greeting will be in English.

```
var me:Person = new Person ("Cesare");
trace(me.greet()); // prints Hello Cesare
trace(me.greet("it")); // prints Ciao Cesare
```

The only rule to follow when using optional parameters in method signatures is to put them after required ones. So the first line below is allowed and the second throws a compiler error.

```
public function greet(p1:String, p2:String="") { ... }
public function greet(p1:String="", p2:String) { ... }
```

Static versus Instance

Besides visibility, methods and variables also have another specifier: instance or static. So far all the methods and variables that we have defined are of instance. This means that different instances have *their own* values and methods. Sometimes you might want to set up your class in a way that an instance is not needed to access a value or call a method. In those cases you need a static method or property. For example, let's say you need a way to sort a list of people by different parameters. The first thing you might want to do is to create a class, PeopleSorter, which takes an array of people and a sort criterion and outputs a sorted list. So the sort method might look something like this:

```
//Method of Sorter.as
public function sort (list:Array, crit:int):Array {
    // Sort code here
}
```

Fine. What do you need to do when you want to use it? Simple: Create an instance and call the sort method with parameters.

```
var s:Sorter = new Sorter();
s.sort(myList, 1);
```

Let's say you need to do it in many places of your code. Do you really want to overpopulate your application's memory with sorters? In this scenario a static method comes in handy. Let's just refactor your method as follows:

```
public static function sort (l:Array, crit:int):Array
{
    // Sort code here ...
}
```

We did something really simple—added a keyword—but its value saves us from instantiating many sorters and allows us to type the following code:

```
Sorter.sort(myList, 1);
```

This is much more simple and clean from a design viewpoint. Again, addressing when and why a method/variable is better to be static is outside the scope of this book. We invite you to get more details by studying some object-oriented design books. Static can be combined with an accessibility specifier so all the following declarations are allowed:

```
public static function sort ( ... ) { ... }
private static function ( ... ) { ... }
protected static function ( ... ) { ... }
private static var: ...
public static var: ...
```

Let's try with a var. Let's say we want to keep track of how many instances of people have been created. Here a static variable comes in handy. We can review our implementation by adding a counter that gets incremented each time we create a new instance (i.e., in the constructor).

```
public class Person {
    public static var total:Number = 0;
    public function Person() {
        total++;
    }
}
```

Whenever we want we can access the counter value of the class itself.

```
var p:Person = new Person("Cesare");
trace ("total is " +Person.total);
var p2:Person = new Person();
trace ("total is " +Person.total);

// Outputs
// total is 1
// total is 2
```

Getters and Setters

Getters and setters are special methods to access private variables. The `getter` is the method that retrieves a value, whereas the `setter` stores it. Within the class they are defined as methods, though when used they look like a property. Let's assume one of the requirements for the Person class is the following: A person cannot have a name shorter than two letters. How could we implement this? We have to check this constraint before setting the property name. Of course, we can declare the property as public and check by means of an `if` statement if the requirement is met. Do we want to do it every time we set the variable? What if the requirement changes in the future? We have to modify a lot of code in many places!

An easier way is to check the requirement in the setter. If the requirement changes we only have to put hands in one method! In object-oriented terminology this is called *encapsulation*—that is, the ability to expose functionalities (like getting and setting a value) without worrying about what happens anytime getting or setting happens. So we can refactor out the Person class as follows.

```
public class Person {
    private var _name:String;
    public function Person() { }
    // getter
    public function get name ():String {
        return _name;
    }
    // setter
    public function set name (name:String):void {
        this._name = name;
    }
}
```

As you can see, in the code `getter` and `setter` have a special syntax, similar to a function but with "get" and "set" keywords. Of course, `getter` does not need a parameter because it just reads, whereas `setter` needs the new value as a parameter. Another trivial remark is that the property has to be private, otherwise the implementation of `getter` and `setter` makes no sense. As we said, `getter` and `setter` are used as if they were properties; in fact, we can write the following code:

```
var me:Person = new Person();
me.name = "Cesare";

trace(me.name); // Outputs Cesare
```

In the `setter` we can now implement the name length requirement:

```
public function set name (name:String):void {

    if (name.length > 1)
        this._name = name;
}
```

In the future, if the requirement changes, you have to update just this line of code. Are you starting to like object-oriented programming? You should! Say that you want to log some operation to have statistics: one of the actions to be logged is when a property is the read operation. Just add the logging code in the `getter` and you are done! Another advantage of encapsulation will be presented when we talk about events.

Object-Oriented Support in Flash Builder

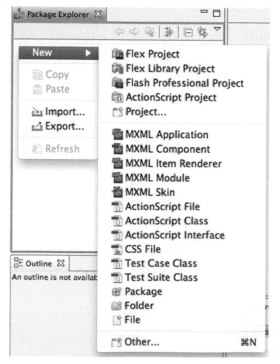

Figure 1.19 Creating a new ActionScript project.

Now that we know the basics it is time to have a look at how Flash Builder can assist us in creating and manipulating ActionScript classes. To not get confused, we will keep things simple and we will create just an ActionScript project. Just keep in mind that everything we show in this example can be done also in a Flex project. Right-click on the package explorer and select "ActionScript Project." See Figure 1.19. An alternative way is to select "New" from the File menu. See Figure 1.20.

This will open a wizard. We just type the name of the project, "MyProject," and hit "Finish." Flash Builder has already set up a project for us, creating a class MyProject.as as the entry point. If you have a Java background this class is like the one that contains the *main* method.

Now we want to add a new class to the project. According to what we said above we can open the corresponding folder of the project, create the directories for the package, and then create the ActionScript file, which includes the class definition. This is legitimate, and if you

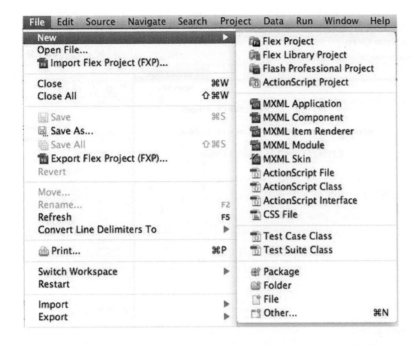

Figure 1.20 Creating a new ActionScript project: "File > New."

like you can do it, but there is a much shorter way. Just exploit the wizard of Flash Builder!

Let's say we want to create a class named Person in the package `com.studiomagnolia.model`. We right-click on the project and select "New > ActionScript Class" (Figure 1.21). A pretty clear

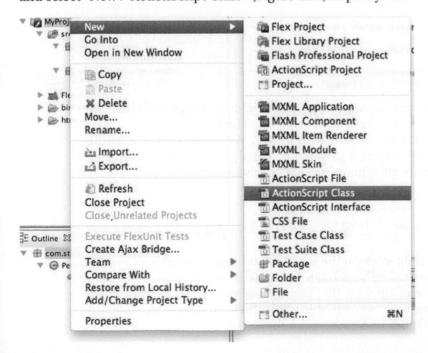

Figure 1.21 Creating a new ActionScript class.

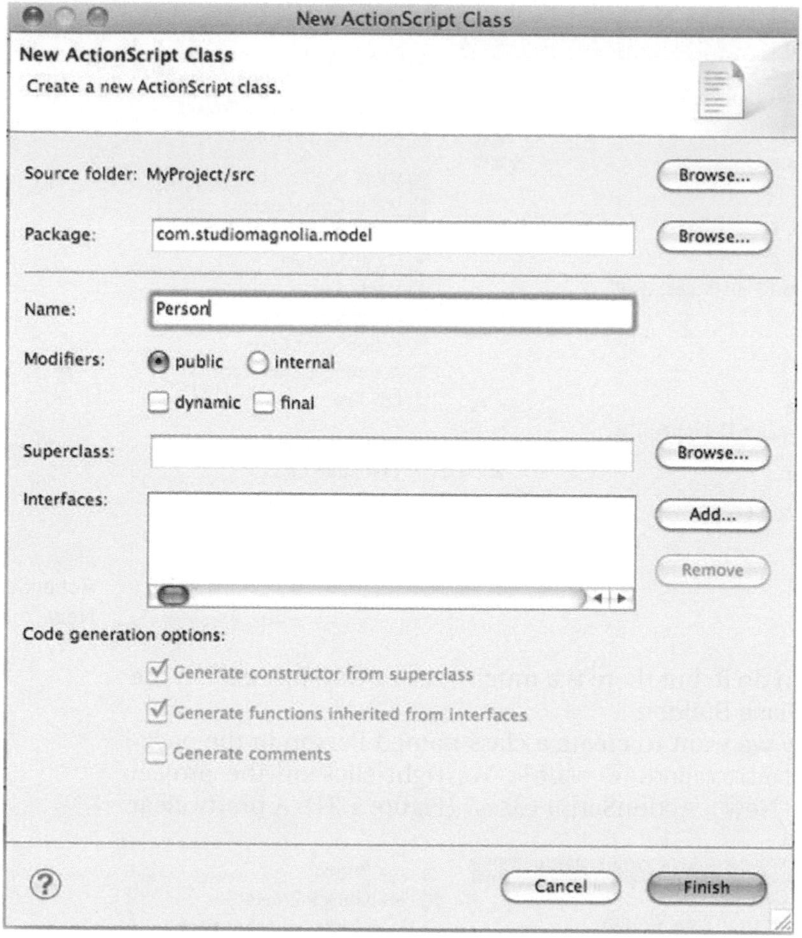

Figure 1.22 Defining an
ActionScript class.

modal wizard opens up. We fill two fields, package and class, and
we hit "Finish." The class is ready! See Figure 1.22.

Now let's populate it with a field. We want some encapsulation, so we declare a private `var` with `getter` and `setter`. Here
comes more good news: just add a private `var` as follows:

```
public class Person {
    private var _name:String;
    public function Person() { }
}
```

Now we right-click on the variable and select "Source > Generate
Getter/Setter" (Figure 1.23). The label is pretty explanatory and
you will end up with this menu that allows you to personalize
`getter` and `setter`: variable name, method names, accessibility,
etc. See Figure 1.24.

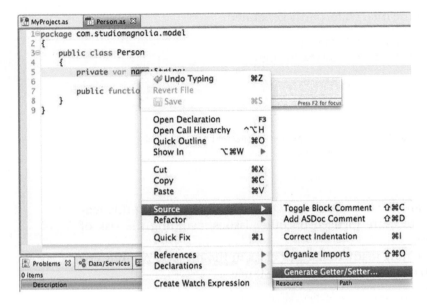

Figure 1.23 Generating getter and setter.

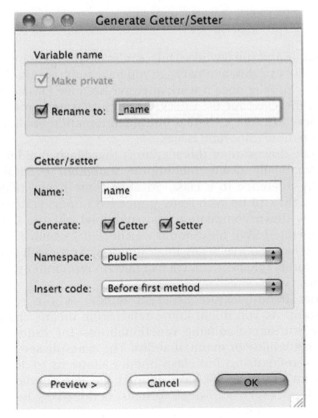

Figure 1.24 Configure getter and setter.

This is the final code, partly generated:

```
public class Person {
    private var _name:String;
    public function Person() { }
    public function get name ():String {
        return _name;
    }
    public function set name (name:String):void {
        this._name = name;
    }
}
```

As you can see, it is pretty easy to use it. By exploiting this feature we are more focused on other issues, avoiding the risk of mistyping.

We are now ready to use our class in the project. We move to the main class and we create an instance.

```
public function MyProject() {
    var me:Person = new Person();
    me.name = "Cesare";

    trace("My name is " + me.name);
}
```

If we compile and run it works. Did we miss anything? Remember: to use a class in a different package you have to import it. Did we import it? No. Why does it work anyway? Because Flash Builder imported the class for us! Check the import statements if you don't believe me. Again, there is built-in automation to allow you to focus on more important issues.

The only downside of this feature is that Flash Builder does not automatically delete the import statement even if you delete any reference to a class. So after some heavy refactoring you might end up with some unneeded import statements, which slow down compilation and (possibly) enlarge the size of the generated SWF file. Should we check it by hand? No. We can just select "Source > Organize Imports" and Flash Builder will do it for us (Figure 1.25). We just have to remember to run it sometimes.

Another handy feature of Flash Builder is the refactoring assistant. As you might know, refactoring means changing the code without modifying functionalities—for example, to improve readability or maintainability. The example seen above is a sort of refactoring, but Flash Builder allows us to do more. Let's see an example. We have defined the Person class with a method, prettyPrint, which formats as the string name and surname.

Do you prefer to switch between keyboard and mouse as few times as possible? Just configure a key shortcut and getter and setter will be generated just by hitting the key combination you defined.

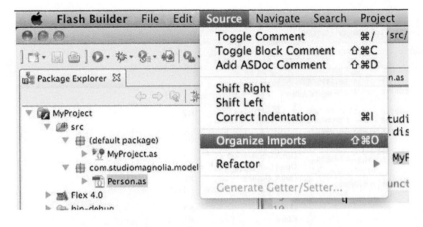

Figure 1.25 Flash Builder organizes imports.

```
public class Person {

    public var name:String;
    public var surname:String;

    public function Person() {}

    public function prettyPrint ():String {

        return "---------------------\n" +
            "Name: " + name +
            "\nSurname: " + surname;
    }
}
```

We use this class in our main method.

```
var me:Person = new Person();
me.name = "Cesare";
me.surname = "Rocchi";

trace(me.prettyPrint());
// Outputs

---------------------
Name: Cesare
Surname: Rocchi
---------------------
```

The method `prettyPrint` has a generic name, which might not reflect its functionality. At the beginning of the project we did not care, but the project has grown and now we need more clarity. To improve code readability we want to rename it to `lineSeparatedFormat`. In this example we have just one method call, so you might think it is not a big deal to rename it by hand, but in real projects method calls will be spread all over the source code and renaming by hand can get very tedious. To open the refactor assistant we select the method and right-click (Figure 1.26).

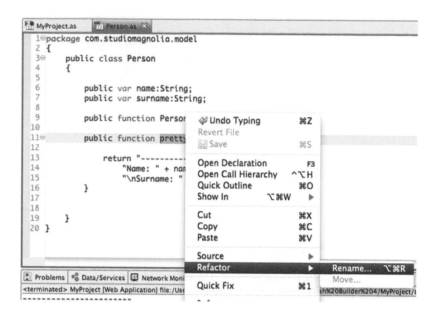

Figure 1.26 Opening the refactor assistant.

This prompts a dialog window that allows us to rename our method. It is important that "Update References" is checked, otherwise the renaming does not update all the method calls, but just the class definition. See Figure 1.27.

If you click "Preview" something very interesting happens. Flash Builder fetches *all* the project files affected by the change and for each file you can preview all the changes (see Figure 1.28). This feature is very useful, especially when you refactor something crucial to your code and you want to preview all the changes to your code (Figure 1.28). Once all the changes are approved, you can run the application and it will work, because the reference in the MyProject class has also been updated.

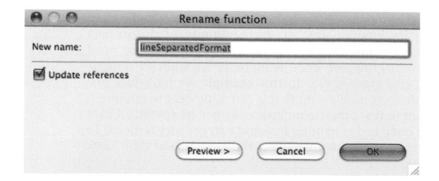

Figure 1.27 Renaming the method.

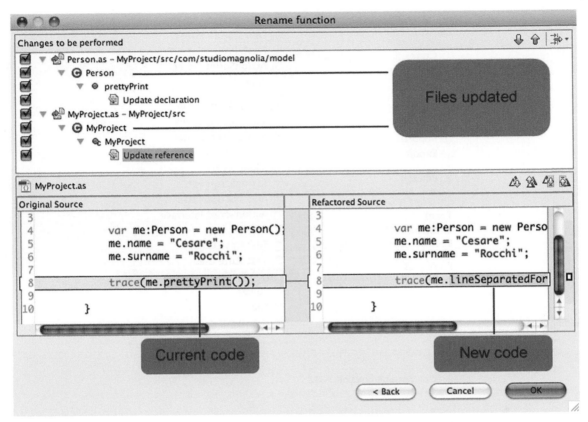

Figure 1.28 Previewing changes during refactoring.

Flash Builder is even more powerful because it allows you to also change the package to classes. For example, to be more specific, we want to move the Person class to a new package: `com.studiomagnolia.model.people`. First of all, we have to create the new package (right-click on the `src` folder and select "New > Package"; see Figure 1.29). Then we select the class name (or the constructor), right-click, and choose "Refactor > Move" (Figure 1.30). This opens up a dialog that allows us to select the new destination package.

Again, remember to check "Update References" and Flash Builder will take care to change source files that refer to the class. If we run our project it works as expected, thanks to this essential feature.

Inheritance

The principal feature of object-oriented programming is inheritance. Inheritance allows defining new classes by using already-defined ones. This features enables developers to:

Figure 1.29 Adding a new package.

Figure 1.30 Moving to the new package.

- Reuse code
- Build on top of existing code (e.g., libraries)

Inheriting from a class means creating a new class that extends the definition of the previous class—for example, by adding new properties/behaviors or overriding existing behaviors. In fact, the keyword to implement inheritance is *extends*. The existing class is called *superclass*, whereas the new one is called *subclass*. From the examples above we already have seen the class Person, with two properties (name and surname) and a method (prettyPrint). We rewrite the code here for convenience.

```
public class Person {

    public var name:String;
    public var surname:String;

    public function Person () {}

    public function prettyPrint():String {
        return "----------------------\n" +
                "Name: " + name +
                "\nSurname: " + surname;
    }
}
```

Now let's assume our project needs a new class, Employee, which has the same features of Person, but needs an extra property, say badgeID, which is shown in the string generated by the prettyPrint method. One way is to duplicate the source code of Person, rename it appropriately, and add missing features. This would work but there is a much more convenient way—that is, extending (inheriting from) the Person class, as in the following code.

```
public class Employee extends Person {
    public function Employee() {}
}
```

At this point we have a new class (the subclass), named Employee, which has exactly the same features as the Person class (its superclass). This code can also be generated automatically by Flash Builder. You just need to run the New ActionScript Class wizard and fill it as in Figure 1.31.

As we said, the requirement is to add a new feature, so let's write it.

```
public class Employee extends Person {
    public var badgeID:Number;
    public function Employee() {}
}
```

At this point we can go back to the project and use the newly created class.

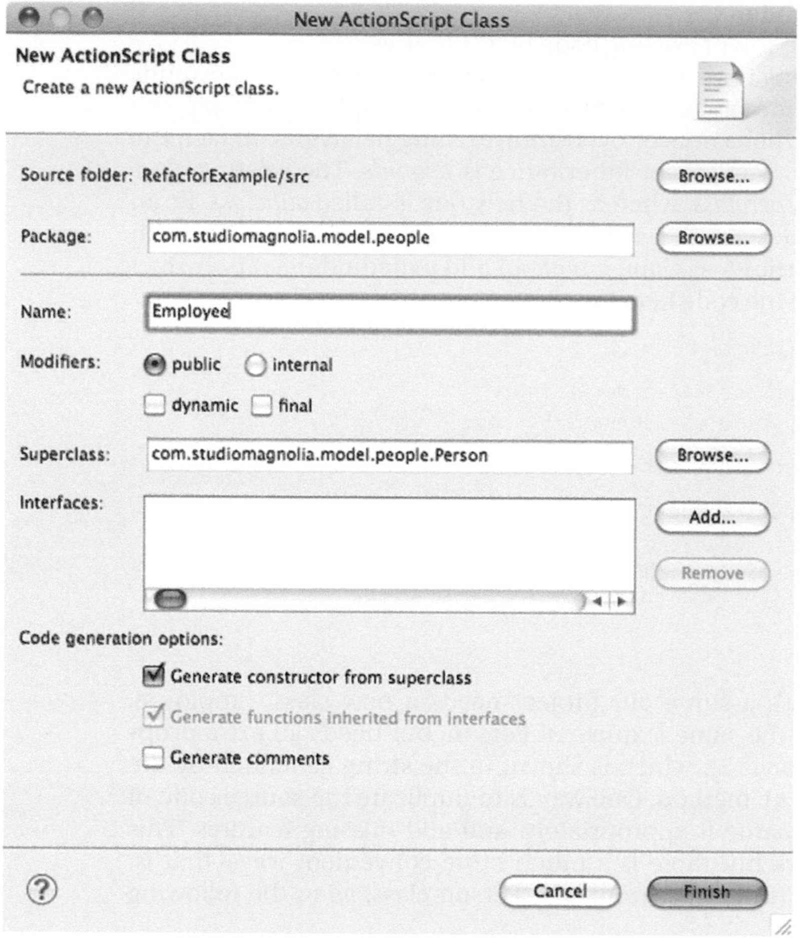

Figure 1.31 Extending a class via the New ActionScript Class wizard.

```
public function MyProject() {

    var me:Employee = new Employee();
    me.name = "Cesare";
    me.surname = "Rocchi";
    me.badgeId = 001;

    trace(me.prettyPrint());

}
// Outputs

-----------------------
Name: Cesare
Surname: Rocchi
```

As you can see we are almost done, the only thing missing is the modification of the print method to include the newly added feature, badgeId. While so far we have been just extending the

Person class, in this case we are overriding one of its behaviors— that is, the mechanism that outputs its string format. As above, the keyword *override* recalls the action performed. The new method is defined by the following syntax.

```
override public function prettyPrint():String {
    // new code here
}
```

As in the example above, we might be tempted to redefine all the methods by writing the following code.

```
override public function prettyPrint():String {

    return "----------------------\n" +
            "Name: " + name +
            "\nSurname: " + surname +
            "ID: " + badgeId;

}
```

From a functional viewpoint this is legitimate and it will work as expected, printing the new feature. But let's suppose that a new requirement is to change the separator (line of dashes) with a new character. At this point there are two classes to be changed, Person and Employee. Are you thinking, "Not a big deal, just two modifications"? In this specific case you probably are right, but let's report this example to a real-world scale, and you will find you are wrong.

The project has been started a few months ago, there are ten classes inheriting from Person, and the line of dashes as separator is spread over five methods, which you extended as above. Now, how many lines of code do you have to change? Fifty! Now do you see the big deal? One of the tricks of object-oriented programming is to exploit inheritance as much as possible. For example, if dashes were all in the Person class we would need just five modifications. Is it possible? Yes. The trick is to define the `prettyPrint` method as follows.

```
override public function prettyPrint():String {

    return super.prettyPrint() +
            "\nID: " + badgeId;
}
```

Here we don't entirely rewrite the method. We call the same method of the superclass and we concatenate the new feature. The behavior of the application remains the same but the source code is much more maintainable, reusable, and readable.

The example about inheritance presented so far is very basic and introductory. We should recall that it works because of the following reasons:

> Expert object-oriented developers would even do more. They would put a separator as a static variable of the Person class. In this case, when the requirement changes, they would change just one line of code.

- `prettyPrint` is public. It could have been protected or internal. You cannot override private methods.
- The overridden version `prettyPrint` maintains the same accessibility (public/protected/internal), the same number and type of parameters (none in this case), and the same return type (`String` in this case).

All the following examples are not implementable and will throw a compilation error of which the description is "Incompatible override."

```
// changes accessibility, prettyPrint has to be public
override internal function prettyPrint():String { ... }

// changes signature, prettyPrint has no parameters
override public function prettyPrint(p1:int):String{}

// changes signature, prettyPrint returns a String
override public function prettyPrint():Number {...}
```

For sake of completeness we should mention that another important concept in object-oriented programming is the one of interfaces (not to be confused with user interfaces, or UI). Interfaces are a way to specify the behavior of a class (read its methods) with no need to provide a specific implementation. Such a concept is out of the scope of this book and will not be introduced further. If you want to know more about interfaces in ActionScript you can have a look at Yard et al.'s book, *Object-Oriented ActionScript 3.0.*

Binding

One of the most powerful tools in Flex is binding. In the introduction to this section we mentioned that the Flex framework embeds solutions to deal with common problems in UI development. How many times have you had to refresh the value of a component according to an interaction or the state of another component? Binding does exactly this: it allows us to bind an *object* to another one, so that whenever the first value (*source*) changes, the second (*target*) is updated accordingly.

For example, we want to build a UI that allows the configuration of a button's label. To keep it simple, we will have a text input widget, which allows typing the new label, and a button. To improve the user experience of our application, we want the user to see changes in real time, as he or she types in the text input. In the terms introduced above, the text input is the source and the button label is the target. This is easily implementable in Flex by exploiting binding and the design view. In general, it is simpler to start by declaring the source. So we drag a text input component

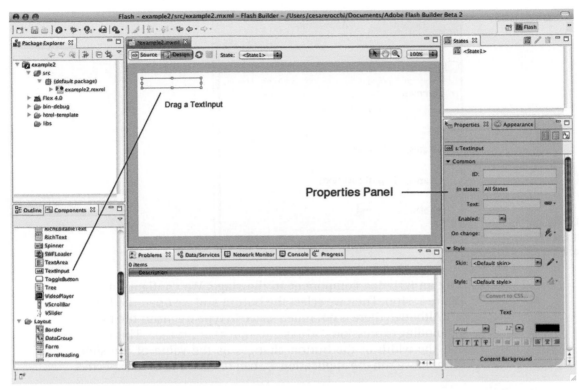

Figure 1.32 Setting the ID of the text input.

from the list. Once selected, we set its ID to `inputLabel` by using the Properties panel (Figure 1.32).

If you check the source view this has generated the following code:

```
<s:TextInput id="inputLabel"/>
```

This allows us to refer to this component by just indicating its ID. In this case, the ID is needed to refer to the source.

We can now drag an instance of the button. You might notice that the system already provides a default value ("Button") for the label. We can delete it and change it with a binding expression. A binding expression is wrapped by curly braces and evaluates the expression embedded. In our case we specify `{input Label.text}`, which means "the value of the text property of the component named `inputLabel` (Figure 1.33).

If we run the application, we will see that the button's label gets updated whenever we modify the text in the input field.

Let's now extend this example by creating a way to configure height and width of the button. We open the design view and we

Each component in Flex can have an ID. This property, which has to have a unique value, allows us to build a map of references to the component. This way, to access a component, we do not need to write a find procedure, we just refer to it by ID.

Figure 1.33 Configuring a binding expression in the Properties panel.

drag an `HSlider` component to the stage. We configure it as in Figure 1.34(a). Then we select the button and we open the Layout tab. Although there is not much space to type we insert the following binding expression: `{widthConfigurator.value}`. This means that the width of the button changes as the value of the slider varies. If we run the application we can test if it works as expected.

Figure 1.34 Configuration of the (a) `HSlider` and (b) button width.

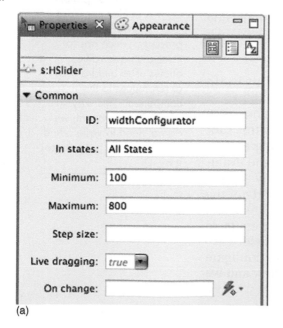

(a)

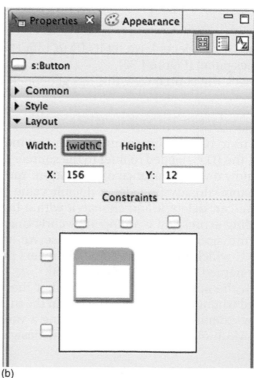

(b)

Instead of "wiring" components' properties with binding you can define a binding expression by means of a tag, as follows.

```
<fx:Binding
    destination="button.label"
    source="inputLabel.text"/>

<s:TextInput id="inputLabel"/>
<s:Button id="button" x="147" y="1"/>
```

Note that, in this case, you need to define an ID for both the components involved in the binding expression. Note also that binding involves properties of components (label for the button, text for the label).

A new feature introduced in Flex 4 in bidirectional binding is that two components' properties are the destination and source for each other.

```
<fx:Binding
    destination="inputLabel.text"
    source="inputLabel2.text"
    twoWay="true"/>

<s:TextInput id="inputLabel"/>
<s:TextInput id="inputLabel2"/>
```

This way `inputLabel` is updated by `inputLabel2` and vice versa. An alternative way is to use the @ symbol directly in the property definition.

```
<s:TextInput
    id="inputLabel"
    text="@{inputLabel2.text}"/>

<s:TextInput id="inputLabel2"/>
```

It is also possible to bind values defined in MXML and ActionScript code. In this case we use the directive `[Bindable]`.

```
<fx:Script>
  <![CDATA[

    [Bindable]
    private var myName:String = "Cesare";

  ]]>
</fx:Script>
<s:Button label="Email {myName}"/>
```

Let's illustrate a pretty common scenario. We have a class, Person, which represents the data model. We want to bind the label of a button to one property of the class (name) in order to dynamically build the label (e.g., "Email Cesare"). We should redefine the class as follows.

> You might have noticed that the properties of `HSlider` include a "Live Dragging" parameter, set to True by default. This way the width of the button is updated *while* we drag the head of the slider. If we change the parameter to False the width is updated when the mouse is *released*.

```
public class Person {

    [Bindable]
    public var name:String;

    ...

    public function Person() {}

}
```

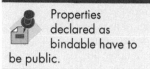

Properties declared as bindable have to be public.

Here the property name has been defined as a potential source of a binding expression.

Now we can use it in our code.

```
<fx:Script>
    <![CDATA[

    [Bindable]
    private var me:Person = new Person();

    private function init():void {

        me.name = "Cesare";

    }
    ]]>
</fx:Script>

<s:Button label="Email {me.name}"/>
```

Notice that also the instance of Person has to be declared [Bindable].

As we will see binding will be used a lot in Flex development because it enables us to easily update parts of the application when the user interacts with it or when data to be displayed change.

Binding—Under the Hood

You might wonder about the magic behind binding. At the moment we do not have all the elements to understand it so we will provide a naïve explanation. Whenever we create a binding expression we sort of undersign a contract between two components, where the source "promises" to notify the target when there are changes. This is done by means of events. We will provide further explanations when we present events.

Very First Piece of GUI in Flash Builder

Now we have enough knowledge to create our first piece of GUI in Flash Builder. Since the book is about data visualization, and data are often loaded from login-protected locations, we will start from a very much-needed component, a login form.

In this example, we will see how to use some of the components of Flex (buttons, text inputs) and containers (panel and form).

Let's create a new project, LoginForm, and move to the design view of the LoginForm.mxml. We drag a Panel container. Within the panel we drag a Form container. In the Form we drag two text input components and a button. We rename them appropriately and we should end up with a view similar to Figure 1.35.

At this point the structure of the MXML should be the following (geometrical properties omitted for clarity).

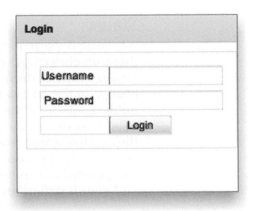

Figure 1.35 Design of the LoginForm.

```
<s:Panel title="Login">
    <mx:Form >
        <mx:FormItem label="Login">
            <s:TextInput/>
        </mx:FormItem>
        <mx:FormItem label="Password">
            <s:TextInput/>
        </mx:FormItem>
        <mx:FormItem >
            <s:Button label="Login"/>
        </mx:FormItem>
    </mx:Form>
</s:Panel>
```

One thing that is not doable in the design view is to declare the second text input as a password field. So we switch to the code view and we update the corresponding component with a Boolean feature, as follows.

```
<mx:FormItem label="Password">
    <s:TextInput displayAsPassword="true" />
</mx:FormItem>
```

This way the input of the label is shown as dots. For the rest, the UI is done! We just need to hook it up to the login web service, which will return a right or wrong message according to the data we entered. Before getting there let's focus a bit more on the UI. Is anything missing? What if somebody wants to register? Our application has to offer this possibility. As in the case of inheritance presented above, we might be tempted to create a copy of the login panel and modify it to add new fields for the registration procedure. As above, we can do it and it will work, but there is a more convenient way to implement it, by using states.

States

A state is a sort of static picture of a UI: a button here, a combo there, on-click trigger this action, etc. Of course, any Flex application can work perfectly as expected without using states. But any change to the UI has to be managed according to user actions, notifications from the server, etc. Wouldn't it be nice to identify a finite set of states and switch between them? With reference to the example above, wouldn't it be nice to define two states (`login` and `register`) instead of manipulating the display of each single component? Here is how we can achieve this result.

A state is defined by means of the following syntax.

```
<s:states>
    <s:State name="State1"/>
    <s:State name="State2"/>
</s:states>
```

So far we have just created two logical elements. Now we need to arrange components according to the different states. If you have worked with Flex 3 states you will notice a big shift. States in Flex 3 were arranged according to the following paradigm: *Provide changes to be performed when switching to a new state.*

For example, when you change states, you have to specify which elements have to be added (and where) or removed. In Flex 4 the approach has been changed to a declarative paradigm. According to this new perspective you just have to define which components are included (or excluded) in a given state. This can be done by using the following syntax.

```
<mx:FormItem includeIn="register" >
    <s:TextInput />
</mx:FormItem>
```

This component will appear only when the selected state is `register`, otherwise it will be invisible, and the framework will handle the rendering. The same can be applied to properties.

```
<mx:FormItem
    label.register="Register"
    label.login="Login">

    <s:TextInput />

</mx:FormItem>
```

In this case, the label of the form item will change according to the state selected. As we will see next, working with Flex 4 states is easy and effective, and developers can focus primarily on appearance rather than code.

Login and Register with States

Now let's go back to our previous example. We already have set up part of the application, but we will rearrange it by adopting the following strategy. We will put on stage all the components needed by both the login and register states. Then we will duplicate the state and finally we will add include/ exclude statements to the specific components. First of all, we have to rearrange the previous example as in Figure 1.36.

This is a blend of all the components needed by both states. We have added an email field and an extra password field. At the bottom we have added a Link button, which allows switching between states. At this point our code should look as follows.

Figure 1.36 Design of the Login/ Register panel.

```
<!-- Geometrical properties omitted for clarity -->

<s:Panel title="Login">

  <mx:Form>

      <mx:FormItem label="Username">
        <s:TextInput/>
      </mx:FormItem>

      <mx:FormItem label="Email">
        <s:TextInput/>
      </mx:FormItem>

      <mx:FormItem label="Password">
        <s:TextInput displayAsPassword="true" />
      </mx:FormItem>

      <mx:FormItem label="Password">
        <s:TextInput displayAsPassword="true" />
      </mx:FormItem>

      <mx:FormItem >
        <s:Button label="Login"/>
      </mx:FormItem>

  </mx:Form>

  <mx:LinkButton label="Create Account"/>

</s:Panel>
```

Now we can go back to the design view to create a new state. In the panel on the top right we click on the New State button (Figure 1.37). This opens up the following dialog, where we specify a name for the new state, register (Figure 1.38).

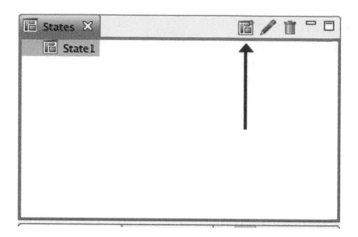

Figure 1.37 New State button.

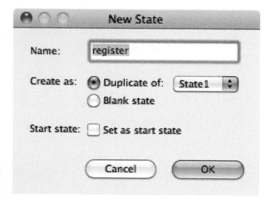

Figure 1.38 New State wizard.

Now we have two states—that is, two logical elements representing a different configuration of the UI. Let's rename state 1 as `login`, to have a more meaningful name. If we check the source code, there is a new tag defining the states.

```
<s:states>
    <s:State name="login"/>
    <s:State name="register"/>
</s:states>
```

We are left with the most important task—choosing what has to be shown according to the state. The email item has to be shown only in the `register` state, and the same holds for the second password field.

```
<mx:FormItem label="Email" includeIn="register">
    <s:TextInput/>
</mx:FormItem>

<mx:FormItem label="Password">
    <s:TextInput displayAsPassword="true" />
</mx:FormItem>

<mx:FormItem label="Password" includeIn="register">
    <s:TextInput displayAsPassword="true" />
</mx:FormItem>
```

Essentially we are pretty much done. Let's attach the switch code to the Link button to see the effect.

```
<mx:LinkButton label="Create Account"
        click.register="currentState = 'login'"
        click.login="currentState = 'register'"/>
```

As you can see, the same component can perform different actions according to the state of the UI.

We are left with finishing touches. The panel has two different titles:

```
<s:Panel title="Login" title.register="Register">
```

So does the Form button:

```
<mx:FormItem >
    <s:Button label="Login" label.register="Register"/>
</mx:FormItem>
```

And the Link button:

```
<mx:LinkButton
        label="Create Account"
        label.register="Back to Login"
        click.register="currentState = 'login'"
        click.login="currentState = 'register'"
/>
```

If we build the application, it works as in Figure 1.39.

Congratulations! You have built your first panel with a double functionality, login and registration.

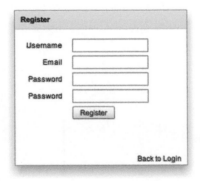

Figure 1.39 Final result of Login/Register panel.

Loading Data from Remote Locations

Rich Internet Applications (RIAs) are made of two key elements: user interface and backend. So far we have seen how to manipulate UI elements to implement layout and interaction. In this section we will have a look at the interaction with the backend, to load and manipulate data.

If you have worked with Flex 3 (and Flex Builder) you might be aware that it is not immediate to set up a connection for loading remote data. You have to learn how to use classes and callbacks, and the only way to implement data-loading procedures is to write MXML/ActionScript 3 code. One of the new additions to Flash Builder is the Data/Services tab and its companion, Network Monitor. In the standard layout they are both located at the bottom. The first is a very useful addition, for it allows us to interactively browse web services and create automatically generated code to interact with those services. If you have ever built an RIA you know how tedious this part of the development is: read documentation, find which URL to call, find which parameter to pass, parse the content, and, finally, render the loaded content. As a designer you are much more focused on the UI and everything that simplifies the "load and parse" phase is very welcome. The Data/Services feature has been implemented with this scenario in mind.

Figure 1.40 Data/Services and Network Monitor tabs.

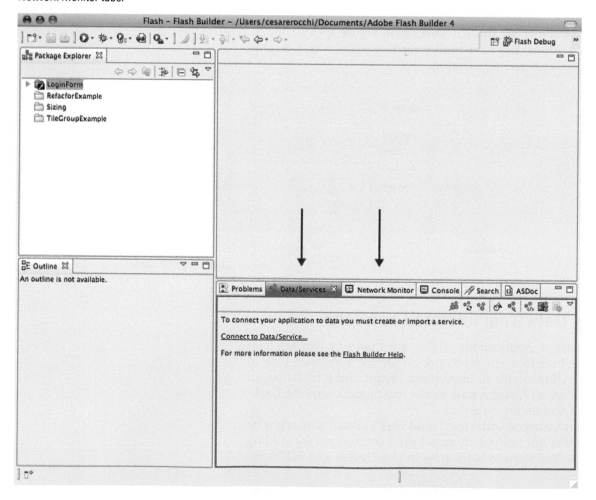

Importing a Service

Let's first have a look at the Data/Services feature. As you probably know, loading data from a remote location might require authentication. To start with a simple example, we will load an RSS (Really Simple Syndication) feed, which is public and does not require any authentication.

Let's go to the Yahoo Finance RSS Generator at *http://finance. yahoo.com/rssindex*. This page allows us to dynamically create RSS feeds that include information about the financial situation of a company. We enter the symbol of Adobe (ADBE) and we get different links. See Figure 1.41.

We are interested in the RSS type of link, *http://finance.yahoo. com/rss/headline?s=ADBE*. Let's examine it.

We call what is before the "?" the *entry point*—that is, the root URL that allows the retrieval of news headlines in RSS format. After the "?" there are parameters, in this case just one. Parameters are in the format of key/value, separated by a "=". In RIAs, when

RSS is an XML-based format used to describe items on the Web (e.g., blog posts, videos, etc.). There are different variants. To know more you can consult the corresponding definition on Wikipedia. Note that by means of the Data/Services wizard you can easily set up a data-driven application, with almost no need to study the variants of RSS.

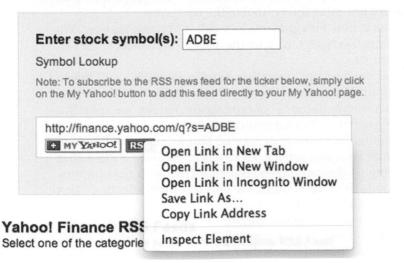

Figure 1.41 Create an RSS for Adobe.

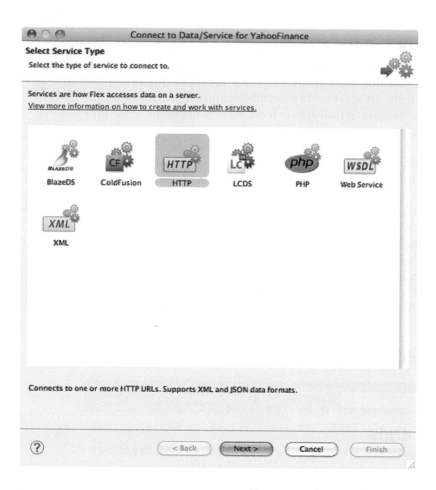

Figure 1.42 Format of the service.

loading remote data, we can change the URL and parameters. We will now see an example in which we vary the "s" parameter—that is, the one representing the symbol of the company.

We create a new Flex project; let's call it "YahooFinance." We open the Data/Services tab, start the wizard, and select "HTTP," as in Figure 1.42.

Now we rename the operation "getFinanceInfo" and paste the entry point URL, *http://finance.yahoo.com/rss/headline*. Then we add a parameter name "s" of type string. Finally, we specify a name for the service: "YahooFinanceInfo," as in Figure 1.43.

Flash Builder has already generated some code, which is useful to interact with the service. In essence, we have a class that takes a string as the parameter, builds a URL with that parameter, and loads the remote data. We can test it by selecting "Test Operation." See Figure 1.44.

This opens a new tab where we can provide a symbol of a company (e.g., ADBE) and test the result. When we click "Test" the system invokes the URL and shows the result as a tree. See Figure 1.45.

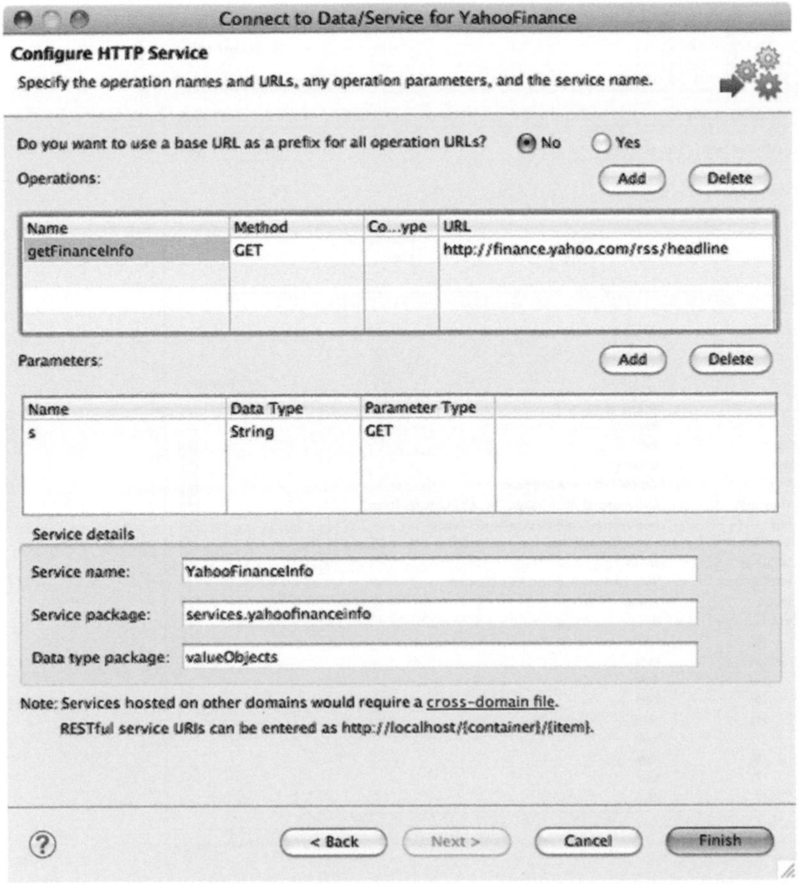

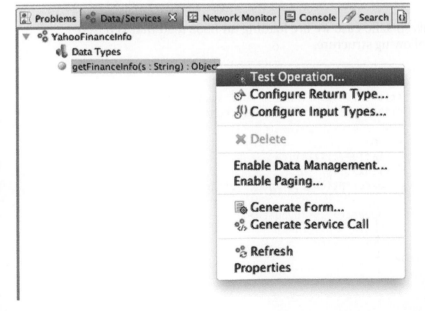

Figure 1.43 Defining the finance service.

Figure 1.44 Running a test of the load operation.

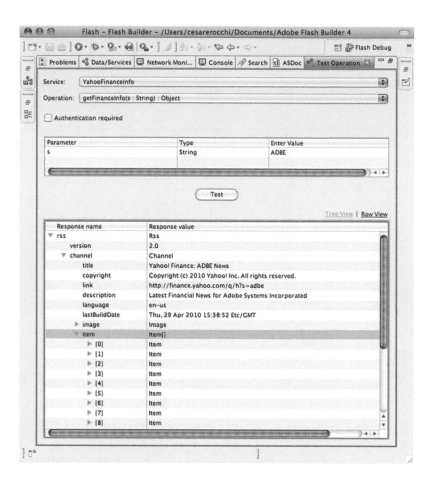

Figure 1.45 Result for the symbol ADBE.

In this specific case we are loading an RSS2 feed that is based on the following structure.

```
<rss version="2.0">
  <channel>
  <title>Yahoo! Finance: ADBE News</title>
  <link>http://finance.yahoo.com/q/h?s=adbe</link>
  ...
  <item>
    <title>...</title>
    <link>...</link>
    <description>...</description>
    ...
    <pubDate>...</pubDate>
  </item>
  <item>...</item>
</rss>
```

If you check the tree generated by the Test operation it corresponds exactly to this structure. We are now left with the second part: building a model to represent data returned by the web service.

Building a Data Model

If you looked closely at Figure 1.45 the web service has no return type associated to it. We create it by selecting "Configure Return Type" (Figure 1.46).

This opens a wizard that will assist us in defining the classes to represent our data. We will let the wizard autodetect the type by inspecting the result of a web service call (Figure 1.47).

To allow inspection we need to provide a value and retrieve real data. We enter the Adobe symbol, ADBE. See Figure 1.48.

The system analyzes data for us and prompts a set of choices: the name of data types and the root to start from. Note that if we have already defined some data type, we can associate them to XML nodes (Figure 1.49).

If we look at the project explorer a lot has changed. We have new packages and classes that represent the type of data returned by the web service, and it is all automatically generated. We skipped all the tedious part of building a representation

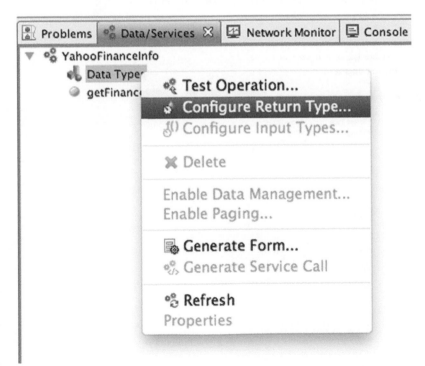

Figure 1.46 Configuration of the return type.

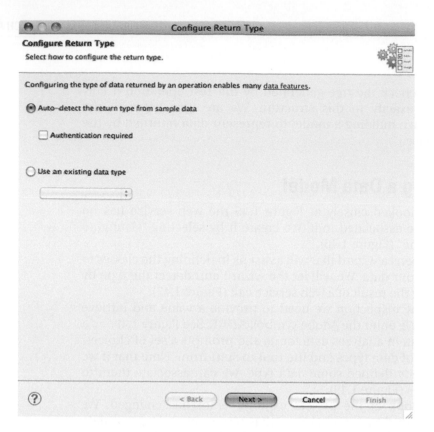

Figure 1.47 Autodetection of data type.

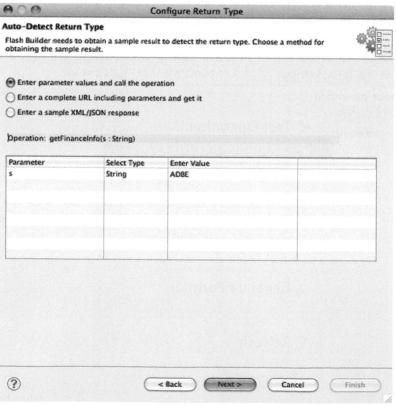

Figure 1.48 Providing parameters for a web service call.

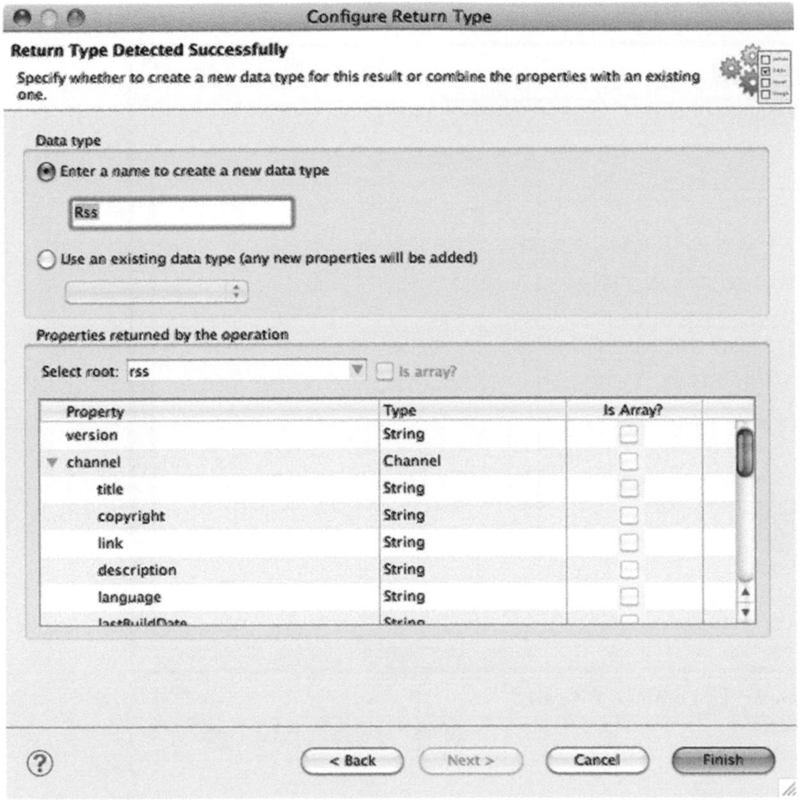

Figure 1.49 Associating/creating data types to XML nodes.

model, choosing the type of variables, etc. This is particularly useful if we want to build a working prototype quickly or if we cannot afford the work of a developer to build the code to query web services.

At this point we are ready to use the web service in our application. We have all the elements needed: procedures to load remote data, to pass parameters, and to represent returned data. Let's say we want to show titles of news in a list. Even if we do not realize it, we are few steps away from such a result.

We open our MXML application and switch to the design view. We drag a list component and arrange it as we like. A list component shows a set of items arranged vertically, much like the Select form in HTML. To populate the list with data retrieved from the server, instead of writing code, we drag and drop the operation node onto the list. See Figure 1.50.

We are prompted with the last choices:

- Which XML nodes have to populate the list? The answer: the Item node.
- Which part of the Item node has to be shown in the list? The answer: the Title.

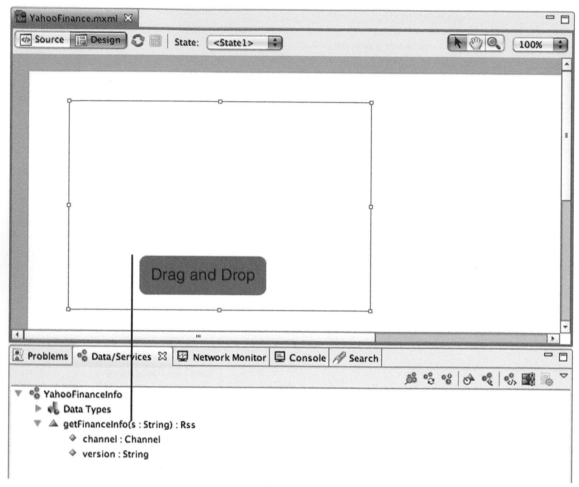

Figure 1.50 Associate load operation to visual component.

Flash Builder now switches automatically to the source view and shows the following code.

```
<!-- some code refactored for readability-->
<fx:Script>
<![CDATA[

    protected function listCreated(event:FlexEvent):voi
d {
      onInfoReceived.token =
        yahooFinanceInfo.getFinanceInfo("ADBE");
    }
]]>

</fx:Script>

<fx:Declarations>
    <s:CallResponder id="onInfoReceived"/>
    <yahoofinanceinfo:YahooFinanceInfo
      id="yahooFinanceInfo"
```

```
       fault="Alert.show(event.fault.faultString + '\n' +
              event.fault.faultDetail)"
       showBusyCursor="true"/>

</fx:Declarations>

<s:List id="list"
    creationComplete="listCreated(event)"
    labelField="title">

    <s:AsyncListView
      list="{TypeUtility.convertToCollection(
           onInfoReceived.lastResult.channel.item)
           }"/>

</s:List>
```

The Flash Builder hints for us to provide a parameter for the function `getFinanceInfo`. Let's enter "ADBE" here. We run the application and it shows Adobe's headlines in the list as expected (Figure 1.51).

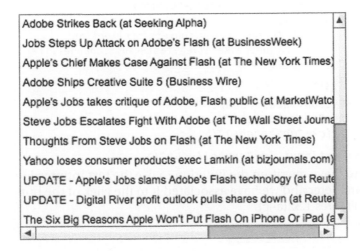

Figure 1.51 The FinanceYahoo working as expected.

Refining the Application

Probably an application that loads data about one company is not very useful. Let's try to extend it to allow specifying symbols in a text input, much like a search engine. We need the following modifications:

- Add one button and one text input area.
- Associate the load operation to the click of the button.
- Associate the parameter of the `getFinanceInfo` operation to the value of the text input area.

Whether we do it in the design or source view, we will end up with a code similar to this.

```
<fx:Script>
<![CDATA[

    protected function doSearch():void {
        onInfoReceived.token =
        yahooFinanceInfo.getFinanceInfo(symbolInput.
        text);
    }

]]>
</fx:Script>
<fx:Declarations>
    <s:CallResponder id="onInfoReceived"/>
    <yahoofinanceinfo:YahooFinanceInfo
      id="yahooFinanceInfo"
      fault="Alert.show(event.fault.faultString + '\n' +
              event.fault.faultDetail)"
      showBusyCursor="true"/>

</fx:Declarations>
<s:List id="list" labelField="title">
    <s:AsyncListView
        list="{TypeUtility.convertToCollection(
                onInfoReceived.lastResult.channel.item)
              }"/>

</s:List>
<s:Button label="Search"
    id="searchButton"
    click="doSearch()"/>

<s:TextInput id="symbolInput"/>
```

Here we have rewritten the function to use the text input value as the parameter and we have associated it to the click of the button. See Figures 1.52(a–c).

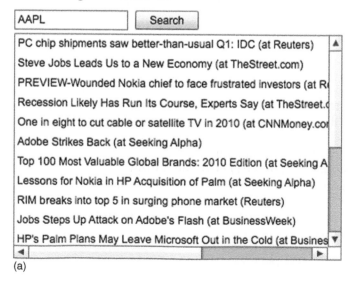

Figure 1.52 (a–c) Examples of the final application.

(a)

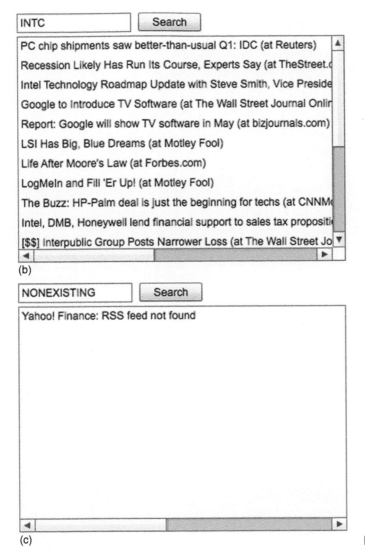

(b)

(c)

Figure 1.52–Continued

Conclusion

In this section we have seen the basics of Flex (MXML and ActionScript 3), some components (layout containers, buttons, text inputs), and some of the handy features included in the new Flash Builder (e.g., Data/Services tab). In the next section, we will dive deeper into the use of other components and learn how to build custom ones.

PROJECT 1: MUSIC STORE BROWSER

Theory is important, but, when consolidated by practical knowledge, it is even better. In this project we will build an example to see in action all the concepts presented throughout this chapter. We will build a Music Store application, which enables users to search for artists, retrieve information about songs, and switch to different stores. We will see in action the following concepts: components layout, interaction with web services, binding between components, and configuration of states.

Description of the Project

The project will be a Flex application that allows searching for a list of songs by a given artist. For each song the user can visualize the corresponding album cover, singles price, and album price. Moreover, the user will be able to switch to different worldwide stores to compare prices in different currencies. The application will be built on top of the free iTunes Search API,[1] which perfectly fits this scenario and supports all the remote operations needed by our application. The visual elements of the application will be the following:

- A text input to type in the name of the artist.
- A combo box to choose a store.
- A button to trigger the search.
- An interactive list to show the retrieved list of songs.
- An image to visualize the cover of the album.
- A form to display information about a single song when selected on the list.

The application will have different states according to the action currently performed by the user, as described in Table 1.1.

---

[1]The full documentation of the API is available at *http://www.apple.com/itunes/ affiliates/resources/documentation/itunes-store-web-service-search-api.html*.

Table 1.1 Description of the Application's States

State	Description
startup	The application has been loaded for the first time. A text input, a combo box, and a button are displayed.
searching	The user has run a search. A "searching" message is displayed. Input area, combo box, and Search button are disabled.
searchSuccessful	The list of songs retrieved is displayed in the list. The "searching" message is hidden.
searchError	An error message is displayed.

Creating the Layout

We already know how to work with the design view. The suggested dimension of the application is 550 pixels (width) × 450 pixels (height). Once we have put all the elements on the stage our design should look like Figure 1.1.

To keep things simple we opted for a "free" layout, so each component is explicitly positioned on the stage. The following is the code corresponding to the layout in Figure 1.1.

```
<s:Application ...
  width="550" height="450">

<s:Label x="174" y="21"
    text="Music Store"
    fontSize="36" fontWeight="bold"/>
```

Figure 1.1 First design of the Music Store application.

```
<s:TextInput x="52" y="108"
    width="160" height="25"/>

<s:ComboBox x="220" y="108"
    width="60" height="25"/>

<s:List x="51" y="164"
    width="201" height="246"></s:List>

<mx:Image x="273" y="164"
    width="100" height="100"/>
<mx:Form x="273" y="272"
    width="229" height="140">
    <mx:FormHeading label="Details"/>
    <mx:FormItem label="Album name">
        <s:Label/>
    </mx:FormItem>

    <mx:FormItem label="Track price">
        <s:Label />
    </mx:FormItem>

    <mx:FormItem label="Album price">
        <s:Label />
    </mx:FormItem>

</mx:Form>
<s:Button x="303" y="108"
    label="Search" height="25"/>

</s:Application>
```

There are a couple of elements left to be added to this layout. First, we need a way to provide feedback during a search. Second, the application needs a way to tell the user about errors. We put a label to fulfill both needs and change its text accordingly. We position it right below the text input field, so the code will be the following.

```
<s:Label x="52" y="144"
    text="Searching ..."
    width="160"/>
```

Now we have all the components needed to meet all the requirements of the application. Let's move to the configuration of states.

Adding States

The graphical interface of the application has to arrange visual components according to the requirements previously defined (see Table 1.1). In essence, components have to appear or disappear in relation to the actions triggered by the user. For example, while a search is ongoing, only input field, combo box, and button have to be visible and disabled. When the search is successful the list has to be visible (and populated); when a list item is clicked the image and details have to be visible; and so on. To implement this we start from the only state currently defined in our application and we arrange components accordingly.

Let's start by creating a clone of the current state. We move to the design view and right-click on State1 (Figure 1.2). The new state will be called searching (Figure 1.3). To keep names consistent, we rename State1 as startup (Figure 1.4). We follow the procedure above until we have four states, as in Figure 1.5.

Once done, Flash Builder has added the following code to the one illustrated before.

```
<s:states>
  <s:State name="startup"/>
  <s:State name="searching"/>
  <s:State name="searchSuccessful"/>
  <s:State name="searchError"/>
</s:states>
```

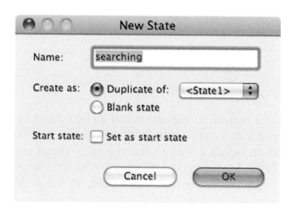

Figure 1.3 Creating the searching state.

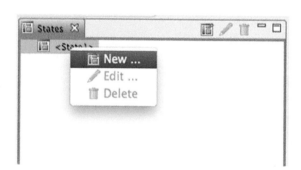

Figure 1.2 Duplicating the current state.

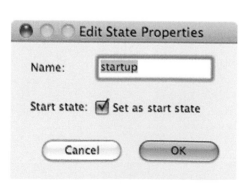

Figure 1.4 Renaming the initial state.

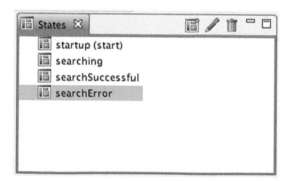

Figure 1.5 The full list of states.

Now we have a stack of four states, which are identical. We can move on to the configuration. With the `startup` state selected in the list we pick the list, the image, and the form, and we press the Delete or Canc button on the keyboard. This does not mean that we have deleted our carefully placed elements; we have just excluded them from the `startup` state because they are not needed. We have to do the same in the `searching` and `searchError` states, because in those cases we will display only a label. If you check our code now you should notice the following modifications.

```
<s:List
  x="51" y="164"
  width="201" height="246"
  includeIn="searchSuccessful">

</s:List>

<mx:Image x="273" y="164"
  width="100" height="100"
  includeIn="searchSuccessful"/>

<mx:Form x="273" y="272"
  width="229" height="140"
  includeIn="searchSuccessful">
    ...

</mx:Form>
```

Flash Builder has inserted specifications for components according to the state. Now we can go on with the rest. The feedback label has to be deleted from the `startup` and `searchSuccessful` states. In the `searchError` state the text of the label has to be changed to `Error in searching`. After these changes, the code for the label will be the following (additions shown in italics).

```
<s:Label
    x="52" y="144"
    text="Searching ..." width="160"
    includeIn="searchError,searching"
    text.searchError="Error in searching."/>
```

Finally, in the "searching" state, we mark as disabled the input text, the combo box, and the Search button. So far, the code for the whole application looks like the following (changes shown in italics).

```
<s:Application ...
    width="550" height="450"
    currentState="startup">

    <s:states>
        <s:State name="startup"/>
        <s:State name="searching"/>
```

```
            <s:State name="searchSuccessful"/>
            <s:State name="searchError"/>
        </s:states>

        <s:Label x="174" y="21"
            text="Music Store"
            fontSize="36" fontWeight="bold"/>

        <s:TextInput x="52" y="108"
            width="160" height="25"
            enabled.searching="false"/>

        <s:ComboBox x="220" y="108"
            width="60" height="25"
            enabled.searching="false"/>

        <s:List x="51" y="164"
            width="201" height="246"
            includeIn="searchSuccessful">

        </s:List>

        <mx:Image x="273" y="164"
            width="100" height="100"
            includeIn="searchSuccessful"/>

        <mx:Form x="273" y="272"
            width="229" height="140"
            includeIn="searchSuccessful">

            <mx:FormHeading label="Details"/>
            <mx:FormItem label="Album name">
                <s:Label/>
            </mx:FormItem>

        <mx:FormItem label="Track price">
            <s:Label />
        </mx:FormItem>

        <mx:FormItem label="Album price">
            <s:Label />
        </mx:FormItem>
        </mx:Form>

        <s:Button x="303" y="108"
            label="Search"
            height="25"
            enabled.searching="false"/>

        <s:Label x="52" y="144"
            text="Loading ..."
            width="160"
            includeIn="searchError,searching"
            text.searchError="Error in searching."/>

    </s:Application>
```

Adding Backend Capabilities

Now that we are ready with the user interface we can start working on the interaction with remote data. As we have said in the presentation of the project we will use iTunes Search API to query the music store database. If we check out the documentation it is easy to find out that we are interested in the following URL: `http://ax.itunes.apple.com/WebObjects/MZStoreServices.woa/wa/wsSearch?term=`*`ARTIST`*`&country=`*`COUNTRYCODE`*.

Values highlighted in italics are to be substituted by "real" values like "Led Zeppelin" and "us"; therefore, the final URL will be like the following: `http://ax.itunes.apple.com/WebObjects/MZStoreServices.woa/wa/wsSearch?term=`*`led+zeppelin`*`&country=`*`us`*. If we paste this URL into a browser we should see some JavaScrip Object Notation (JSON), as in Figure 1.6.

This means that we are on the right track, in that parameters are correct and the web service is working. Let's copy the same URL, for we will use it to build the backend functionality of our application. In the Data/Services tab we start up the wizard to create a new web service and we choose "HTTP," as in Figure 1.7.

We paste the URL in the first table and press "Enter." As you can see the wizard automatically detects the list of parameters. We can customize names of the classes and packages that will be generated, as in Figure 1.8.

Figure 1.6 A successful query to the backend.

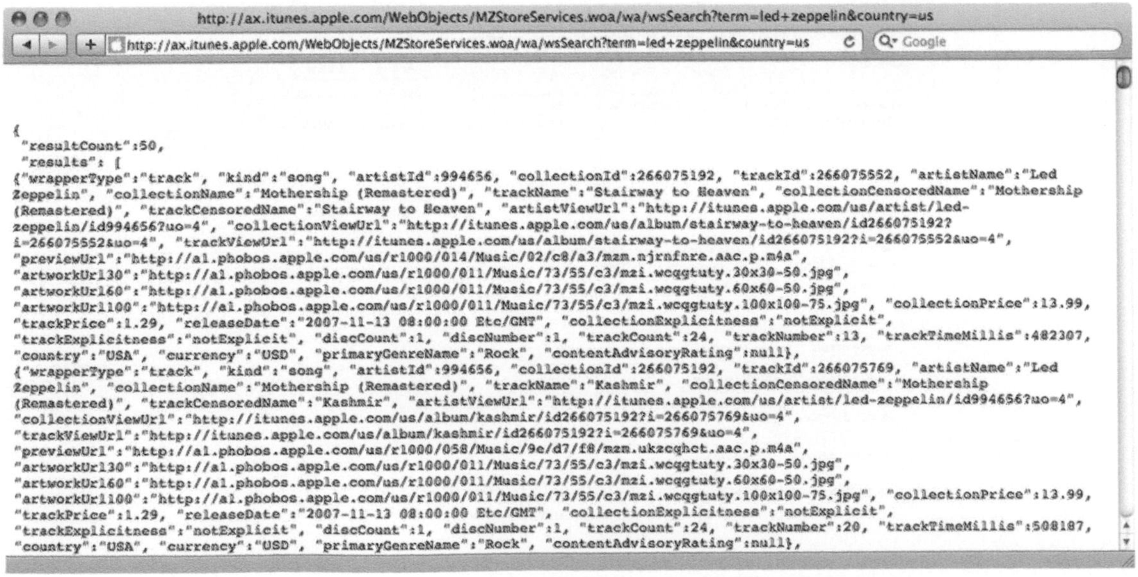
http://ax.itunes.apple.com/WebObjects/MZStoreServices.woa/wa/wsSearch?term=led+zeppelin&country=us
http://ax.itunes.apple.com/WebObjects/MZStoreServices.woa/wa/wsSearch?term=led+zeppelin&country=us
Google
{
"resultCount":50,
"results": [
{"wrapperType":"track", "kind":"song", "artistId":994656, "collectionId":266075192, "trackId":266075552, "artistName":"Led
Zeppelin", "collectionName":"Mothership (Remastered)", "trackName":"Stairway to Heaven", "collectionCensoredName":"Mothership
(Remastered)", "trackCensoredName":"Stairway to Heaven", "artistViewUrl":"http://itunes.apple.com/us/artist/led-
zeppelin/id994656?uo=4", "collectionViewUrl":"http://itunes.apple.com/us/album/stairway-to-heaven/id266075192?
i=266075552&uo=4", "trackViewUrl":"http://itunes.apple.com/us/album/stairway-to-heaven/id266075192?i=266075552&uo=4",
"previewUrl":"http://a1.phobos.apple.com/us/r1000/014/Music/02/c8/a3/mzm.njrnfnre.aac.p.m4a",
"artworkUrl30":"http://a1.phobos.apple.com/us/r1000/011/Music/73/55/c3/mzi.wcqgtuty.30x30-50.jpg",
"artworkUrl60":"http://a1.phobos.apple.com/us/r1000/011/Music/73/55/c3/mzi.wcqgtuty.60x60-50.jpg",
"artworkUrl100":"http://a1.phobos.apple.com/us/r1000/011/Music/73/55/c3/mzi.wcqgtuty.100x100-75.jpg", "collectionPrice":13.99,
"trackPrice":1.29, "releaseDate":"2007-11-13 08:00:00 Etc/GMT", "collectionExplicitness":"notExplicit",
"trackExplicitness":"notExplicit", "discCount":1, "discNumber":1, "trackCount":24, "trackNumber":13, "trackTimeMillis":482307,
"country":"USA", "currency":"USD", "primaryGenreName":"Rock", "contentAdvisoryRating":null},
{"wrapperType":"track", "kind":"song", "artistId":994656, "collectionId":266075192, "trackId":266075769, "artistName":"Led
Zeppelin", "collectionName":"Mothership (Remastered)", "trackName":"Kashmir", "collectionCensoredName":"Mothership
(Remastered)", "trackCensoredName":"Kashmir", "artistViewUrl":"http://itunes.apple.com/us/artist/led-zeppelin/id994656?uo=4",
"collectionViewUrl":"http://itunes.apple.com/us/album/kashmir/id266075192?i=266075769&uo=4",
"trackViewUrl":"http://itunes.apple.com/us/album/kashmir/id266075192?i=266075769&uo=4",
"previewUrl":"http://a1.phobos.apple.com/us/r1000/058/Music/9e/d7/f8/mzm.ukzcqhct.aac.p.m4a",
"artworkUrl30":"http://a1.phobos.apple.com/us/r1000/011/Music/73/55/c3/mzi.wcqgtuty.30x30-50.jpg",
"artworkUrl60":"http://a1.phobos.apple.com/us/r1000/011/Music/73/55/c3/mzi.wcqgtuty.60x60-50.jpg",
"artworkUrl100":"http://a1.phobos.apple.com/us/r1000/011/Music/73/55/c3/mzi.wcqgtuty.100x100-75.jpg", "collectionPrice":13.99,
"trackPrice":1.29, "releaseDate":"2007-11-13 08:00:00 Etc/GMT", "collectionExplicitness":"notExplicit",
"trackExplicitness":"notExplicit", "discCount":1, "discNumber":1, "trackCount":24, "trackNumber":20, "trackTimeMillis":508187,
"country":"USA", "currency":"USD", "primaryGenreName":"Rock", "contentAdvisoryRating":null},

Figure 1.7 First step to configure the iTunes web service.

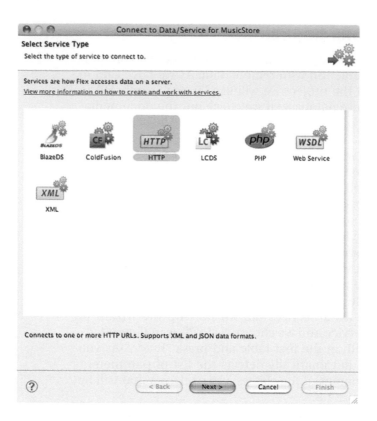

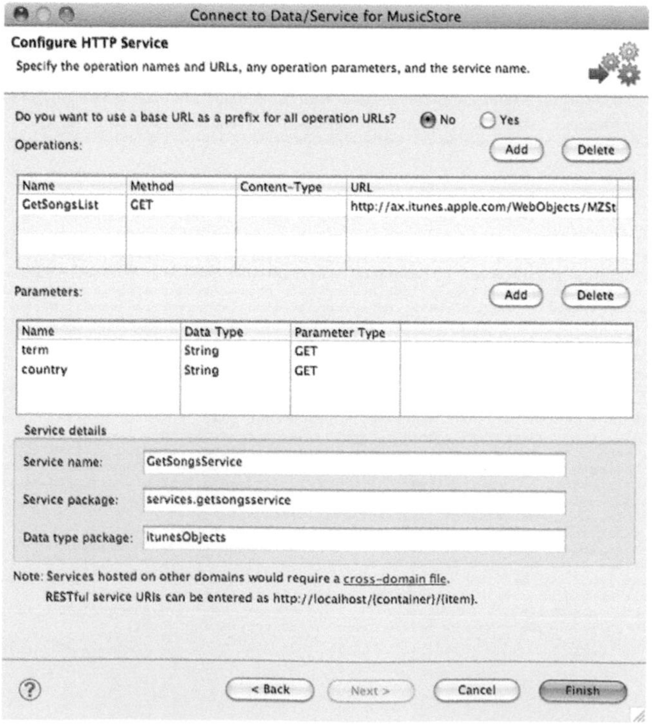

Figure 1.8 Configuring the iTunes web service.

At this point all the code needed to run the web service has been generated and we can test it directly in Flash Builder. Just right-click on the service and select "Test Operation." You can also change values to further verify the correctness of the web service, as in Figure 1.9.

We are getting close to the first run of the application. Though not strictly required it is suggested to also create return type classes, to better manipulate information afterwards. We right-click again on the service and choose "Configure Return Type," as explained earlier. We follow the autodetect procedure by providing two real values, as we did during testing (Figure 1.10).

This will call the actual service and analyze the result. In our case we are interested in the array named "results," which describes the list of songs retrieved. We name the data type "Song" (Figure 1.11).

Now the definition of web services is complete and we hook it up to the user interface.

Figure 1.9 Testing the iTunes web service with different parameters.

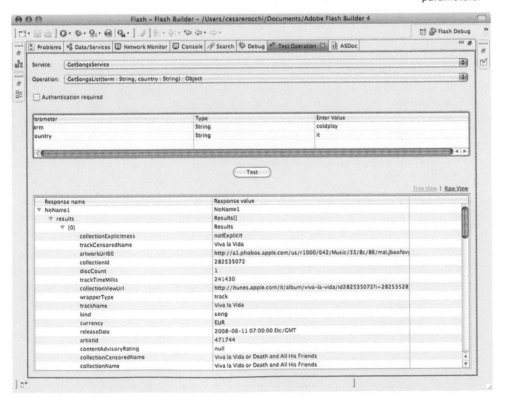

Figure 1.10 Providing values to the return type configurator.

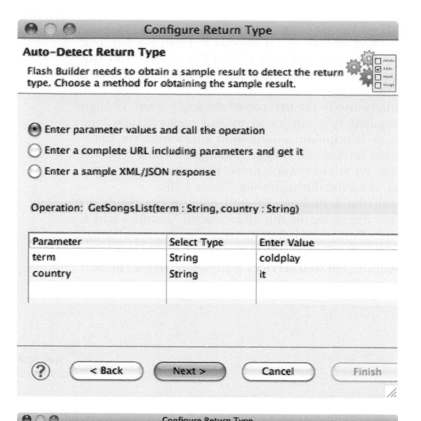

Figure 1.11 Naming the types returned by the web service.

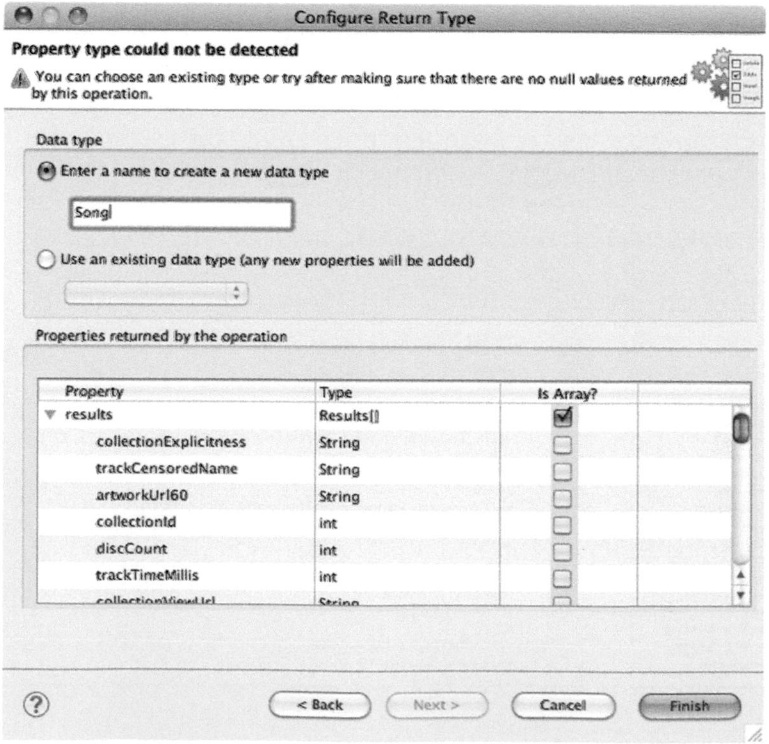

Connecting Backend to User Interface

As explained before there is a real quick way to connect the web service code with the user interface, via drag and drop. We select the `searchSuccessful` state and from the Data/Services tab we drag our "GetSongsList" onto the list component (Figure 1.12).

We have only one service and one operation, already selected for us. As the data provider we select "results," which is the array of songs returned by the server. The items in the list component are displayed by means of a label, to which we assign the field "trackName." Finally, we can click "OK" (Figure 1.13).

This automatic procedure saves some typing but does not exactly do what we do. If you check out the code the search action is triggered by the `creationComplete` event of the list component, whereas we want it to be run when the button is clicked.

```
<s:List ...
  includeIn="searchSuccessful" id="list"
  creationComplete="
    list_creationCompleteHandler(event)"
  labelField="trackName">

  <s:AsyncListView ... />

</s:List>
```

Figure 1.12 Connecting a web service to a component.

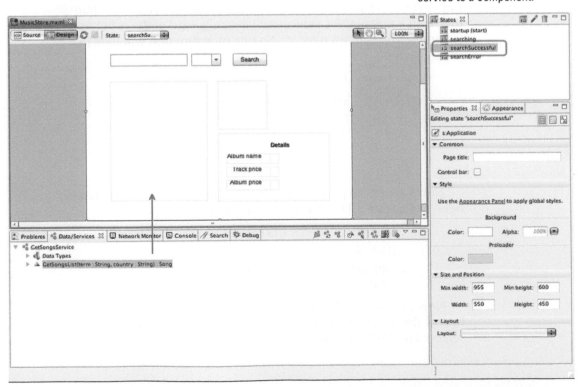

Figure 1.13 Configuring the web service.

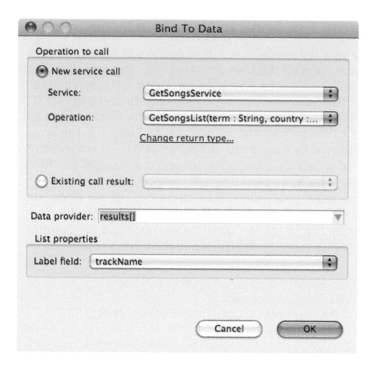

We can associate this function to the click event of the button, but first let's clean it up a bit. We change the name of the handler with a meaningful name, and we can get rid of the event as a parameter (we do not need it). So our new function will look like the following.

```
protected function searchSongs():void {

GetSongsListResult.token =
    getSongsService.GetSongsList(
        /*Enter value(s) for */ term, country
    );

}
```

Now we have to pass two parameters to the function. First, we need to assign an ID to the input components, as follows.

```
<s:TextInput id="artistInput" ...
    enabled.searching="false"/>

<s:ComboBox id="storeCode" ...
    enabled.searching="false"/>
```

Now we can use these references to update our function. The first is the value of the input field, and the second is the value selected in the combo box.

```
protected function searchSongs():void {

GetSongsListResult.token =
    getSongsService.GetSongsList(
        artistInput.text, storeCode.selectedItem);

}
```

At this point, the combo box is empty so we have to populate it with a list of codes, as follows.

```
[Bindable]

private var stores:ArrayCollection =
            new ArrayCollection(['us', 'it', 'au']);

...

<s:ComboBox id="storeCode"
    dataProvider="{stores}" ... />
```

We are pretty much done. The only thing left is the switch between states according to the current operation performed by the application.

Adding State-Switching Logic

If we look at the GetSongsService component we have a hint of the modification we need to do.

```
<getsongsservice:GetSongsService
    id="getSongsService"
    fault="Alert.show(
        event.fault.faultString + '\n' +
        event.fault.faultDetail)"
    showBusyCursor="true"/>
```

Here the fault event (fired when there is an error in searching) shows an alert. We can substitute this handler with the following code.

```
<getsongsservice:GetSongsService
    id="getSongsService"
    fault=" currentState='searchError' "
    showBusyCursor="true"/>
```

The "opposite" event (triggered when the search is successful) is named result. In that case we switch to the searchSuccessful state.

```
<getsongsservice:GetSongsService
    id="getSongsService"
    result=" currentState='searchSuccessful' "
    fault=" currentState='searchError' "
    showBusyCursor="true"/>
```

Our application is getting to the final form. We only left out the searching state. This is activated when we press the Search button. Instead of using MXML we add the following instructions in the function, right before the call to the web service.

```
protected function searchSongs():void {

    currentState = 'searching';
    GetSongsListResult.token =
        getSongsService.GetSongsList(
            artistInput.text, storeCode.selectedItem);

}
```

This will display the feedback message and will disable input components while the application is interacting with the server.

The final touch is to display information about a song when it is selected from the list. We connect the form and image components to the list by means of some binding expression, as follows.

```
<mx:Image x="273" y="164"
    width="100" height="100"
    includeIn="searchSuccessful"
    source="{list.selectedItem.artworkUrl100}"/>

<mx:Form x="273" y="272"
    width="250" height="140"
    includeIn="searchSuccessful">

    <mx:FormHeading label="Details"/>

    <mx:FormItem label="Album name">
      <s:Label
        text="{list.selectedItem.
        collectionName}"/>
    </mx:FormItem>

    <mx:FormItem label="Track price">
      <s:Label
        text="{list.selectedItem.trackName}" />
    </mx:FormItem>

    <mx:FormItem label="Album price">
      <s:Label
        text="{list.selectedItem.
        collectionPrice}"/>
    </mx:FormItem>
</mx:Form>
```

Now our application is complete. We can run and see that it works as expected. At startup we have just the input components (Figure 1.14). During the search process we have the correct feedback (Figure 1.15). Results are rendered by title. When we select a song details and the album's image are correctly displayed (Figure 1.16). Errors are shown by means of a label (Figure 1.17).

Figure 1.14 Music Store application at startup.

Figure 1.15 Feedback during the search.

Figure 1.16 Details about a song.

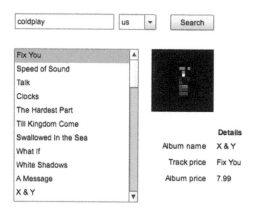

Figure 1.17 Notification of an error.

Possible Improvements

The project described in this chapter can be improved in a number of ways to enhance also your knowledge of Flash Builder and the Flex library. Here is a suggested list of changes:

- Detect when the input is empty.
- Enable the Search button only when the input field is not empty.
- Add a loading state (or a preloader) to the album image.
- Build a similar example and, instead of using the design view, edit states via MXML code.
- Detect when the list of results is empty and provide feedback accordingly.

BUILDING USER INTERACTION

Learning events and components behavior is essential to build and deploy effective Rich Internet applications (RIAs) in Flex. In this section we will have a more detailed look at components and the way we can use them in our projects. After an introduction to events and key elements in Flex applications, we will learn how to use containers and states. We will see a full example of how to implement a login panel that provides feedback according to the response on the server side. We will also illustrate how to use validators and to use the debugger.

Events

As we have seen in Section 1, a component in Flex has many features like size, style, and behavior. A key feature of Flex components is the ability to dispatch and/or listen to events.

An event is something that happens. Whether initiated by the user (e.g., a click) or by the system (e.g., an image is loaded) an event is a data structure used to notify that something has happened. Following is a list of events:

- The user resized a window.
- The login information is wrong.
- The Flex application has started.
- The user interface (UI) of the Flex application has been rendered.
- The user changed the value of a text input.
- The URL specified does not exist.
- The application is going to be closed.

Events are not specific of Flex. In fact, they were already included in ActionScript version 1. Although changed and refined since then, events still remain a key component of the Flash platform and client web programming in general.

When we program for the Web we have to keep in mind that it is an asynchronous "world." This means there is wait time. For example, when you need to log in to a service, the following happens "under the hood" (roughly):

- Read data provided (login and password).
- Ask the backend to validate data.
- Show the result (correct or wrong).

The second operation, ask the backend, is the asynchronous one. In this case you ask something and you wait for the response. This does not mean that your application is blocked. Indeed, all the parts that do not depend on the result of the asynchronous operation can be executed (e.g., banner at the bottom, news from the blog, etc.). This is an advantage in that it shows the user that not everything is "stuck." The downside of this approach is that the programmer has to deal with asynchronous programming and notifications. For example, each asynchronous operation can have at least a positive and a negative result. As a developer/designer it is a good practice to specify both and to notify the user accordingly. Moreover, in the HTTP world, things can go wrong for many reasons, so it is not unusual to notify specific errors or situations. For example, the application cannot log in because of the following errors:

- Username does not exist.
- Wrong combination of username and password.
- No Internet connection.
- Login service unavailable.

Although all these situations are similar to the final user ("Can't login") there are differences that we might want to signal at the UI level. That means for each of these events we can provide a UI behavior (e.g., pop up a message). Events in Flash are important not just because we know when something happens, but because we can associate one or more actions to an event. In fact, when you talk about an event there are two key actions associated: listening and reacting. Let's try to start with an example.

The Login Scenario

In Section 1 we learned how to build the UI of a login form. Let's resume from there. When the user clicks the button the application sends data to the backend and waits for a response. At this point the developer has to have already specified all the behaviors of the UI in the different cases. To start, let's just consider two generic cases, *success* and *failure*.

First of all, it is a good practice to notify the user that something is happening. When he or she clicks the login button we should show a spinner or some "ongoing-activity" signal, and we should remember to remove it whether the procedure is a success or a failure. Wait a second ... aren't these states? Yes! Then we could arrange our logic in term of states. How? We listen to the login service on the backend and we display the UI panel accordingly.

States and Events for Login Scenario

We can dispose our application according to Table 2.1. The first event is triggered by the user and the second and third are generated by the backend. The UI can react to all of these events and switch to the correspondent state. First let's set up the UI. Following is part of the code developed in Section 1. The graphical counterpart is shown in Figure 2.1.

Table 2.1 Correspondence between Events and States in Our Application

Event	State
Login button click	Logging
LogIn success	LoggedIn
Login failure	ErrorInLogging

```
<s:Application
 xmlns:fx="http://ns.adobe.com/mxml/2009"
... >

 <s:Panel x="211" y="99" title="Login">
        <mx:Form >

     <mx:FormItem label="Username">
      <s:TextInput/>
     </mx:FormItem>

     <mx:FormItem label="Password">
      <s:TextInput
 displayAsPassword="true"/>
     </mx:FormItem>

     <mx:FormItem >
      <s:Button label="Login"/>
     </mx:FormItem>

    </mx:Form>
   </s:Panel>
 </s:Application>
```

Figure 2.1 The Flash login form.

We will follow the same method adopted in Section 1: we first create the needed elements and then arrange them according to the state. To the current implementation we need to add a label and a rectangle. Table 2.2 shows how these elements are used.

In the `Initial` state the new label and the rectangle are hidden. In the first, we have to show just the label and set its text. The second and the third are similar and display both the rectangle and the label. We have already seen how to work with states in Flash Builder (see Section 1), so we simply report the code you should end up with.

Table 2.2 Login Form: Events, States, and UI Appearance

Event	State	UI
Login button click	Logging	Label = "Authenticating ..."; Rectangle = invisible
Login success	LoggedIn	Label = "Login Successful"; Rectangle = green
Login failure	ErrorInLogging	Label = "Error in Logging In"; Rectangle = red

```
<s:Application ...
  minWidth="955" minHeight="600">

<s:states>
  <s:State name="Initial"/>
  <s:State name="Logging"/>
  <s:State name="LoggedIn"/>
  <s:State name="ErrorInLogging"/>
</s:states>

<s:Panel x="211" y="99" title="Login">
  <mx:Form >
    <mx:FormItem label="Username">
      <s:TextInput/>
    </mx:FormItem>

    <mx:FormItem label="Password">
      <s:TextInput displayAsPassword="true"/>
    </mx:FormItem>

    <mx:FormItem >
      <s:Button label="Login"/>
    </mx:FormItem>

    <mx:FormItem >
      <s:Label />
    </mx:FormItem>
  </mx:Form>
```

```
<s:Rect
    height="20" width="20"
    x="200" y="99">

  <s:fill>
      <mx:SolidColor />
  </s:fill>

</s:Rect>

</s:Panel>
</s:Application>
```

If you preview this, you will notice that the label is empty and the rectangle is black (default color). Now we have to declare where to include these elements and how their properties (color and text) vary according to states. Let's start with the label.

```
<mx:FormItem >
  <s:Label
    excludeFrom="Initial"
    text.Logging="Authenticating..."
    text.LoggedIn="Login Successful"
    text.ErrorInLogging="Error in Logging In"
  />
</mx:FormItem>
```

Instead of including it in three states, we exclude it from the `Initial` state. Setting text is pretty intuitive. Now we can move on to the rectangle.

```
<s:Rect
  excludeFrom="Initial,Logging">
  <s:fill>
    <mx:SolidColor
      color.LoggedIn="0x608e34"
      color.ErrorInLogging="0x8e3434"
  />

  </s:fill>
</s:Rect>
```

The UI is now ready to react according to different events. Let's see how we can listen to events and associate an action each time we catch one.

Login Web Service

Here we illustrate a simple web service that *simulates* login. Please do not consider it as good backend programming. It is just a way to show how the UI works in case of success and failure. We will do it in PHP, just because we think it is easier to set up locally.

 In this example our Flash application is going to "speak" XML with the backend, so we could implement a backend based on a different technology/ language (e.g., Java, .net, Lisp, etc.). As long as the XML is the same our Flash application will continue to work with no need of modifications.

In our example we have set up MAMP,[1] a bundle that allows installing the Apache web server, with PHP and MySQL configured, on a local machine.[2] Let's have a look at the code.

```php
<?php
if(($_POST['username'] != "") AND
  ($_POST['password'] != ""))
{
$u=$_POST['username'];
$p=$_POST['password'];

  if($u == "cesare" AND $p == "password")

    echo "<login>ok</login>";

  }
  else {

    echo "<login>wrong</login>";

  }
}
else {
        echo "<login>nodata</login>";
}?>
```

The output of this service is always in XML format. It is an "ok" string if the username and the password are matched, and "wrong" otherwise. A third case is detected when no values are passed (nodata). Parameters are passed as POST variables, named 'username' and 'password'.[3] These are two arbitrary names, which can be changed as you wish. It is important that they are the same both on the client (Flash) and the server (PHP in this case). If there is no match the application might not work as expected, so it is strongly suggested that developers agree on the names of variables on the frontend and backend.

Hooking UI to Web Service

Now we will see how to connect the UI to the web service we have just set up. We already know how to do it by using the Data/Services wizard of Flash Builder (see Section 1). Since we should now feel more comfortable with this code tab, we will build this example by typing code. We need one Flex element we have not introduced so far: HTTPService. This is a class that allows

---

[1] See *http://www.mamp.info.*

[2] There is also a Microsoft Windows version at *http://www.wampserver.com/en/*

[3] The difference between GET and POST is out of the scope of the book. To learn the difference, see *http://wiki.answers.com/Q/What_is_the_difference:between_get_and_post_method_in_HTTP.*

loading a specific URL via the HTTP protocol. The minimal elements to provide in order to make it work are a URL and a call to its method, `send()`.

```
<mx:HTTPService
  id="loginService"
  url="http://localhost/dvbook/login.php"
          >
  . . .
    loginService.send();
```

These two pieces of code would be enough to load a URL. Usually when you load a URL you want to manipulate loaded data or notify whether something went wrong. What enables this in Flash? Events! If you check out the completion of HTTPService there are lots of properties, some of which have an orange icon. Those are events.[4] In our scenario we are interested in two events, `fault` and `result`. The names are pretty intuitive but they need some explanation anyway.

The `result` event is fired when the URL is correctly loaded. This does not mean that the login is successful every time we receive that event. For example, if we submit the wrong combination of username and password the URL is correctly retrieved but the login is not successful. The same happens when we do not provide data in the `POST` variables. So we need a way to detect not just the type of event but also its content. There is more on this later.

When is the `fault` event fired? When the web service is not available, or when your client is not connected to the Internet. In general, when there is a communication problem between the service and the client. In this case we could notify it on the UI.

Now we know what the *hooks* are to use information provided by the HTTPService class. But, what are the fillers of event properties? Methods. Technically, a function can also be a filler for an event property, though it is a widely adopted (and correct) practice to use methods. Let's see some code.

```
<mx:HTTPService
  id="loginService"
  result="onResult(event)"
  fault="onFault(event)"
  url="http://localhost/dvbook/login.php"
  method="POST"
>
```

[4] You can check out documentation about events of HTTPService at *http://help.adobe .com/en_US/FlashPlatform/reference/actionscript/3/mx/rpc/http/mxml/HTTPService .html#eventSummary.*

On lines 3–4 we specify two methods, `onResult` and `onFault`, which will be called when the service loads correctly or not. We should remember to specify a formal parameter, `event` in this case, which will hold the content of the event (e.g., "ok" or "wrong" strings defined in the web service). The URL is the same as above, while we should remember to specify that it is a `POST` request, for the default value is `GET`.

As we said before, parameters are to be passed to the server for verification. HTTPService has been defined to specify parameters as children, as follows.

```
<mx:HTTPService
  id="loginService"
  result="onResult(event)"
  fault="onFault(event)"
  url="http://localhost/dvbook/login.php"
  method="POST"
>
  <mx:request>

    <username>{userInput.text}</username>
    <password>{passwordInput.text}</password>

  </mx:request>

</mx:HTTPService>
```

Here we can see another useful usage of binding, which allows us to dynamically read the values of the form and send them directly to the web service. We are now left with the definition of methods. These, when executed as responses to an event, are commonly referred to as *callbacks*.

```
<fx:Script>
<![CDATA[

  import mx.rpc.events.FaultEvent;
  import mx.rpc.events.ResultEvent;

  private function onResult(event:ResultEvent):void {
// Code when successful
  }
  private function onFault(event:FaultEvent):void {
    // Code when failure
  }
]]>

</fx:Script>
```

We should be already familiar with this syntax. The only important aspect to highlight is that events are typed (`ResultEvent` and `FaultEvent`) and those classes need to be imported.

Now it is time to associate some event to the UI states defined above. If we receive a `fault` event we can set the UI to the `ErrorInLogging` state, as follows.

```
private function onFault(event:FaultEvent):void {
    this.currentState = 'ErrorInLogging';
}
```

The `result` case is a bit more complex, because we need to identify the reason of the callback. We will define the method as follows.

```
private function onResult(event:ResultEvent):void {

var res:Boolean =
String(event.result.login) == "ok";

    if (res)
        this.currentState = 'LoggedIn';

else
  this.currentState = 'ErrorInLogging';
}
```

To identify the reason of the callback we have to check the content of the `result` property of the event, which stores the values as we have defined them on the server. The only positive case is when such a value is equal to "ok," which is associated to the `LoggedIn` state (green square). All the rest are equal to a negative feedback.

The last step is to trigger the send procedure when the button is pressed. To be more clear, we will define another function and associate it to the click of the button.

```
private function authenticate():void {
    this.currentState = 'Logging';
    loginService.send();
}
...
<mx:FormItem >
  <s:Button label="Login"
click="authenticate()"/>
</mx:FormItem>
```

Now we are ready to test our application. If you test it locally you probably won't notice the switch from the `Initial` state to the authenticating phase, but as soon as the service will be online, you and your user will appreciate that feedback. Figures 2.2 and 2.3 are, respectively, two screenshots when the login is successful or not.

Figure 2.2 Login correct.

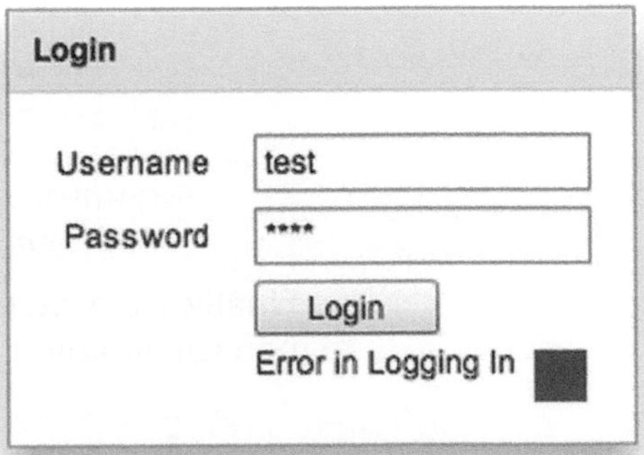

Figure 2.3 Login wrong.

Events in ActionScript 3

In this section we will see how to use events in ActionScript code. If you check the source code generated during the previous example you might get a glimpse of how to handle events in ActionScript 3. Here we will rebuild part of the previous example in ActionScript 3. We will specifically rewrite the declaration of the services and its hooks to the UI. Here are the steps to do.

We can delete the ⟨fx:Declarations⟩ tag and its content. We create an instance variable of HTTPService as follows.

```
private var loginService:HTTPService =
    new HTTPService();
```

Although the name is the same, there are two HTTPService classes: the one used in the first example is from the package mx.rpc.http.mxml.HTTPService, whereas this is part of mx.rpc.http.HTTPService. The functionality is the same.

We then declare a function to set up the attributes of the loginService variable. We will call this function init.

```
private function init():void {

  loginService.url = "http://localhost/dvbook/login.
  php";
  loginService.method = "POST";

  loginService.addEventListener(
      ResultEvent.RESULT,
      onResult);

  loginService.addEventListener(
      FaultEvent.FAULT,
      onFault);
}
```

We will execute this function when the application is ready, so we will attach it to the creationComplete event, as follows.

```
<s:Application
    xmlns:fx="http://ns.adobe.com/mxml/2009"
    xmlns:s="library://ns.adobe.com/flex/spark"
    xmlns:mx="library://ns.adobe.com/flex/mx"
    minWidth="955" minHeight="600"
    creationComplete="init()">
```

Finally, we have to slightly modify the authenticate function to manage parameters.

```
private function authenticate():void {

  this.currentState = 'Logging';

  var r:Object = new Object();
  r.username = userInput.text;
```

```
    r.password = passwordInput.text;
    loginService.send(r);
}
```

And here is the end of our "porting" to ActionScript 3. This will have the same functionality of the application built above. You might wonder: Why did we see both versions? Because in real-life projects you will meet many situations and it is better to know how to write/modify both MXML and ActionScript 3 code. For example, later in this section we will see how to decouple logic and UI in the login example.

To consult the documentation, go to the Help item in the menu of the Flash Builder and choose "Flash Builder Help." This opens an Adobe AIR application that shows documentation, examples, and a lot more information related to ActionScript 3, Flex, and Flash Builder.

Custom Events

Every component of the Flex library has an associated set of events. To find which events pertain to a component you can check the documentation. For example, Figure 2.4 shows a portion of the documentation related to the Button class.

As you can see, each event has a name and a description about when it is dispatched. Although there are already many events defined for each component you might want to define a new type of event, with its own data structure, for your application. For example, your boss might ask you to do the following: *Whenever the button is clicked dispatch an event that carries the label of the button and a timestamp.*

The first step is to start the wizard to add a new class. We already know how to do it. In this case, we extend the class

Figure 2.4 Events for the Button class.

Protected Methods

▶ Show Inherited Protected Methods

Method	Defined By
clickHandler(event:MouseEvent):void The default handler for the MouseEvent.CLICK event.	Button
mouseDownHandler(event:MouseEvent):void The default handler for the MouseEvent.MOUSE_DOWN event.	Button
mouseUpHandler(event:MouseEvent):void The default handler for the MouseEvent.MOUSE_UP event.	Button
rollOutHandler(event:MouseEvent):void The default handler for the MouseEvent.ROLL_OUT event.	Button
rollOverHandler(event:MouseEvent):void The default handler for the MouseEvent.ROLL_OVER event.	Button

Events

▶ Show Inherited Events

Event	Summary	Defined By
buttonDown	Dispatched when the user presses the Button control.	Button
change	Dispatched when the selected property changes for a toggle Button control.	Button
dataChange	Dispatched when the data property changes.	Button

flash.events.Event. The wizard saves us some typing and we should end up with the following code.

```
package com.studiomagnolia.events
{
 import flash.events.Event;
 public class MyCustomEvent extends Event
 {

  public function MyCustomEvent(type:String,
      bubbles:Boolean=false,
      cancelable:Boolean=false){
    super(type, bubbles, cancelable);
 }
```

Now the requirement is to have a custom event that carries some extra information with respect to the base class event. Let's add two variables to hold such information.

```
public class MyCustomEvent extends Event
{
    public var label:String;
    public var timestamp:Date;

    public function MyCustomEvent(...) {...}
}
```

It is a good practice to add also a static constant to identify the event. As we will see, an event requires a string to identify its type. Of course, you can provide the string on-the-fly when you create the event like the following code.

```
var e = new MyCustomEvent("myCustomEvent"...);
```

Since the event type is just a string it is easy to mistype and the compiler will not tell you anything about possible errors. A widely known convention has spread: the name of the event is specified only as a constant in the class declaration, as follows.

```
public class MyCustomEvent extends Event {

    public static const MYCUSTOMEVENTTYPE:String =
                "myCustomEventType";
    public var label:String;
    public var timestamp:Date;

    public function MyCustomEvent(...) { ...}
}
```

This way it is almost impossible to mistype the event type, since we will create it by using the constant.

```
new MyCustomEvent(MyCustomEvent.MYCUSTOMEVENTTYPE,...)
```

In essence, we are done. We can create an event and attach the information required when the button is clicked.

```
var e:MyCustomEvent = new MyCustomEvent(
        MyCustomEvent.MYCUSTOMEVENTTYPE);
e.label = myButton.label;
e.timestamp = new Date();

// code to dispatch e
```

As an alternative, we can modify the constructor to store values directly at instantiation time.

```
public function MyCustomEvent(
        type:String,
        label:String,
        timestamp:Date,
        bubbles:Boolean=false,
        cancelable:Boolean=false)
{
    super(type, bubbles, cancelable);
    this.label = label;
    this.timestamp = timestamp;
}
```

In this case we can create the event all in one line of code.

```
var e:MyCustomEvent = new MyCustomEvent(
        MyCustomEvent.t MYCUSTOMEVENTTYPE,
        "Label",
        new Date());
```

Let's see how we can use the event in a Flex application.

```
<s:Application ... >

<fx:Script>
<![CDATA[

import com.studiomagnolia.events.MyCustomEvent;

protected function onMyClick(event:MouseEvent):void {

  var e:MyCustomEvent = new MyCustomEvent(
        MyCustomEvent.MYCUSTOMEVENTTYPE,
        e.label,
        new Date());

  this.dispatchEvent(e); // notification of new event

}

]]>
</fx:Script>
```

```
<s:Button
    id="myButton"
    click="onMyClick(event)"
    label="My Button"/>

</s:Application>
```

Consuming Custom Events

Now that we know how to build custom events we probably want to see the other flip of the coin: how to listen to custom events. Let's do more than that. We will build a full example based on a refactoring of the login application implemented above. From an architectural viewpoint this example has a problem: it is all done in one class. Mixing up logic and UI code is not a good practice, especially if you like to reuse your code in other projects. To favor this practice it is important to isolate similar functionalities and encapsulate them in classes/components. For example, in the login example above, we can isolate the UI from the logic—that is, the code that handles the communication with the backend. In other words, out of the code above, we can build a UILogin and an Authenticator class. One step at a time.

Let's start with the logic. We will embed the communication with the backend in a single class. This is the skeleton of the class.

```
public class Authenticator
{
  private var loginService:HTTPService =
      new HTTPService();

  public function Authenticator()
  {

    // set up some property

  }

  private function onResult(event:ResultEvent):void
  {

    // handle the result event

  }

  private function onFault(event:FaultEvent):void
  {

    // handle the fault event
  }
  public function authenticate(username:String,
                  password:String):void
  {
    // start the authentication process
  }
}
```

In the constructor we set up some of the functionalities of the class. We then handle two types of events (result and false). Instances of this class can be used by means of the authenticate function. In the constructor we decorate the instance of loginService.

```
public function Authenticator()
{
loginService.url =
    "http://localhost/dvbook/login.php";

loginService.method = "POST";
loginService.addEventListener(
    ResultEvent.RESULT, onResult
    );

loginService.addEventListener(
    FaultEvent.FAULT, onFault
    );
}
```

The authenticate function builds the parameters list and calls the service.

```
public function authenticate(username:String,
    password:String):void
{
    var credentials:Object = new Object();
    credentials.username = username;
    credentials.password = password;

    loginService.send(credentials);

}
```

In the two handlers we manipulate data returned by the server and dispatch new events accordingly. The onResult handler is defined as follows.

```
private function onResult(event:ResultEvent):void
{
    var res:Boolean =
        String(event.result.login) == "ok";

    var time:Date = new Date();

    if (res)
    {
      dispatchEvent(
          new LoginEvent(
            LoginEvent.LOGINSUCCESSFUL,
            time)
    );
    }
```

```
              else
              {
                dispatchEvent(
                  new LoginEvent(LoginEvent.LOGINFAILED,
                  time)
                  );
              }
            }
```

Assuming events are already implemented, if we compile now we get a compilation error: "Call to a possibly undefined method dispatchEvent." This is due to the fact that an ActionScript class cannot dispatch an event per se. The previous example worked because we were in a <Application> context, which is part of a hierarchy of classes that either extend the EventDispatcher class or implement the IEventDispatcher interface. In our case it is enough to make the Authenticator class to extend EventDispatcher to be allowed to call the dispatchEvent method. As you can see there is no more reference to UI elements—Authenticator just calls a URL and dispatches the event. Whenever you happen to meet a situation like this you are in front of well-architected (and reusable) code.

Now let's see how the LoginEvent is defined.

```
        public class LoginEvent extends Event
        {
            public static const LOGINSUCCESSFULL:String =
                             "loginSuccessFull";

            public static const LOGINFAILED:String =
                             "loginFailed";

            public var timestamp:Date;

            public function LoginEvent(
                         type:String,
                         timestamp:Date,
                         bubbles:Boolean=false,
                         cancelable:Boolean=false
                         )
            {
                super(type, bubbles, cancelable);
                this.timestamp = timestamp;
            }
        }
```

In this case one class is enough. We just use the event type to distinguish whether it is successful or not. Now we can plug our new class into the previous Flex application. We substitute the code with the following.

```
private var loginService:Authenticator =
        new Authenticator();

protected function init():void
{
        loginService.addEventListener(
                LoginEvent.LOGINSUCCESSFULL,
                onSuccess);

  loginService.addEventListener(
          LoginEvent.LOGINFAILED,
          onFailure);
}

private function authenticate():void
{

  this.currentState = 'Logging';

  loginService.authenticate(
          userInput.text,
          passwordInput.text);

}
private function onSuccess (event:LoginEvent):void
{
        this.currentState = 'LoggedIn';
}

private function onFailure (event:LoginEvent):void
{
        this.currentState = 'ErrorInLogging';
}
```

See how much cleaner it is? We have a setup phase in the `init` function and we react to two events (`success` and `failure`), which respectively change the UI into positive or negative feedback. In the previous example the Flex application did everything: logic, UI, and connection between the two. Now we have isolated logic in a class, so the application still does both UI and connection. We want to achieve a situation where the application connects just UI and logic. To get to such a scenario we have to isolate UI in a visual component.

Building a Custom Component

So far we have seen how to use Flex's built-in components. We will now learn how to create our custom components. The procedure is pretty similar to the creation of a new ActionScript class. We are helped by a wizard dialog, which can be started by right-clicking on the project, as in Figure 2.5.

The wizard helps us in the definition of the features for the new component. First we have to specify a package. To be consistent with the rest we add the component to a new package called

In this case we are building a new component in the sense of a "conglomerate" of single components. Sometimes, building a custom component also refers to the construction of a new Flex component from scratch. This is out of the scope of this book.

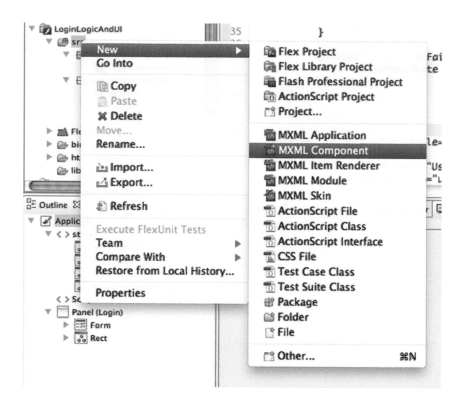

Figure 2.5 How to start the creation of a new component.

com.studiomagnolia.view. We call the component LoginPanel and we specify is has a basic layout, extending the Panel class (see Figure 2.6). We end up with a code similar to this one.

```
<s:Panel
    xmlns:fx="http://ns.adobe.com/mxml/2009"
    xmlns:s="library://ns.adobe.com/flex/spark"
    xmlns:mx="library://ns.adobe.com/flex/mx">

    <s:layout>
        <s:BasicLayout/>
    </s:layout>

</s:Panel>
```

Now we can literally cut and paste the definition of states, which was originally included in the Flex application. States, in fact, pertain to UI.

```
<s:Panel ... >

<s:states>
    <s:State name="Initial"/>
    <s:State name="Logging"/>
    <s:State name="LoggedIn"/>
```

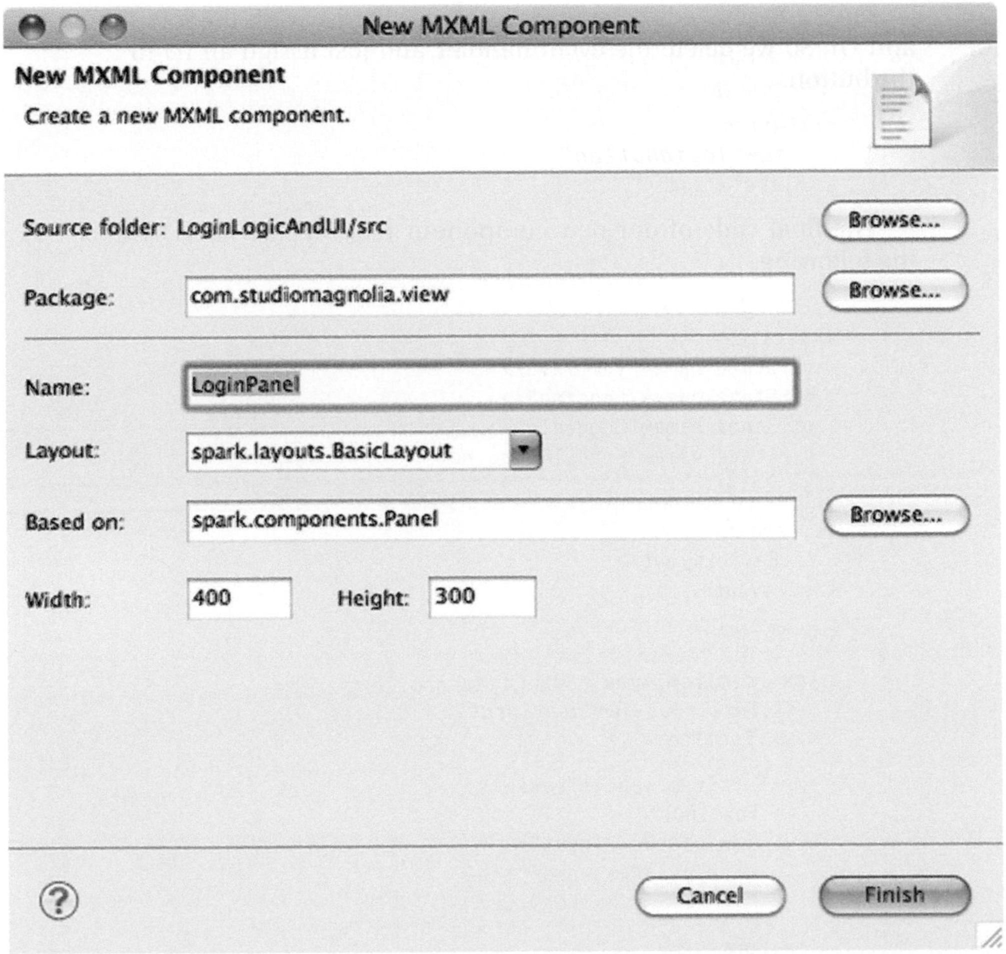

Figure 2.6 Details of the new component.

```
    <s:State name="ErrorInLogging"/>
</s:states>

<s:layout>
    <s:BasicLayout/>
</s:layout>

</s:Panel>
```

We can also cut and paste the code that draws the form, but we need a small modification to expose the Login button. As you probably remember, the `authenticate` action was directly wired to the click event of the button.

```
<s:Button
    label="Login"
    click="authenticate()"/>
```

This is exactly what we want to avoid, hard-wiring the login and UI. So we delete the event handler and just assign an ID to the button.

```
<s:Button
    id="loginButton"
    label="Login"/>
```

The final code of our new component (LoginPanel.mxml) is the following.

```
<s:Panel ... >
<s:states>
  <s:State name="Initial"/>
  <s:State name="Logging"/>
  <s:State name="LoggedIn"/>
  <s:State name="ErrorInLogging"/>
</s:states>

<s:layout>
  <s:BasicLayout/>
</s:layout>

<mx:Form >

  <mx:FormItem label="Username">
    <s:TextInput id="userInput"/>
  </mx:FormItem>

  <mx:FormItem label="Password">
    <s:TextInput
        id="passwordInput"
        displayAsPassword="true" />
              </mx:FormItem>

  <mx:FormItem>
    <s:Button
        id="loginButton"
        label="Login"/>
  </mx:FormItem>

  <mx:FormItem>
    <s:Label
      excludeFrom="Initial"
      text.Logging="Authenticating ..."
      text.LoggedIn="Login Successful"
      text.ErrorInLogging="Error in
            Logging In"
                                  />

  </mx:FormItem>
</mx:Form>

<s:Rect
  height="20" width="20"
  x="200" y="99"
```

```
      excludeFrom="Initial, Logging"
      >

      <s:fill>
        <mx:SolidColor
            color.LoggedIn="0x608e34"
            color.ErrorInLogging="0x8e3434"
        />
      </s:fill>

    </s:Rect>
</s:Panel>
```

We are almost done: We have isolated the logic (`Authenticator` class) and the UI (`LoginPanel` component). At the moment, unlike the previous implementation, they "ignore" each other, in that there is no reference to the view in the Authenticator and vice versa. Now the task of the Flex application is to just create a bridge between an instance of the Authenticator class and an instance of the newly created `LoginPanel`.

We substitute all the MXML code with the following few lines.

```
<view:LoginPanel
        id="loginPanel"
        x="211" y="99"
        title="Login"/>
```

All the view is here. We need to update the `init` function to wire the click of the button to the `authenticate` function.

```
protected function init():void
{

    loginService.addEventListener(
            LoginEvent.LOGINSUCCESSFULL,
            onSuccess);

    loginService.addEventListener(
            LoginEvent.LOGINFAILED,
            onFailure);

    loginPanel.loginButton.addEventListener(
            MouseEvent.CLICK,
            authenticate);

}
```

Finally, we make a slight modification of the `authenticate` function, to point to the text input fields embedded in the login panel.

```
private function authenticate(event:MouseEvent):void {

  loginPanel.currentState = 'Logging';

  loginService.authenticate(
          loginPanel.userInput.text,
          loginPanel.passwordInput.text);

}
```

Here is the complete code after the redesign.

```
<s:Application
  ...
  creationComplete="init()"
  xmlns:view="com.studiomagnolia.view.*">

  <fx:Script>
  <![CDATA[
  import com.studiomagnolia.backend.Authenticator;
  import com.studiomagnolia.events.LoginEvent;

  private var loginService:Authenticator =
              new Authenticator();

  protected function init():void
  {
        loginService.addEventListener(
              LoginEvent.LOGINSUCCESSFULL,
              onSuccess);

    loginService.addEventListener(
          LoginEvent.LOGINFAILED,
          onFailure);

    loginPanel.loginButton.addEventListener(
          MouseEvent.CLICK,
          authenticate);
  }

  private function authenticate(
              event:MouseEvent):void
  {
    loginPanel.currentState = 'Logging';

    loginService.authenticate(
          loginPanel.userInput.text,
          loginPanel.passwordInput.text);

  }
  private function onSuccess (
          event:LoginEvent):void
  {

    loginPanel.currentState = 'LoggedIn';
  }
        private function onFailure (
                    event:LoginEvent):void
     {
    loginPanel.currentState = 'ErrorInLogging';
  }
  ]]>

  </fx:Script>

  <view:LoginPanel
```

```
      id="loginPanel"
      x="211" y="99"
      title="Login"/>

 </s:Application>
```

As you can see, the code is much more understandable and organized, while the functionality is exactly the same as the previous
implementation.

Flex 4 Components

In this section we illustrate some components that can be
immediately useful for your first application: DataGroup and validators. While learning how to use DataGroup we will also explain
how a data-driven component works by illustrating its key features: dataProvider and itemRenderer.

DataGroup

DataGroup is a new layout component introduced in the Flex
4 library. It is one of the simplest and most lightweight ways to
layout and render list-based elements.

Whenever you want to build a simple and easy list-based layout you are encouraged to give DataGroup a try. This is the minimum information you have to specify to create a DataGroup: a
dataProvider, an itemRenderer, and a layout.

```
<s:DataGroup
    dataProvider="{myList}"
    itemRenderer=
      "spark.skins.spark.DefaultItemRenderer" >

<s:layout>

  <s:VerticalLayout/>

</s:layout>

</s:DataGroup>
```

> DataGroup is
> "lightweight"
> because it uses
> virtualization—that is, a
> technique that creates only
> the objects needed to
> render the items displayed.
> For example, if you have a
> list of 40 elements but only
> 10 visible at a time,
> virtualization allows the
> application to have in
> memory only 10 objects
> (instead of 40).

This is a recurrent schema in data-driven components:
dataProvider, itemRenderer, layout. So if you learn it correctly,
working with components is pretty easy. The dataProvider can
be anything that implements the IList interface. If you do not
want to check the documentation to find out which class implements IList, just remember that an ArrayList is fine. For example,
we can populate our DataGroup with a simple list of numbers.

```
for (var i:int = 0; i < 100; i++) {
    myList.addItem(i);
}
```

The `itemRenderer` is the graphical element that displays the information associated to each element of the data list. We already are familiar with the notion of `layout`. Wrapping up the complete code for the example is the following.

```
<s:Application
  creationComplete="init()">

<fx:Script>
<![CDATA[
  import mx.collections.ArrayList;

[Bindable]
private var myList:ArrayList = new ArrayList();

private function init():void
{

  for (var i:int = 0; i < 100; i++) {

      myList.addItem(i);

  }
}
]]>

</fx:Script>

<s:DataGroup
  dataProvider="{myList}"
  itemRenderer=
    "spark.skins.spark.DefaultItemRenderer" >

  <s:layout>
    <s:VerticalLayout/>

  </s:layout>
</s:DataGroup>
</s:Application>
```

Besides being lightweight the DataGroup is also flexible, in that it allows us to render complex objects by means of custom renderers. Let's see an example. We build a simple model, a Person class, with two fields, `name` and `surname`.

```
    package com.studiomagnolia.model
{

  public class Person
  {

    public var name:String;
    public var surname:String;

    public function Person(name:String,
          surname:String)
    {

      this.name = name;
```

```
      this.surname = surname;
    }
  }
}
```

We would like to show information about the person by means of two horizontal labels in the form: Name: <name> Surname: <surname>. The creation of a custom item renderer is similar to the creation of a custom component, as we did above: Just select the corresponding voice from the "New" menu. See Figure 2.7. We put the new renderer in the view package and we call it PersonRenderer. See Figure 2.8.

To the code generated we add information about the layout and the labels, as follows.

```
<s:ItemRenderer ...>

  <s:layout>
   <s:HorizontalLayout/>
  </s:layout>

  <s:Label text="Name: {data.name}" />
  <s:Label text="Surname: {data.surname}" />
</s:ItemRenderer>
```

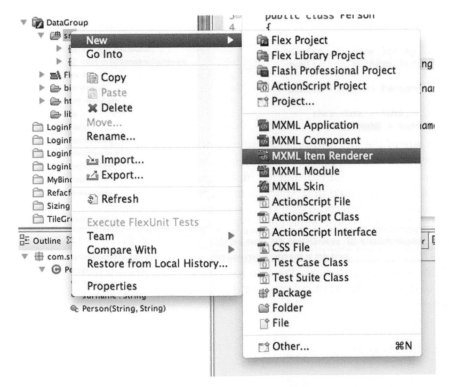

Figure 2.7 The creation of a custom item renderer.

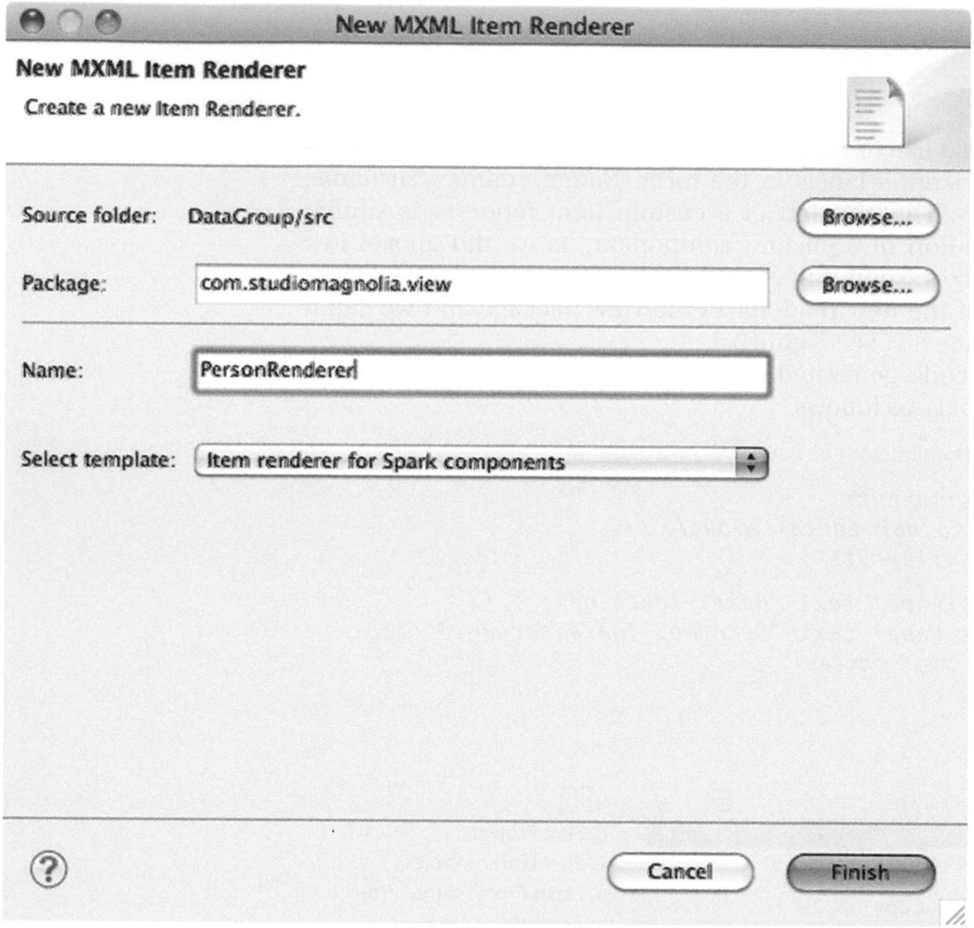

Figure 2.8 We provide details about the custom item renderer.

Here one of the key points is to understand the use of "data." It is the keyword used to refer to the object of which the properties (e.g., name or surname) are displayed in the instance of the render. It is important to notice that "data" is not typed, so if we mistype the name of the property (e.g., data.nsme) the compiler does not complain. Just be careful when you type it, otherwise you can get some unexpected behavior like empty labels.

Let's personalize a bit of the appearance, just to show the capabilities of this approach. We add two states, one of which is meant to define a different color when the mouse hovers over the renderer.

```
<s:ItemRenderer ... >

  <s:states>
    <s:State name="normal"/>
```

```
    <s:State name="hovered"/>
  </s:states>

  <s:layout>
    <s:HorizontalLayout/>
  </s:layout>

  <s:Label
    text="Name: {data.name}"
    color.hovered="#ff0000"/>

  <s:Label
    text="Surname: {data.surname}"
    color.hovered="#ff0000" />

</s:ItemRenderer>
```

Now let's go back to the first version of the application and update it accordingly. Here is the final result.

```
<s:Application ...
  creationComplete="init()">

<fx:Script>
<![CDATA[

  import com.studiomagnolia.model.Person;
  import mx.collections.ArrayList;

  [Bindable]
  private var myList:ArrayList = new ArrayList();

  private function init():void
  {

    for (var i:int = 0; i < 100; i++)
    {
      myList.addItem(new Person(
              "name"+i,
              "surname"+i)
        );
    }
  }
]]>
</fx:Script>

<s:DataGroup
  dataProvider="{myList}"
  itemRenderer=
    "com.studiomagnolia.view.PersonRenderer">

  <s:layout>
    <s:VerticalLayout/>
  </s:layout>

</s:DataGroup>

</s:Application>
```

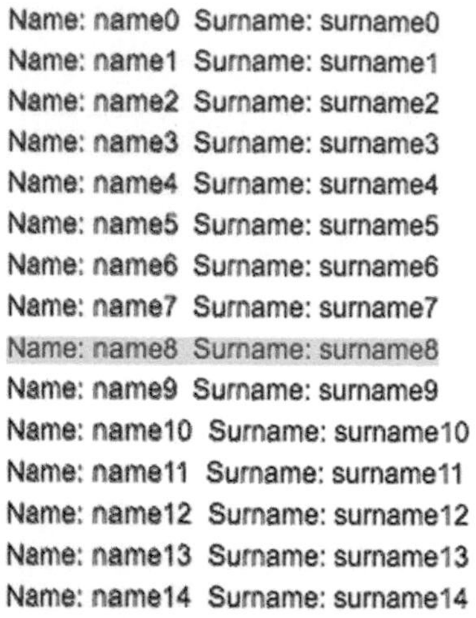

Name: name0 Surname: surname0
Name: name1 Surname: surname1
Name: name2 Surname: surname2
Name: name3 Surname: surname3
Name: name4 Surname: surname4
Name: name5 Surname: surname5
Name: name6 Surname: surname6
Name: name7 Surname: surname7
Name: name8 Surname: surname8
Name: name9 Surname: surname9
Name: name10 Surname: surname10
Name: name11 Surname: surname11
Name: name12 Surname: surname12
Name: name13 Surname: surname13
Name: name14 Surname: surname14

Figure 2.9 DataGroup with custom item renderers.

As you can see, we made a few changes: imported the new Person class, modified the population of the `dataProvider`, and, the most important, changed the class used as renderer in the DataGroup. The final result is shown in Figure 2.9.

The same mechanism applies to all the components that support data-driven rendering like `DataGrid`, `List`, `ComboBox`, etc.

Validating Data

An important aspect of data visualization application is data entry. Whenever you want to update your data it is a good practice to check whether data entered by the user are "valid" with respect to the data model. For example, if we talk about personal information about a user we might require that name and surname must be provided. The same applies for more "formal" data like phone or credit card number, which have specific requirements.

The Flex library comes with built-in validators that ease the task of developers when it's time to validate data entered by users. A validator usually checks a property of a component. In fact, these are the two features to specify in order to make a validator work: an instance of a component and a name of a property, like in the following example.

```
<fx:Declarations>
  <mx:StringValidator
      source="{myTextInput}"
      property="text"
      />

</fx:Declarations>

<s:TextInput id="myTextInput" />
```

First of all, we should notice that validators are not visual components, so they have to be embedded in the Declarations tag. The code above will check the validity of the *text* entered in the `myTextInput` component. Let's now add some constraint.

```
<mx:StringValidator
    source="{myTextInput}"
  property="text"
  tooShortError=
    "This string is too short. Minimum allowed
    length is 4. "

  tooLongError=
    "This string is too long. Maximum allowed
    length is 10."

  minLength="4" maxLength="10"
/>
```

Here we have provided two constraints on the length and their respective error message. If we enter a nonvalid string we can see the effect of validation, as shown in Figure 2.10.

A more common example is the following, where validation is made upon the click of a button.

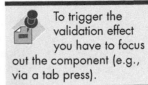

To trigger the validation effect you have to focus out the component (e.g., via a tab press).

ss| This string is too short. Minimum allowed length is 4.

Figure 2.10 DataGroup with custom item renderers.

```
<fx:Declarations>
  <mx:StringValidator
    source="{myTextInput}"
    property="text"

    tooShortError="This string is too short.
        Minimum allowed length is 4. "

    tooLongError="This string is too long.
        Maximum allowed length is 10."

    minLength="4" maxLength="10"å
    trigger="{myButton}"
    triggerEvent="click"

    valid="fLabel.text = 'Validation Succeeded!'"/>
</fx:Declarations>
<s:TextInput id="myTextInput"/>
<s:Button id="myButton" label="Validate" />
<s:Label id="fLabel"/>
```

Besides, with basic string validation components there are also more specific validators for credit card, date, zip code, currency, and regular expressions. For more information you are invited to check out the documentation, especially the mx.validators package at: *http://help.adobe.com/en_US/FlashPlatform/reference/actionscript/3/mx/validators/package-detail.html*

Debugging

We are getting more acquainted with Flex development and Flash Builder. Unfortunately, not all of the code you write works as expected since the beginning: There can be bugs or unexpected behaviors. To find out where problems are generated and how to fix them Flash Builder provides two crucial tools: debugger and stepper. Let's see how to use them.

Debugging is a mode of running a Flex application. It is not the final mode, in which users will interact with your application; rather, it is a special mode in which you can hunt bugs or misbehaviors. To debug a Flex application you need a debug version of the Flash player and a debug version of the SWF file you want to check.

When you click on the Debug button of the Flash Builder a lot of things happen:

Remember: When you update the Flash player on your machine, if you want to debug your applications, you have to install the debug version of the Flash player. For a complete list of the Flash players, go to *http://www.adobe.com/support/flashplayer/downloads.html.*

- A debug version of the application is generated.
- An instance of the browser is started.
- The first time you are asked to switch perspective.
- Trace statements (if any) appear in the console window.
- Errors, if any, appear in the console window as well.

Let's reproduce an error to see the debugger in action. A typical runtime error is thrown when some piece of code tries to access an object that does not exist yet. For example, the following code tries to access a property of a color picker before it is instanciated (pre-initialize).

```
<s:Application
    preinitialize="init()">

        <fx:Script>
            <![CDATA[
                private function init():void {
                trace("picker" +picker.
                selectedColor);
                }

            ]]>
        </fx:Script>

        <mx:ColorPicker id="picker"/>
</s:Application>
```

If we run this code in debug mode we should end up with the Flash Builder arranged as in Figure 2.11 (if we did not do any personalization of the debug perspective).

Figure 2.11 The result of a runtime error in debug mode.

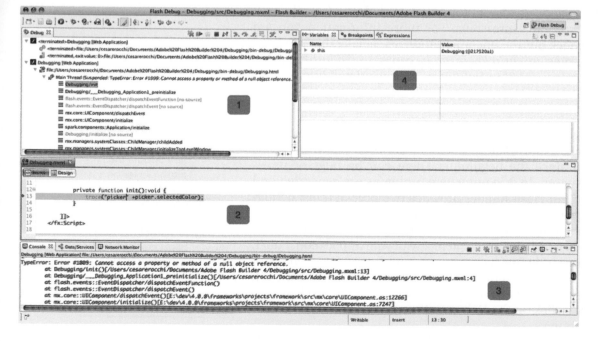

On the upper left in the figure we see the list of function calls until the error is generated (1). In the middle is the source code, already scrolled to the line that generated the error (2). At the bottom is the console with a textual description of the error (3). On the right an interactive list of variables with their current values (4). This will particularly be helpful when we use the stepper.

Stepping

To interrupt the execution of an application and inspect it we have to place a breakpoint. Let's say we have the following piece of code, which stores in a variable the number of times that the user changes color.

```
<s:Application...>
   <fx:Script>
   <![CDATA[

     private var _times:int = 0;

     private function onChange():void {

       _times++;
     }
   ]]>
   </fx:Script>
   <mx:ColorPicker
       id="picker"
       change="onChange()" />

</s:Application>
```

We want to inspect the value of times whenever it changes. We place a breakpoint on the corresponding line, as in Figure 2.12. To place a breakpoint we can double-click the corresponding line or right-click and choose "Toggle breakpoint."

Now if we run in debug mode and we change the selection in the picker the execution halts at that line. At this point we can inspect the value of the _times variable by hovering the mouse on it, or using the Variables tab (Figure 2.13).

> The same operations are required to remove a breakpoint.

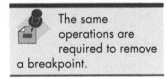

Figure 2.12 A breakpoint.

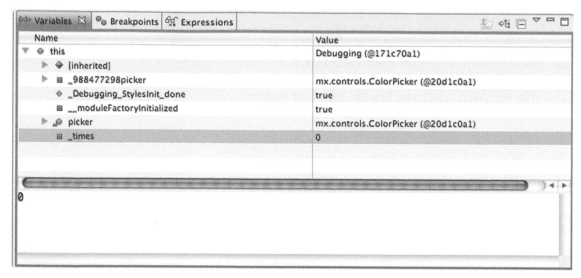

Figure 2.13 The Variables tab.

In this example, Step Into will not work because the operation `_times++` is atomic—that is, it is not defined by any other ActionScript code.

To proceed along the code execution step-by-step we can use the commands in the Debug tab, as shown in Figure 2.14.

Resume will go on with the execution of the code, until another breakpoint is met. Terminate stops the application and the debugger. Step Over will execute the next line of code. Step Into will inspect the code corresponding to the current line. Step Return is the opposite of Step Into.

Figure 2.14 Debug commands.

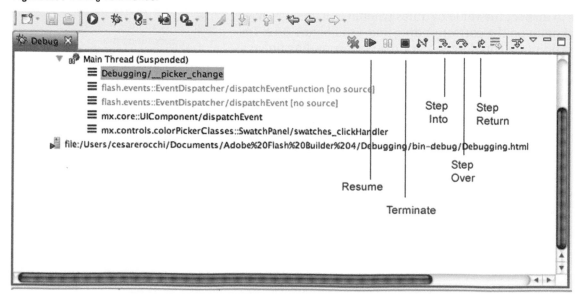

Conditional Breakpoints

An interesting feature has been added to the new Flash Builder 4: conditional breakpoints. Let's suppose you are in the middle of a for loop, which creates some problem when a variable has a value greater than 4. It can be boring (and time consuming) to step over four times whenever we want to achieve the critical situation of our code. In Flash Builder we can now enable the condition that has to be met to stop at a given breakpoint by right-clicking on the circle and selecting "Breakpoint properties" (see Figure 2.15). This opens a window that allows defining when the execution has to pause (see Figure 2.16).

This is a terrific new feature that is now included in Flash Builder 4.

Figure 2.15 To enable conditional breakpoints.

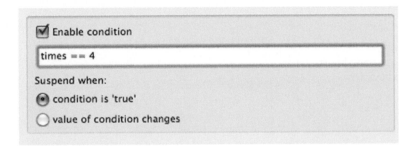

Figure 2.16 The condition to stop the execution.

Conclusion

In this section we have introduced events and we have seen how to manipulate them and how to build custom ones. We have learned states and have also seen how events can be used to decouple logic from UI. We have illustrated a full implementation of a login panel, which provides feedback according to the response on the server side. Finally, we have seen how to use validators and to inspect our code execution by means of the debugger.

PROJECT 2: TWEETS ON A MAP

We will build an application that shows tweets on a map according to the geolocation of a Twitter message. The user will be able to perform a search on Twitter and the results will be displayed on a map accordingly. The development of this project will help us to get acquainted with the usage of web services, events managed in ActionScript, and third-party Flex libraries.

Description of the Project

This kind of application is usually referred to as "mashup," in that it couples information from two different services displayed on the same visual interface. Two services will be used: Twitter Search API and Google Maps. Using the application, the user will be able to search tweets containing a given string and created around a given location. For example, we could search the term "traffic" in the area around New York.

The visual elements of the application will be the following:
- A text input to type in the string to be searched.
- An interactive map where tweets are placed.
- An interactive set of icons that show the message when clicked.

The description of the implementation will cover the building of the layout, the configuration of web services, and the population of the data map. With respect to the project described in Section 1, we will make a more extensive use of ActionScript.

Building the Layout

The layout of the application is quite simple. We have to accommodate a text input, a button, a feedback label, and a map. We put all the elements, except the map, in a form so it is easier to arrange layout. We also set up three states: startup, searching, and error. At the end we should end up with the following code.

```
<s:Application ...
    currentState="startup">

  <s:layout>
    <s:VerticalLayout/>
  </s:layout>

  <s:states>
    <s:State name="startup"/>
    <s:State name="searching"/>
    <s:State name="error"/>
  </s:states>

  <mx:Form
      enabled.searching="false"
      height="55" width="100%">

    <mx:FormItem
        direction="horizontal">

      <s:TextInput id="keywordInput"/>

      <s:Button
          enabled="{keywordInput.text != ''}"
          label="Search"/>

      <s:Label
          text="Searching..."
          text.error="Error in searching"
          paddingTop="7"
          includeIn="searching,error"/>

    </mx:FormItem>
  </mx:Form>

</s:Application>
```

The application is in the `startup` state when it is run. The form, and its children components, are all disabled when the state is `searching`. The button is enabled only when some text has been entered in the input component. An error message is shown when something goes wrong.

Atom is an XML-based format that is commonly used to exchange data represented in plain text. For more details, check the Wikipedia entry: *http://en.wikipedia.org/wiki/Atom_(standard)*.

Configuring Twitter Web Service

We will use the search functionality of the Twitter API. The documentation for the search function is available at `http://dev.twitter.com/doc/get/search`. The URL that we need has the following form (parameters' values uppercased): `http://search.twitter.com/search.FORMAT?geocode=LATITUDE,LONGITUDE,RADIUS&q=STRING`. The first parameter is the return format. For this project we will use Atom.

The second parameter is made of a list of three comma-separated values, which express latitude, longitude, and radius (the dimension of the circled area of which the center is the point defined by latitude and longitude). The third is the string that we want to search on Twitter. For example, if we want to search who is tweeting about "lunch" in the area of New York (1 mile around Times Square) we can use the following URL: `http://search.twitter.com/search.atom?geocode=40.736072,-73.992062,1mi&q=lunch`.

Now let's feed this example into Flash Builder to create the code to interact with the Twitter Search API. We are already familiar with this process so we just show the settings in Figure 2.1. Then we configure the return type as in Figure 2.2.

To find out the coordinates of a point on a map you can use the tooltip feature of Google maps: *http://maps.google.com/maps?showlabs=1*.

Connect to Data/Service for TweetsOnAMap

Configure HTTP Service
Specify the operation names and URLs, any operation parameters, and the service name.

Do you want to use a base URL as a prefix for all operation URLs? ● No ○ Yes

Operations: [Add] [Delete]

Name	Method	Content-Type	URL
TwitterGeoSearch	GET		http://search.twitter.com/search.json?geocode=4

Parameters: [Add] [Delete]

Name	Data Type	Parameter Type	
geocode	String	GET	
q	String	GET	

Service details

Service name: | TwitterSearchService |

Service package: | services.twittersearchservice |

Data type package: | tweets |

Note: Services hosted on other domains would require a cross-domain file.
     RESTful service URIs can be entered as http://localhost/{container}/{item}.

(?)   [< Back] [Next >] [Cancel] [Finish]

Figure 2.1 Configuration of the Twitter Search service.

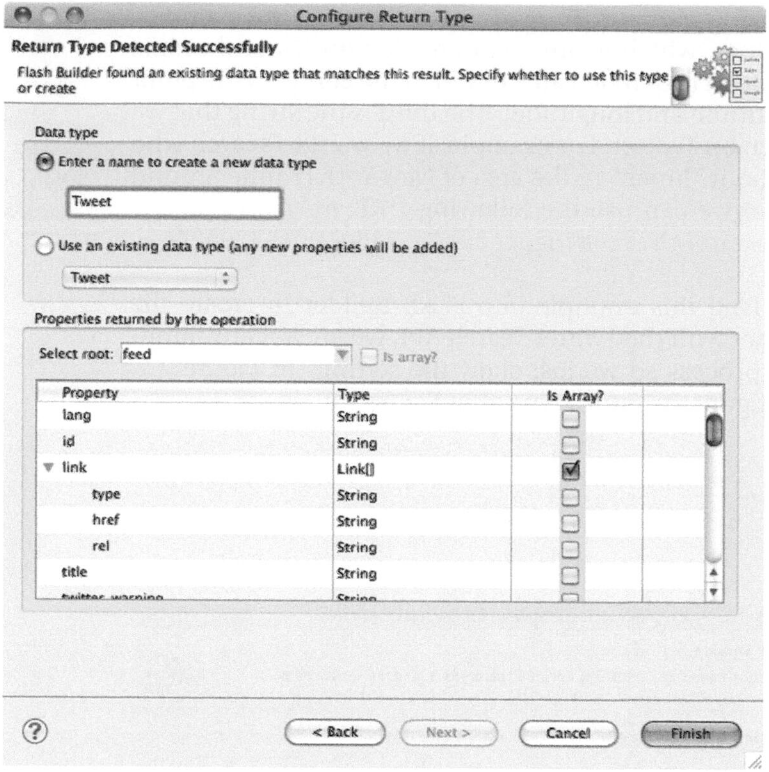

Figure 2.2 Configuration of the Twitter Search return type.

Searching on Twitter

Now we can set up the Twitter search and some listener to update the application according to its current state. We add a `Declarations` tag to our application, to hold our web services, and we create an instance of the `twittersearchservice`.

```
<s:Application ...
  xmlns:twittersearchservice=
        "services.twittersearchservice.*"
>

  ...

<fx:Declarations>
  <twittersearchservice:TwitterSearchService
      id="twitterSearch"
      fault="currentState = 'error'"
      result="onTwitterResult(event)"/>

</fx:Declarations>
```

As you can see Flash Builder automatically imports a new namespace (highlighted in italics). We configure the web service by assigning an ID and two listeners. In case of error we switch to the corresponding state; in case of successful result we execute a callback defined as follows.

```
private function onTwitterResult(
                    event:ResultEvent):void {
    var twitterResult:ArrayCollection =
              event.result.entry as ArrayCollection;

}
```

At the moment the callback just stores in a variable the result of the web service call. We will update this code later, to make it interact with the Google Maps component.

Now that we have an instance of the Twitter Search service we connect it to the input components: the button and the input text. To keep things simple we set up a default location that identifies the Manhattan area in New York. All our searches will be focused around this point in a 25-mile area.

```
private var lat:Number = 40.736072;
private var longit:Number = -73.992062;
private var rad:Number = 25;
```

We then create a function to run a search and assign it to the click event of the button.

```
private function doSearch():void {

  var geoLocation:String =
        lat.toString()+","+
        longit.toString()+","+
        rad.toString()+"mi";

  twitterSearch.doGeoSearch(geoLocation,
                      keywordInput.text);

}

...

<mx:Form
    enabled.searching="false"
    height="55" width="100%">

    ...

  <s:Button
      enabled="{keywordInput.text != ''}"
      label="Search"
      click="doSearch()"/>

    ...

</mx:Form>
```

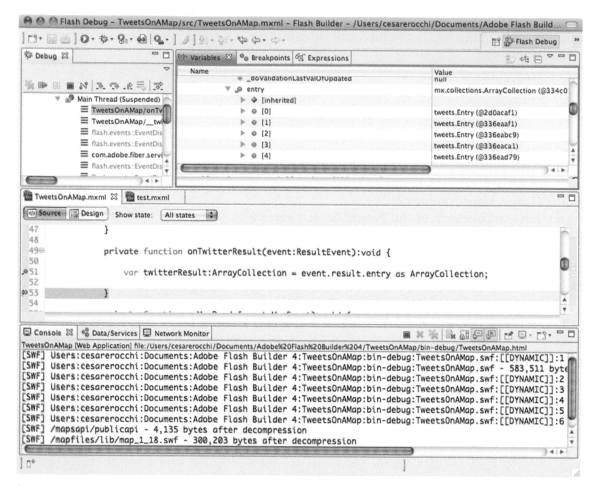

Figure 2.3 Checking the Twitter Search web service.

At this point we can check whether our code is working so far. We place a break point at the end of the `onTwitterResult` callback and we run the application in debug mode. If the web service call is successful we should end up with a situation similar to Figure 2.3, where the variable `twitterResult` is populated with a list of tweets.

We will integrate this part of the code after the setup of the Google Maps web service.

An SWC file is an archived format that contains components, classes, or assets. It is commonly referred to as a library. Unlike SWF, SWC files cannot be run standalone in the Flash player. To use its components the SWC file needs to be imported in a project.

Configuring Google Maps Web Service

To use the Google Maps service we need to add a third-party library to our project. The library is available at *http://maps .googleapis.com/maps/flash/release/sdk.zip*. If you unzip the file there is a Lib folder containing two SWC files.

The first file is built for Flash IDE projects. We are interested in the second file, built for Flex-based applications (Figure 2.4). At the time of this writing the latest version available is 1.18.

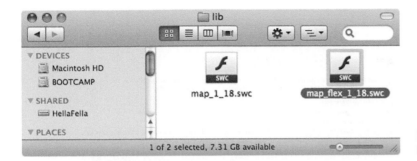

Figure 2.4 Google Maps libraries.

To import a library in a project just drag and drop the SWC file onto the Lib folder in the Package Explorer, so that it appears as in Figure 2.5.

If we did everything correctly we should see that the code completion hints at Google Maps components; we start typing "map" (Figure 2.6).

Figure 2.5 SWC library imported in the project.

Figure 2.6 Code completion recognizes we have imported a new library.

To use the Google Maps service we need an API key, which enables our application to make use of this functionality. To obtain the license we visit *http://code.google.com/apis/maps/signup.html*, and we provide a web site that will host our application (Figure 2.7).

This returns a page with a very long code (86 digits), which we will use as follows. We add an instance of the Map component to our application and we set up some property.

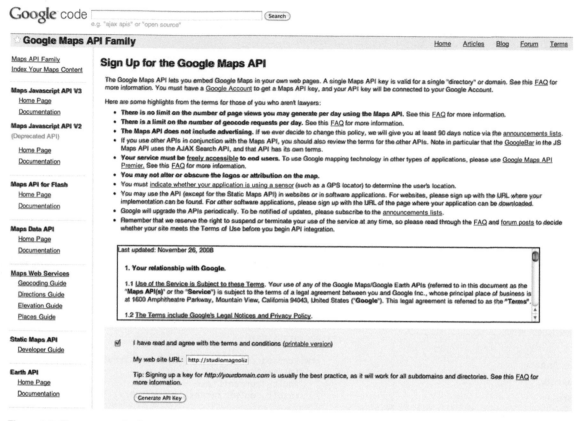

Figure 2.7 The page to obtain a
Google Maps API key.

```
<s:Application ... >

...

    </mx:Form>

    <maps:Map
          id="map"
          key="YOUR_API_KEY"
          width="100%" height="100%"
          mapevent_mapready="onMapReady(event)"
    />

</s:Application>
```

We copy the key into the corresponding property. Since we are
editing the component we also add an ID, some dimensions, and
we set up a listener, onMapReady. This is the function that gets
called when the Map component is loaded. For testing purposes
we create an empty function as follows.

```
    private function onMapReady(event:MapEvent):void {

    }
```

If we run the application now we should see something like in Figure 2.8.

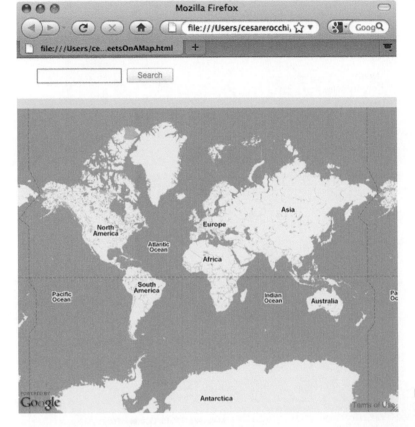

Figure 2.8 A first run of our application.

Since we did not provide any indication, a map of the whole world is displayed. It is already interactive so you can pan by clicking and dragging with the mouse. Since we want to perform a search around a given area we set up the map to focus on the latitude and longitude that we already have in the application. A third parameter to add is the zoom level—that is, how detailed is the map (Figure 2.9). So we update our code as follows.

```
<fx:Script>
    <![CDATA[

import com.google.maps.*;

    ...

private var lat:Number = 40.736072;
```

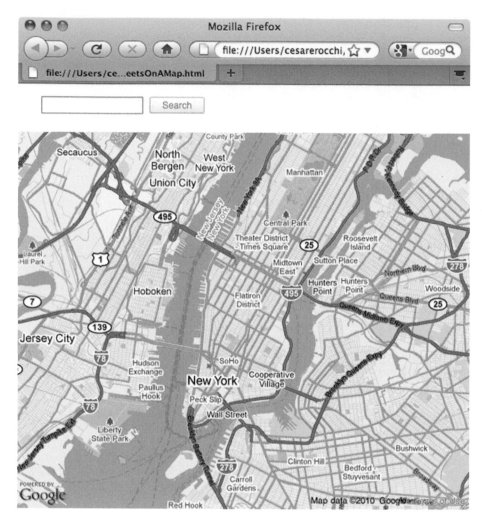

Figure 2.9 The map centered around Times Square in New York City.

```
private var longit:Number = -73.992062;
private var rad:Number = 25;
private var zoomLevel:Number = 12;

  ...

private function onMapReady(event:MapEvent):void {

    map.setCenter(new LatLng(lat,longit),
                  zoomLevel,
                  MapType.NORMAL_MAP_TYPE);

}

]]>

</fx:Script>
```

Displaying Information on a Map

Now the map is ready to display information. We can wire together the two services to position tweets on the map according to the geolocation property. The flow will be the following:

- We run a search on Twitter.
- If the search is successful for each result, we trigger a geocode action, performed by the Google service.
- If the geocode action is successful, we display an icon in that position.

We should pay attention because we have different events and callbacks and some are chained. To avoid confusion we will proceed step by step.

Enabling Geocoding

The first step is to extend each instance of the Entry class to support geocoding. If we check out the documentation of Google Maps services,[1] one of the features available is geocoding, which allows identifying a point on a map given a set of coordinates. The example in the documentation is pretty straightforward.

```
var geocoder:ClientGeocoder = new ClientGeocoder();

geocoder.addEventListener(
            GeocodingEvent.GEOCODING_SUCCESS,
            handleGeocodingSuccess);

geocoder.addEventListener(
            GeocodingEvent.GEOCODING_FAILURE,
            handleGeocodingFailure);
```

We need to create an instance of `ClientGeocoder` and listen for two events, `failure` or `success`. In case of `success`, the returned object will contain information to correctly display an element (e.g., an icon) on our map. We will add this functionality to the Entry class, created during the configuration of the Twitter web service. The class already has some code generated, and we should be careful to not break it. These are the modifications that we will make:

- Add an instance of `ClientGeocoder`.
- Add a function `doGeocode`.
- Add two listeners to dispatch geocoding events.
- Add a helper function to remove listeners.
  Here is the final code with changes highlighted in italics.

```
import com.adobe.fiber.core.model_internal;
import com.google.maps.services.*;
import events.TweetGeocodeEvent;
```

---

[1] See *http://code.google.com/apis/maps/documentation/flash/services.html#Geocoding_Object.*

```
public class Entry extends _Super_Entry {

  private var geoCoder:ClientGeocoder =
                    new ClientGeocoder();

public static function _initRemoteClassAlias():void{

  ...

}

...

/**END OF DO NOT MODIFY SECTION **/

public function doGeocode():void {

   geoCoder.addEventListener(
           GeocodingEvent.GEOCODING_SUCCESS,
           onGeocodeSuccess);

   geoCoder.addEventListener(
           GeocodingEvent.GEOCODING_FAILURE,
           onGeocodeFailure);

   geoCoder.geocode(google_location);

}

private function
       onGeocodeSuccess(event:GeocodingEvent):void{

   var e:TweetGeocodeEvent = new
         TweetGeocodeEvent(
         TweetGeocodeEvent.GEOCODE_SUCCESS);

   e.response = event.response;
   dispatchEvent(e);
   removeListeners();

}

private function
     onGeocodeFailure(event:GeocodingEvent):void {

   trace("geocoding failed. Status: "+event.status);
   removeListeners();

}

private function removeListeners():void {

  geoCoder.removeEventListener(
          GeocodingEvent.GEOCODING_SUCCESS,
          onGeocodeSuccess);

  geoCoder.removeEventListener(
          GeocodingEvent.GEOCODING_FAILURE,
          onGeocodeFailure);

}
```

This code enables each instance of the Entry class to call the geocoding web service of Google Maps and wait for a response. The property passed to the web services is `google_location`, set up when we generated the class by using the wizard. In case the result is successful the instance creates a custom event, `TweetGeocodeEvent`, dumps in it the data of the response, and dispatches it to other (possible) listeners. One of the listeners will be our application, but first let's see how the custom event is defined.

```
package events {

  import flash.events.Event;

  public class TweetGeocodeEvent extends Event {
    public static const GEOCODE_SUCCESS:String =
                            "tweetGeocodeSuccess";
    public var response:Object;

    public function TweetGeocodeEvent(type:String) {

        super(type);

    }

  }

}
```

This is a pretty standard way to create a custom event, by following these rules of thumb:
- Extend the Event class.
- Add a constant to identify the type of event.
- Add public variables to carry data (e.g., response).

Using Geocoding

Now we have a class that embeds the functionality to geocode tweets. When the Twitter search is successful we have already set up an array to collect the result. For each element of the array we can call the `doGeocode` function and listen for a response, as follows.

```
private function
        onTwitterResult(event:ResultEvent):void {

var twitterResult:ArrayCollection =
        event.result.entry as ArrayCollection;

for each (var o:Entry in twitterResult) {

    o.addEventListener(
        TweetGeocodeEvent.GEOCODE_SUCCESS,
        onTweetGeocoded);

    o.doGeocode();

  }

}
```

For sake of completeness we should mention that this is a simplified way to create custom events. For further details, you can check the documentation at *http://livedocs.adobe. com/flex/3/html/help. html?content= createevents_1.html.*

If you remember the custom event includes a custom property named `response`. This property contains the data that we need to add an icon on the map. In particular, we are interested in a property called `placemarks`, which is an array of placemark instances.

```
private function onTweetGeocoded
                    (e:TweetGeocodeEvent):void {

    var m:Placemark = e.response.placemarks[0];

}
```

In our scenario we assume that the placemark is just one, since a tweet can have just one location. We extract this value by accessing the first element of the array. We can set up a break point to check its internal structure, as in Figure 2.10.

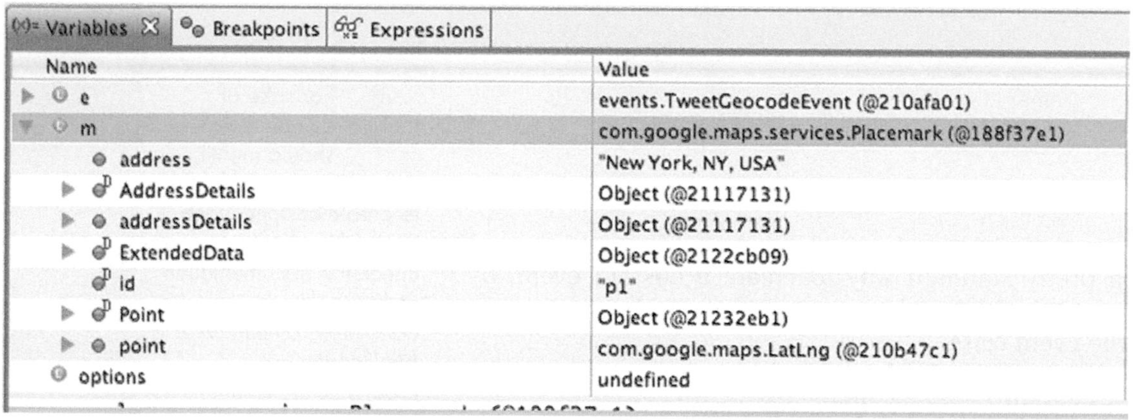

Figure 2.10 The structure of a placemark instance.

Name	Value
▶ ⓔ e	events.TweetGeocodeEvent (@210afa01)
▼ ⓜ m	com.google.maps.services.Placemark (@188f37e1)
ⓞ address	"New York, NY, USA"
▶ AddressDetails	Object (@21117131)
▶ ⓞ addressDetails	Object (@21117131)
▶ ExtendedData	Object (@2122cb09)
id	"p1"
▶ Point	Object (@21232eb1)
▶ ⓞ point	com.google.maps.LatLng (@210b47c1)
ⓞ options	undefined

This is what we need to correctly place the icon on the maps. What we have called so far an "icon" is indeed an instance of Marker, which is another custom class included in the Google Maps library. A *marker* is, for example, a red pin that is displayed to indicate a point when we use Google Maps via the web site, as the one in Figure 2.11.

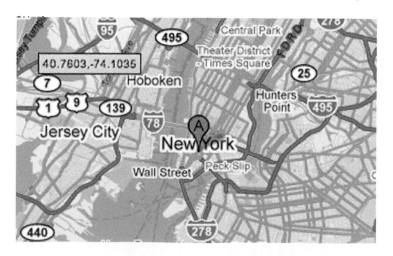

Figure 2.11 An example of a standard marker.

In our case we want something custom, for example, an icon of Twitter. To create a custom marker we use the following code.

```
private function onTweetGeocoded
            (e:TweetGeocodeEvent):void {

var m:Placemark = e.response.placemarks[0];
var options:MarkerOptions = new
        MarkerOptions({hasShadow: true,
                    icon: new TwitterIcon()});
var marker:Marker = new Marker(m.point, options);
map.addOverlay(marker);

}
```

We create an option object that specifies the appearance of the marker and we pass it to the constructor of the Marker class, together with the details about the placemark. Once we have an instance of Marker we can add it to the map and the component will take care of the rest. Notice that in the options we have specified an instance of `twitterIcon` in the icon property. This is a custom component that is defined as follows.

```
<mx:Image
      xmlns:fx="http://ns.adobe.com/mxml/2009"
      xmlns:s="library://ns.adobe.com/flex/spark"
      xmlns:mx="library://ns.adobe.com/flex/mx"
      source="twitterIcon.png">

</mx:Image>
```

 The icon, which can be found on the Web, should be adjusted to a dimension of 20 × 20 pixels and imported into the project.

If we run the application and perform a search we should see something like in Figure 2.12. Some tweet appears on Manhattan—it looks like we are on the right track.[2]

Interacting with the Map

So far we have achieved a great result by correctly displaying tweets on a map. Let's decorate our application by adding some interactive functionality. First, Google Maps users are used to seeing some command to pilot the map. We can show them by modifying the `onMapReady` callback as follows.

```
private function onMapReady(event:MapEvent):void {

map.setCenter(new LatLng(lat,longit),
            zoomLevel,
            MapType.NORMAL_MAP_TYPE);

map.addControl(new NavigationControl());

}
```

[2]Sometimes it might happen that you do not see any icon displayed. This can be due to two factors: none of the tweets returned have a geolocation property (this is possible though rare), or nobody has tweeted the word you are searching within the area selected.

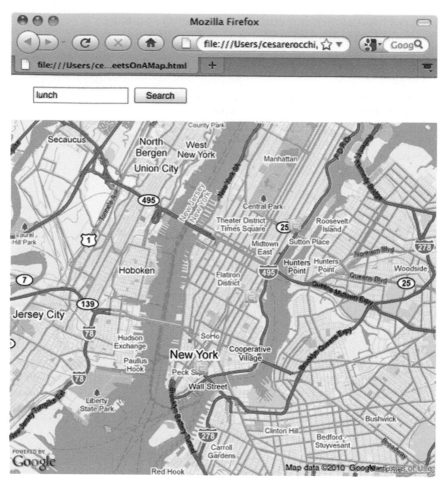

Figure 2.12 A working example of our application.

Second, a common feature of maps-based applications is the possibility to interact with the markers. In our case we can show the content of the Twitter message. To achieve this we need to listen for a mouse event and display the content accordingly.

```
private function onTweetGeocoded
                        (e:TweetGeocodeEvent):void {

var m:Placemark = e.response.placemarks[0];
var options:MarkerOptions =
        new MarkerOptions({hasShadow: true,
                        icon: new TwitterIcon()});
var marker:Marker = new Marker(m.point, options);
map.addOverlay(marker);

marker.addEventListener(MapMouseEvent.CLICK,

 function (event:MapMouseEvent):void {

    marker.openInfoWindow(
        new InfoWindowOptions({
```

```
                    title: "By "+e.target.author.
                    name,
                    content: e.target.title})
            );

        }

    );

}
```

When a marker is clicked a function is called to open an information window in which we can display, for example, the author name and the content of the message, as in Figure 2.13.

Here is the complete code for the main application.

```
<s:Application ...
   currentState="startup"
   xmlns:twittersearchservice=
               "services.twittersearchservice.*"
   xmlns:maps="com.google.maps.*">
```

Figure 2.13 An information window displaying details of a Twitter message.

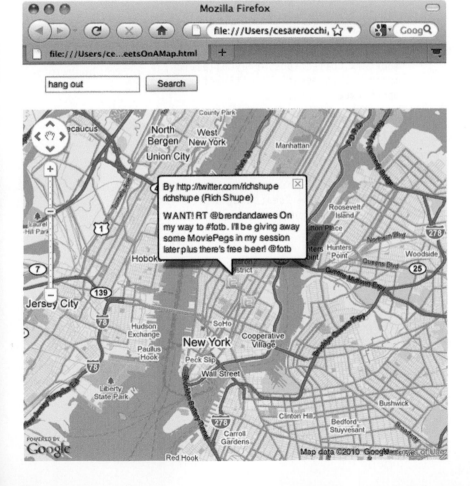

```
<s:layout>
  <s:VerticalLayout/>
</s:layout>

<s:states>
  <s:State name="startup"/>
  <s:State name="searching"/>
  <s:State name="error"/>
</s:states>

<fx:Declarations>

    <twittersearchservice:TwitterSearchService
        id="twitterSearch"
        fault="currentState = 'error'"
        result="onTwitterResult(event)"/>

</fx:Declarations>

<fx:Script>
<![CDATA[

import com.google.maps.*;
import com.google.maps.controls.*;
import com.google.maps.overlays.*;
import com.google.maps.services.*;

import events.TweetGeocodeEvent;
import mx.collections.ArrayCollection;
import mx.rpc.events.ResultEvent;
import tweets.Entry;

private var lat:Number = 40.736072;
private var longit:Number = -73.992062;
private var rad:Number = 25;
private var zoomLevel:Number = 12;

private function doSearch():void {
    currentState = "searching";
    var geoLocation:String = lat.toString()+","+
                             longit.toString()+","+
                             rad.toString()+"mi";

    twitterSearch.doGeoSearch(geoLocation,
                             keywordInput.text);

    }

    private function
        onTwitterResult(event:ResultEvent):void {
      currentState = "";
      var twitterResult:ArrayCollection =
            event.result.entry as ArrayCollection;

      for each (var o:Entry in twitterResult) {

          o.addEventListener(
                TweetGeocodeEvent.GEOCODE_SUCCESS,
```

```
                            onTweetGeocoded);
            o.doGeocode();
        }
    }

    private function onTweetGeocoded
                    (e:TweetGeocodeEvent):void {

    var m:Placemark = e.response.placemarks[0];
    var options:MarkerOptions =
        new MarkerOptions({hasShadow: true,
                        icon: new TwitterIcon()});
    var marker:Marker = new Marker(
                            m.point, options);
    map.addOverlay(marker);

    marker.addEventListener(MapMouseEvent.CLICK,

        function (event:MapMouseEvent):void {

        marker.openInfoWindow(
            new InfoWindowOptions({
                title: "By "+e.target.author.name,
                content: e.target.title
            })
        );
        }
    );

    }

    private function
                onMapReady(event:MapEvent):void {
        map.setCenter(new LatLng(lat,longit),
                    zoomLevel,
                    MapType.NORMAL_MAP_TYPE);
        map.addControl(new NavigationControl());

    }
]]>
</fx:Script>

<mx:Form
    enabled.searching="false"
    height="55" width="100%">

<mx:FormItem
    direction="horizontal">

  <s:TextInput
    id="keywordInput"/>

  <s:Button
    enabled="{keywordInput.text != ''}"
    label="Search"
    click="doSearch()" />
```

```
<s:Label
    text="Searching..."
    text.error="Error in searching"
    paddingTop="7"
    includeIn="searching,error"/>

    </mx:FormItem>
</mx:Form>

<maps:Map
    id="map"
    key="YOUR_API_KEY"
    mapevent_mapready="onMapReady(event)"
    width="100%" height="100%" />

</s:Application>
```

Possible Improvements

This project can be refined by implementing the following features:

- Hide the input components until the map is loaded.
- Provide feedback while the map is loading.
- Clean all the markers before running a search.
- Display the picture of the user beside the content of a message.

CHARTING AND MULTIMEDIA

In this section we explore two more tools for data-driven applications: charts and audio/video. First, we describe the main components of the chart library included in Flash Builder and we will see how to build and customize widely used charts. Second, we focus on the multimedia capabilities of the Flash Builder by illustrating how to manipulate video and audio files.

Building Charts in Flex

Charts are an invaluable tool to visualize data in a significant way. Good and well-organized charts enable people to quickly get an idea of important/critical data and recognize relevant relations among data. In Flex, we can do even more—we can build interactive charts, which enable interacting with data (e.g., filtering, zooming, rendering). In the first part of this section we will learn which types of charts are supported in the Flex built-in library and how to use them. Some third-party libraries that are pretty known in the community are also mentioned. Let's start by showing some chart types.[1]

Chart Types

The following sections outline different chart types and show a sample of each.

Area Chart

Area charts are based on areas, which show totals over time (either percentage or cumulative). For example, in Figure 3.1 we can see a plotting of website visits and the number of pages visualized.

Column/Bar Chart

The column/bar chart is based on lengths, which show observations over time, sometimes in different conditions. It can be

---

[1]See *http://www.sapdesignguild.org/resources/diagram_guidelines/use_charts.html* for more information on using charts.

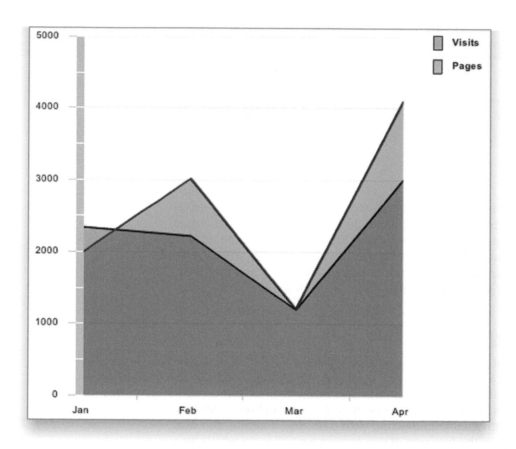

Figure 3.1 Area chart.

arranged vertically (columns) or horizontally (bars). For example, the same data about the website shown in Figure 3.1 can be rendered as in Figure 3.2. There can also be a floating version, as shown in Figure 3.3.

Segmented/Stacked Columns Chart

This kind of chart is based on stacking column lengths to highlight proportional relationships over time. For example, in Figure 3.4 we have the combined number of visits and the number of pages.

Line charts

Line charts are based on the position of data points. They can be used to show trends. Lines can have many forms: normal lines (1), curves (2), steps (3), or noninterpolated lines when data are missing (4). See Figure 3.5 to get an idea of the ways data about our website can be plotted.

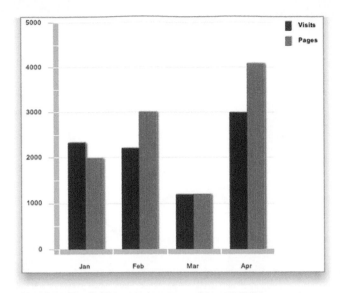

Figure 3.2 Column chart.

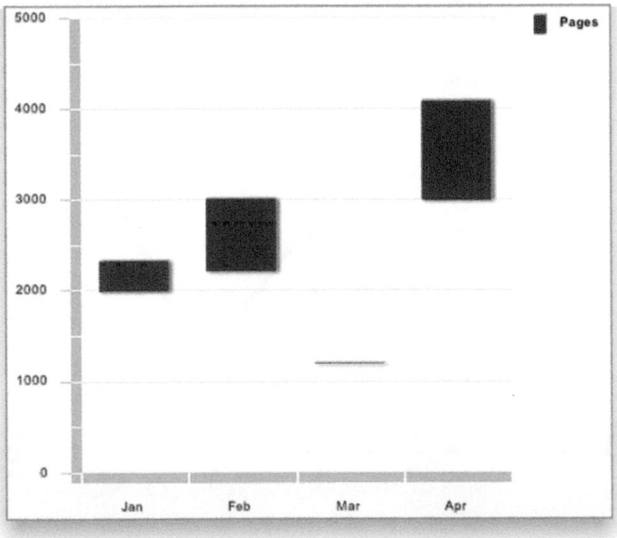

Figure 3.3 Floating column chart.

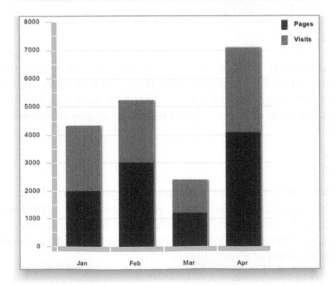

Figure 3.4 Segmented column chart.

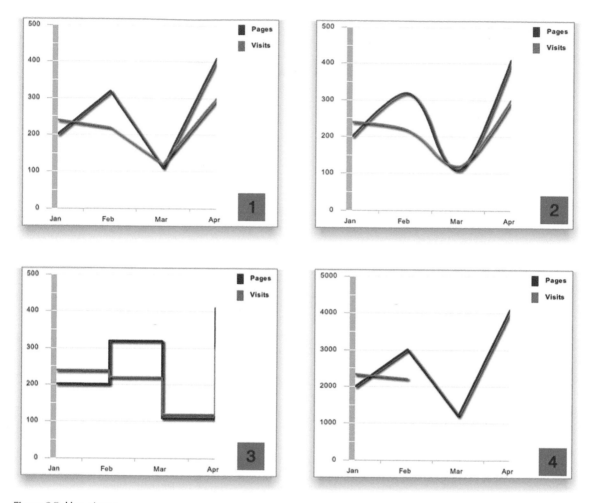

Figure 3.5 Line charts.

Bubble Charts

Besides position, bubble charts show a third dimension: size. This way we can show more complex data. For example, we can show how many pages have been visualized by means of position and render the time spent on all the pages by means of radius, as in Figure 3.6.

Pie Charts

A pie chart is probably the most known type of chart. Data are shown as a sliced circle (like a pie), where each slice represents a subset of data (Figure 3.7). It is ideal to show proportional relationships. There is also an "exploded" version, which is useful to highlight a subset of slices (Figure 3.8).

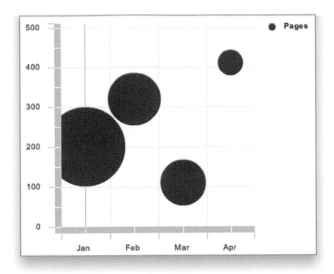

Figure 3.6 Bubble chart.

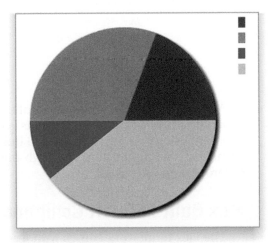

Figure 3.7 Pie chart.

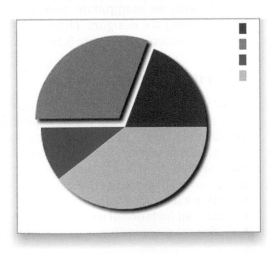

Figure 3.8 Exploded pie chart.

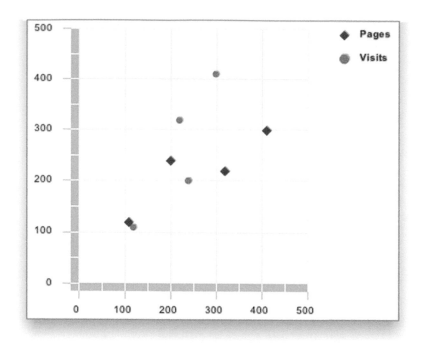

Figure 3.9 Plot chart.

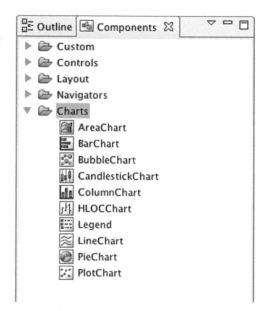

Figure 3.10 Charts in the design view.

Plot Charts

Also referred to as scattered plots, plot charts show the distribution of data points along one or two dimensions (Figure 3.9). Unlike bubble charts, points have no dimension, although they can have different shape and color.

Flex Built-in Chart Components

The Flex framework comes with a set of built-in components to manipulate and render charts. If you are using the designer, charts are grouped into a specific folder, as in Figure 3.10.

My First Chart in Flex

In this section we will build our first chart-based Flex application. We will try to exploit as much as possible the facilities provided by the design view. As we will see, the procedure is pretty similar to the one illustrated in Section 1, when we built a list-based application. The steps are the same:

- Define a data service/source.
- Create an instance of a chart.
- Define the mapping between the data and the chart.

Let's suppose we have data about our websites. More specifically, we have data sets for each month. Each data set contains the number of monthly visits to our websites. Somebody has already set up a web service that takes as input a month and returns data formatted according to the following structure.

```
<sites>

    <site>
        <name>site1.com</name>
        <visits>13000</visits>
    </site>

    <site>
        <name>site2.com</name>
        <visits>9300</visits>
    </site>

    <site>
        <name>site3.com</name>
        <visits>16200</visits>
    </site>

</sites>
```

The root tag contains a list of objects, defined by the `<site>` tag. Each object has two properties: `name` and number of `visits`. To simulate the behavior of a web service, we will put these data in a local file.

We start a new project and save our XML file in the `src` folder. We then start the configuration of a new service, as in Figure 3.11. This opens a configuration wizard, which allows defining where to load data from and how to organize them. We provide the path to our data service (step 1) and we specify we are interested in the `<site>` tag, which has to be considered as an array (step 2; see Figure 3.12).

When we click Finish, the Flash Builder does some magic and we end up with a data service already configured: Site is defined as a data type, with the properties required and `getData` call is ready to load statistics. See Figure 3.13.

The second step is to create an instance of a chart, but that is very easy thanks to the design view. We can drag a column chart on the stage and arrange it as we prefer. The last step is to associate data to the chart. Again, it is a matter of drag and drop: We drag the `getData` function over the chart instance. See Figure 3.14.

 If you have a local or remote web server you can upload the file there. The mechanism is exactly the same.

 You might wonder why we specify `<site>` and not `<sites>` as an array. To some people, it is counterintuitive. When configuring a service in Flash Builder you should answer the following questions: Which is the element to be manipulated? Are there many (i.e., is it an array)? If you follow this tip you should avoid any errors.

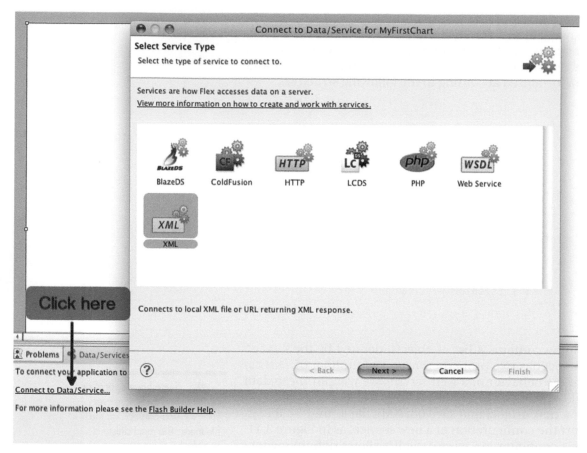

Figure 3.11 Data wizard—step 1.

Now we are asked how to map data to the chart. In this case we just want to show the number of visits for each month. So, on the x axis we place websites and each column shows the number of visits (y axis); see Figure 3.15. Figure 3.16 shows the final result, with data tips already implemented. Just one observation: We did not type any code.

Data Tips

Although charts are meant to be self-explanatory, it is hard to show all the information retrieved by the data service at once. For example, some information might be displayed as users interact with the chart, like hovering on a column (see Figure 3.16). The one shown here is the standard tip, provided by default by the Flex framework. It is possible to customize the message displayed in the data tip, by providing a function that returns a string.

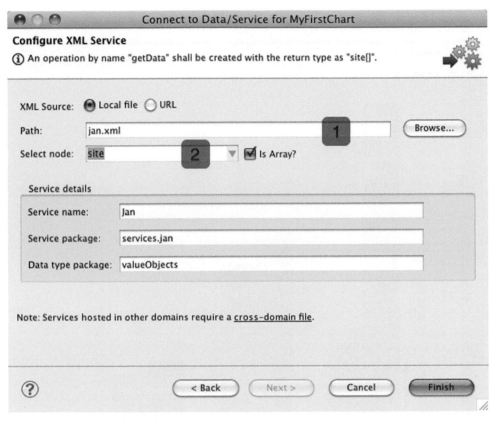

Figure 3.12 Data wizard—step 2.

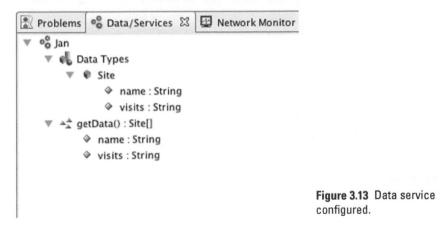

Figure 3.13 Data service configured.

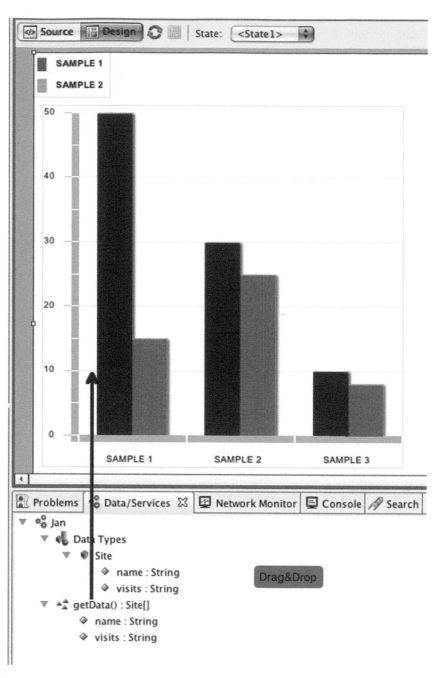

Figure 3.14 Associate service and chart.

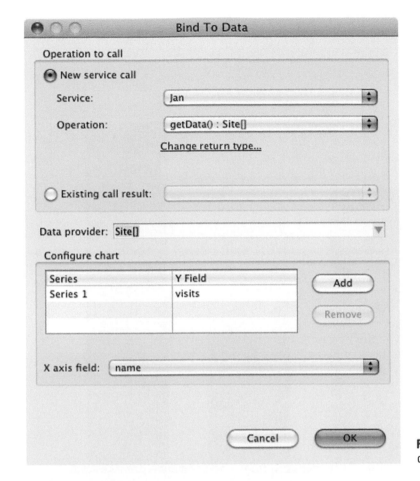

Figure 3.15 Mapping data and chart.

```
<mx:ColumnChart
    ...
    dataTipFunction="myDataTip">
```

The function is required to have a parameter, which is the data associated to the element you are hovering over.

Now you can define your own message to be displayed in the data tip. For example, as opposed to the example above, we can show just the number of visits. In this case we concatenated a string, "visits: ", with the retrieved yValue of the item. This way we obtain the result as in Figure 3.17.

```
private function myDataTip(item:HitData):String {
    return "visits: "+(item.chartItem as
            ColumnSeriesItem).yValue;
}
```

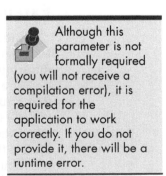

Although this parameter is not formally required (you will not receive a compilation error), it is required for the application to work correctly. If you do not provide it, there will be a runtime error.

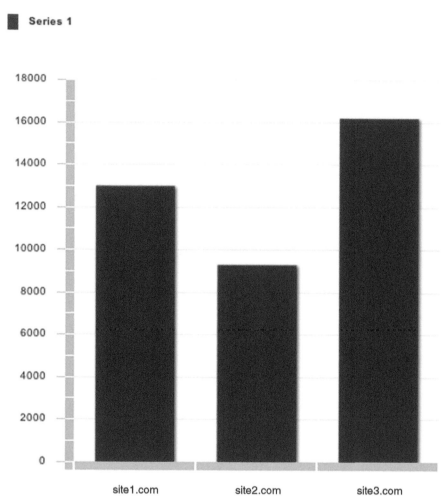

Figure 3.16 Your first chart-based application.

Extending Our First Chart Example

In this section we will extend the first chart we built. We will learn how to rebuild some parts in ActionScript and we will add more interactivity to show the capabilities of the Flex charts library.

More specifically, we will assume that there is a web service that returns data related to the monthly visits of your websites. We will extend our application by adding a combo box that will allow the choice of the month. The application will load and update the chart according to the month selected. Before this, we will rebuild the interaction with the backend in a more developer-oriented way in ActionScript.

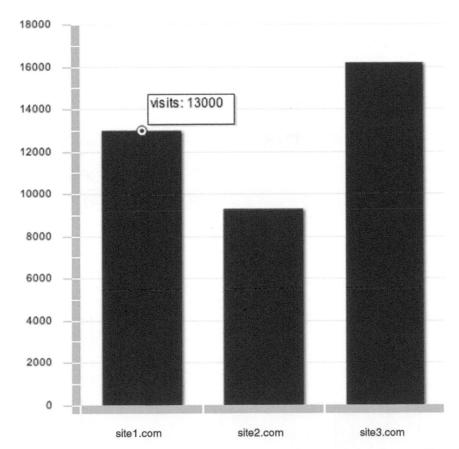

■ Series 1

Figure 3.17 A custom tip.

Building the UI

We already know how the user interface (UI) has to work, so let's place a panel, a combo box, and a column chart on the stage, as in Figure 3.18.

We are already done with the layout. We just provide a title to the panel, "Monthly Visits Chart," and assign an ID to the combo box, to be used later. The code should look like the following.

```
<s:Application ...>

    <s:Panel
        title="Monthly Visits Chart"
        x="10" y="10">

        <mx:ColumnChart >
            <mx:series>

                <mx:ColumnSeries
                        yField=""
```

```
                                      displayName="…"/>
                    </mx:series>
                </mx:ColumnChart>

            </s:Panel>

            <s:ComboBox
                id="monthsList" />

        </s:Application>
```

Let's now focus on the interaction with the backend.

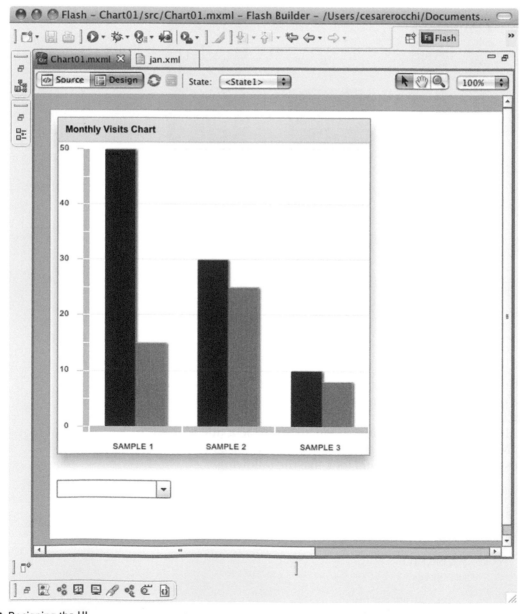

Figure 3.18 Designing the UI.

Backend Interaction

To simulate the behavior of the server we prepare a set of XML files and store them in the local folder. Data are organized according to the same structure presented in the previous example. To load data we will use the HTTPService class. As we already know, such a component has to be placed within the <fx:Declarations> tag, for it is not a visual component. We provide an ID and we specify the E4X format.

This component has to directly react to the changes in the combo box, which we have previously named monthsList. We assume that data will have a URL of the following format:

{month-name}.xml

For example, like jan.xml, feb.xml, etc. The month name will be provided by the item selected in the combo box. To create such a binding we define the URL property of our service as follows.

```
<s:HTTPService
    url="{monthsList.selectedItem}.xml"
    id="dataService"
    resultFormat="e4x"/>
```

This way the URL changes whenever a new item is selected from the combo box component. We just have to write a mental note—remember to tell HTTPService to load the URL when it changes—but we will take care of this later. We already know how to handle loaded data or error: by means of events like result and fault. In the end, our component will look like this.

```
<s:HTTPService
    url="{monthsList.selectedItem}.xml"
    id="dataService"
    result="onResult(event)"
    fault="onFault(event)"
    resultFormat="e4x"/>
```

We need a variable to store data loaded from the server. It will be an XMLList, which perfectly fits our needs, because it simplifies parsing and implements the necessary interfaces to be the data provider of a chart. The list needs to be bindable, for the chart has to change whenever the list is updated. So in code this corresponds to the following listing.

```
<fx:Script>

    import mx.rpc.events.ResultEvent;
    import mx.rpc.events.FaultEvent;

    [Bindable]
    private var monthData:XMLList;

    private function onResult(evt:ResultEvent):void {
```

E4X stands for ECMAScript for XML. It is a specification that simplifies working with XML in ActionScript and Flex.

```
                monthData = evt.result.site;
        }
        private function onFault(evt:FaultEvent):void {
                trace("error");
        }
</fx:Script>
```

Here the magic happens in the onResult handler: The list of websites (elements defined by <site> tags) is parsed and populates our variable. There is no need for further manipulation. If you ever worked on other data-driven technologies you know that this line of code hides a lot of hassles. Before implementing the last part let's do a midpoint recap. The code written so far should look like the following.

```
<s:Application ...>

    <fx:Declarations>

        <s:HTTPService
            url="{monthsList.selectedItem}.xml"
            id="dataService"
            result="onResult(event)"
            fault="onFault(event)"
            resultFormat="e4x"/>

    </fx:Declarations>

    <fx:Script>

        import mx.rpc.events.ResultEvent;
        import mx.rpc.events.FaultEvent;

        [Bindable]
        private var monthData:XMLList;

        private function onResult(ev:ResultEvent):void {

            monthData = ev.result.site;
        }

        private function onFault(ev:FaultEvent):void {
                trace("error");
        }

    </fx:Script>

    <s:Panel title="Monthly Visits Chart"
        x="10" y="10">

        <mx:ColumnChart >

          <mx:series>

            <mx:ColumnSeries
```

```
                    yField="" displayName="..."/>

            </mx:series>

        </mx:ColumnChart>

    </s:Panel>

    <s:ComboBox id="monthsList" />

</s:Application>
```

Displaying Data in the Chart

We are now left with the last step, how to render data in the chart. We already said that the `monthData` list is ready for charting, so let's assign it as the data provider. Since we are editing this tag let's also enable data tips.

```
<mx:ColumnChart
    dataProvider="{monthData}"
    showDataTips="true">

    ...

</mx:ColumnChart>
```

As we decided previously we want the columns to show the number of visits, so we have to specify `visits` as the property to be displayed in the columns. We will also provide a name to be displayed, which will be shown in the data tip.

```
<mx:ColumnChart
    dataProvider="{monthData}"
    showDataTips="true">

    <mx:series>

        <mx:ColumnSeries
            yField="visits"
            displayName="Visits"/>

    </mx:series>

</mx:ColumnChart>
```

On the horizontal axis we will show just the name of the website of which the number of visits is shown in the column.

```
<mx:ColumnChart
    dataProvider="{monthData}"
    showDataTips="true">

    <mx:horizontalAxis>

        <mx:CategoryAxis
            categoryField="name"/>
```

 It is important to remember that fillers provided in `categoryField` and `yField` have to match the name of the tags as specified in the XML retrieved. There is no type check in these cases, so the compiler will not show any error or warning. If there is a mismatch in the names the application will not crash, but your data will not be shown as expected. For example, columns will be equal to 0, the default value.

```
        </mx:horizontalAxis>
    <mx:series>
            <mx:ColumnSeries
                    yField="visits"
                    displayName="Visits"/>
    </mx:series>
</mx:ColumnChart>
```

We are almost ready. Combo box is still empty, so let's populate a list of month names and use it as a data provider.

```
[Bindable]
private var months:ArrayCollection =
        new ArrayCollection(["jan", "feb", "mar"]);

...

<s:ComboBox
    id="monthsList"
    dataProvider="{months}"
    />
```

Remember our mental note above? We have to trigger the loading of a URL whenever it changes. Since the URL is chosen in the combo box, this is a good place to put such a trigger. We will bind it to the change event of the combo box.

```
<s:ComboBox
    change="dataService.send()"
    id="monthsList"
    dataProvider="{months}"
/>
```

Now we are ready to see our new version of the application for the first time. Let's compile and see what happens! If you interact with the application you see it behaves as expected. You might notice that when it loads it does not display anything. If you want it to, just associate a function to the creationComplete event of the application. Here is the final code of our second chart-based application.

```
<s:Application ...
        creationComplete="dataService.send()">

    <fx:Declarations>

        <s:HTTPService
                url="{monthsList.selectedItem}.xml"
                id="dataService"
                result="onResult(event)"
                fault="onFault(event)"
                resultFormat="e4x"/>
```

```
    </fx:Declarations>

    <fx:Script>

      import mx.collections.ArrayCollection;
      import mx.rpc.events.ResultEvent;
      import mx.rpc.events.FaultEvent;

      [Bindable]
      private var monthData:XMLList;

      [Bindable]
      private var months:ArrayCollection = new
              ArrayCollection(["jan", "feb", "mar"]);

      private function onResult(evt:ResultEvent):void {
          monthData = evt.result.site;
      }

      private function onFault(evt:FaultEvent):void {
          trace("error");
      }

    </fx:Script>

    <s:Panel title="Monthly Visits Chart"
        x="10" y="10">

        <mx:ColumnChart
            dataProvider="{monthData}"
            showDataTips="true">

            <mx:horizontalAxis>

                <mx:CategoryAxis categoryField="name"/>

            </mx:horizontalAxis>

            <mx:series>

                <mx:ColumnSeries yField="visits"
                    displayName="Visits"/>

            </mx:series>
        </mx:ColumnChart>

    </s:Panel>

    <s:ComboBox
        change="dataService.send()"
        id="monthsList"
        dataProvider="{months}"
        selectedIndex="0"/>

</s:Application>
```

Figure 3.19 shows a screenshot of the application we have
built.

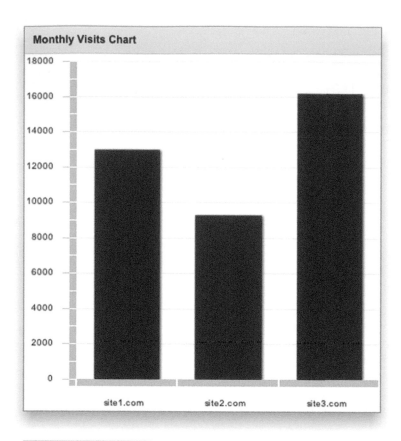

Figure 3.19 Screenshot of our second chart application.

Effects

Although charts provide a rich way to display data, the experience can get even richer if we implement some effects that animate data changes. The application we have built just shows data as static pictures—there is no transition. To highlight data changes we have to provide a value to the `showDataEffect` property, which is implemented in all the `series` elements of charts. To apply such effects we need an instance of chart effect, which has to be bound to the element we want to animate, the column in our case. So we can easily integrate an effect in the application previously built by adding few modifications. We create an instance of effect as follows.

```
<mx:SeriesInterpolate
    id="seriesInterpolate"
    duration="1000" />
```

And we associate it to the column as follows.

```
...
<mx:series>

     <mx:ColumnSeries
          yField="visits"
          displayName="Visits"
          showDataEffect="seriesInterpolate"/>

</mx:series>

...
```

A "resize" effect will highlight each data change. You are invited to discover for yourself other effects like `seriesZoom` and `seriesSlide`.

Styling

Like all the Flex components we can customize the appearance of charts to fit our application's look and feel. The customization happens in the series tag of the chart by varying the `stroke` and `fill` properties.

Specifying Stroke

The `stroke` is the borderline of a component. You can decide its `color`, `weight`, and `alpha` properties. We report here a customized version of the chart built above. The result is shown in Figure 3.20.

```
<s:Panel
    title="Monthly Visits Chart"
    x="10" y="10">
    <mx:ColumnChart dataProvider="{monthData}" >

        <mx:horizontalAxis>
          <mx:CategoryAxis categoryField="name"/>
        </mx:horizontalAxis>

        <mx:series>

          <mx:ColumnSeries
              yField="visits"
              displayName="Visits"
              >

              <mx:stroke>
                <mx:SolidColorStroke
                    color="#953b33"
                    weight="2"
                    alpha="1.0" />

              </mx:stroke>
          </mx:ColumnSeries>
```

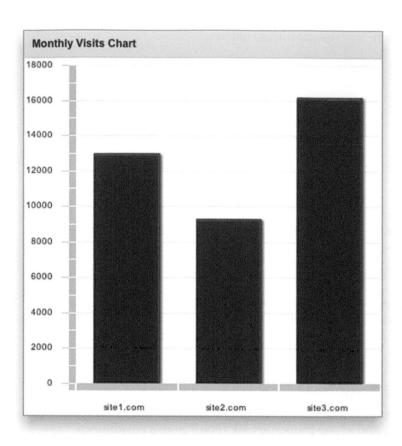

Figure 3.20 Columns with a reddish stroke.

```
            </mx:series>
        </mx:ColumnChart>
    </s:Panel>
```

Change the Fill

We can combine `stroke` and `fill`, much like we are used to with drawing programs like Adobe Illustrator. To overwrite the default color we specify a new fill in the `ColumnSeries` tag. See Figure 3.21 for the final result.

```
<s:Panel
        title="Monthly Visits Chart"
        x="10" y="10">

    <mx:ColumnChart dataProvider="{monthData}" >

        <mx:horizontalAxis>
          <mx:CategoryAxis categoryField="name"/>
        </mx:horizontalAxis>

        <mx:series>
          <mx:ColumnSeries
              yField="visits"
```

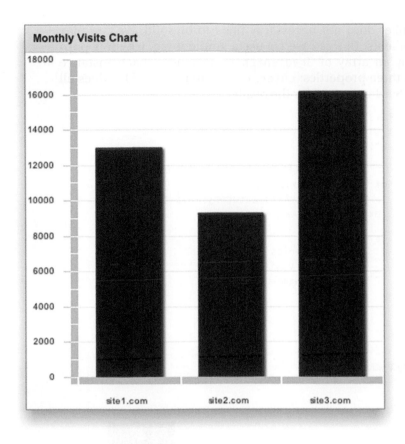

Figure 3.21 Red columns with a reddish stroke.

```
        displayName="Visits"
        >

        <mx:stroke>
          <mx:SolidColorStroke
            color="#953b33"
            weight="2"
            alpha="1.0" />

        </mx:stroke>

        <mx:fill>

          <s:SolidColor
              color="red"
              alpha="1" />

        </mx:fill>

      </mx:ColumnSeries>

    </mx:series>

  </mx:ColumnChart>
</s:Panel>
```

The filler does not necessarily need to be solid. We can play with gradients. In this case we use a gradient tag, which is populated by an array of `GradientEntry` instances. Each instance requires three properties: `color`, `ratio`, and `alpha`. Flex does all the rest. See Figure 3.22 for the result.

```
<s:Panel
    title="Monthly Visits Chart"
    x="10" y="10">

<mx:ColumnChart dataProvider="{monthData}" >
    <mx:horizontalAxis>
        <mx:CategoryAxis categoryField="name"/>
    </mx:horizontalAxis>

    <mx:series>
        <mx:ColumnSeries
            yField="visits"
            displayName="Visits"
            >
```

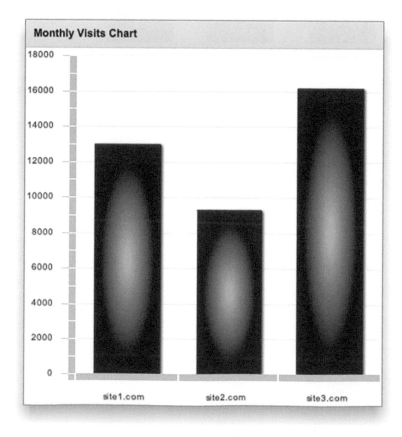

Figure 3.22 Columns with a red/white radial gradient.

```
<mx:stroke>

    <mx:SolidColorStroke
        color="#953b33"
        weight="2"
        alpha="1.0" />

</mx:stroke>

<mx:fill>

    <mx:RadialGradient>
        <mx:entries>
            <fx:Array>

                <s:GradientEntry
                    color="#f9bbb9"
                    ratio="0.1"
                    alpha="1.0" />

                <s:GradientEntry
                    color="#ec322d"
                    ratio="0.9"
                    alpha="1.0" />
            </fx:Array>
        </mx:entries>
    </mx:RadialGradient>

</mx:fill>

        </mx:ColumnSeries>

    </mx:series>
  </mx:ColumnChart>
</s:Panel>
```

Do you want a linear gradient? Easy. Just change the tag from `RadialGradient` to `LinearGradient`, as follows. The result is shown in Figure 3.23.

```
<mx:LinearGradient>
    <mx:entries>
        <fx:Array>

            <s:GradientEntry
                color="#f9bbb9"
                ratio="0.1"
                alpha="1.0" />

            <s:GradientEntry
                color="#ec322d"
                ratio="0.9"
                alpha="1.0" />
        </fx:Array>
    </mx:entries>
</mx:LinearGradient>
```

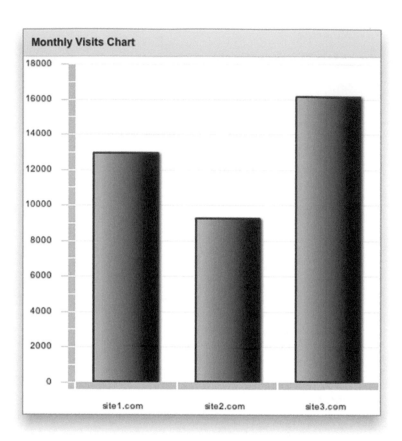

Figure 3.23 Columns with a red/white linear gradient.

As you have probably realized there are endless possibilities to customize the way charts appear. In this section we have tried to give you an overview of how personalization is done.

Other Chart Components

Besides Flex built-in components, there are collections of professional chart components created by third-party companies. Here we present quite an extensive list.

Axiis

Axiis is an open-source framework for data visualization. You download a package, import the library (SWC file) in your project, and you are ready to use it. There are tons of customization possibilities but the resulting code will be clear and concise. Since it is open source you can check what is under the hood and change it as you like. Go to *http://www.axiis.org/* for more information.

ILOG Elixir

ILOG is a complete suite of graphical components that encompass calendars, maps, and charts. It is a commercial product, well suited for enterprise projects, with a professional default look and feel. You can find more information at *http://www.adobe. com/products/flex/ibmilogelixir/*.

Fusion Charts

Fusion Charts is a set of professional components for charting, which includes 3D charts, gauges, funnels, doughnuts, and so on. The focus is on interactivity, compatibility with previous versions of the Flex framework, and printing. You can test its capabilities at *http://www.fusioncharts.com/flex/demos/ChartExplorer/index. html*.

Anychart

Anychart provides a set of components like heat maps, gauges, and interactive charts. It works with Flash and Flex. More information is available at *http://www.anychart.com/home/*.

Working with Video and Audio

In this section we will explore multimedia capabilities of the Flex framework. We will particularly focus on the way we can manipulate streaming videos and audios. In the first part we will check the built-in video components in the Flex library. The second part will be focused on the exploration of audio APIs. This part is aimed at developers, because audio files are mainly manipulated by means of ActionScript code rather than MXML components.

Showing a Video

You probably are getting used to Flash Builder. If you want to build something quickly you drag some component, set some parameter, and it just works. You might wonder: With video, it is harder. Wrong. It is exactly the same philosophy. Drag a video component, set the source file of the video, and you are done (see Figure 3.24).

The result is a simple box, shown in the browser, and the video plays automatically (default setting). The corresponding code is very minimal.

```
<s:VideoDisplay
    x="..." y="..."
    source="myvideo.flv" />
```

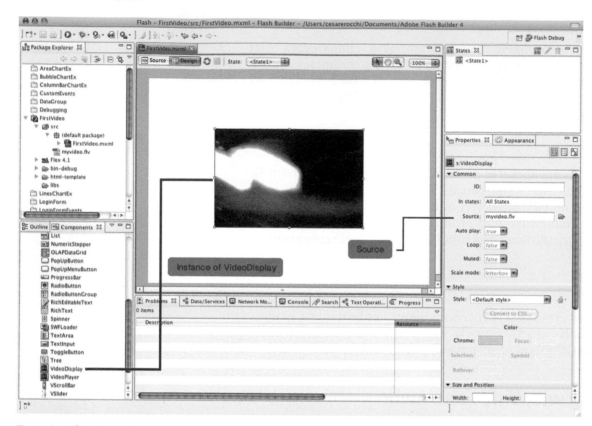

Figure 3.24 Creating a simple video viewer.

Using the `VideoPlayer` Component

Rich Internet applications (RIAs) usually include more than just the ability to show a video. A pretty common requirement is to pilot a video with a set of common actions: play, pause, mute, etc. The Flex library includes a component like that. It is called `VideoPlayer`. Just substitute the tag name in the previous example, as follows.

```
<s:VideoPlayer
    x="..." y="..."
    source="myvideo.flv" />
```

The result is shown in Figure 3.25. There is a play/pause button, a playhead to rewind/forward the video, a current and total time, a volume controller, and a full-screen button. Pretty rich, huh? Again, we didn't type too much. Like every component, it is possible to customize its appearance. We will see how to do that in Section 4.

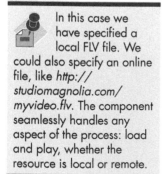

In this case we have specified a local FLV file. We could also specify an online file, like *http:// studiomagnolia.com/ myvideo.flv*. The component seamlessly handles any aspect of the process: load and play, whether the resource is local or remote.

Playing an Audio File

As opposed to video, for which Flex provides ready-to-use built-in components, to work with audio we have to dive deeper into code. In fact, there is no audio player component and we need to get hands dirty with ActionScript code to load, play, and pause an audio file. This is why this section is at the end of the chapter and should be considered pretty advanced, especially if you are a designer.

Let's explore some of the classes that we need to accomplish our task. First of all, we have the `Sound` class, which allows the management of

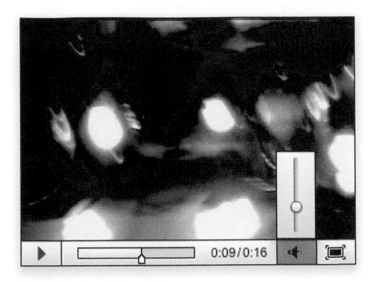

Figure 3.25 Creating a simple video viewer.

basic functionalities related to sound. It works well in combination with the `SoundChannel` class, which is used to control the playback of audio files. Finally, there is the `SoundTransform` class, which enables the manipulation of volume and panning. All these classes are included in the `flash.media` package. To load an audio file the procedure is pretty similar to the one explored in Section 2 regarding loading remote files: You create an object to manage events, and when loading is done you can use an audio file as you wish.

Let's see a simple example. The following happens in the `Script` tag, and the `init` function is called in the `creation Complete` event of the application.

```
<fx:Script>
<![CDATA[

    private var currentAudio:Sound;

    private function init():void {

        var req:URLRequest = new URLRequest("audio.mp3");
        var s:Sound = new Sound();
        s.addEventListener(Event.COMPLETE,
                        onAudioLoaded);

        s.addEventListener(ProgressEvent.PROGRESS,
                        onProgress);

        s.addEventListener(IOErrorEvent.IO_ERROR,
                        onError);
```

```
        s.load(req);
    }

    private function onProgress(e:ProgressEvent):void {
        trace("loaded "+ Math.round(100 *
            (e.bytesLoaded / e.bytesTotal)) + "%");
    }

    private function onError(event:IOErrorEvent):void {
        trace("error in loading");
    }

    private function onAudioLoaded(event:Event):void {
        currentAudio = event.target as Sound;
        currentAudio.play();
    }
]]>
</fx:Script>
```

This is probably the first time we see the `progress` event in this book. It is similar to all other events, but it is called many times during the loading of a source.

As you can see, there are three relevant events: `complete`, `error`, and `progress`. Once the loading is complete we can save the sound in a variable and play.

Managing the Playback

As previously said, the best way to manipulate audio playback is to exploit the `SoundChannel` class. So, instead of saving the loaded file as a `Sound` class we will work with an instance of `SoundChannel`. The code above can be refactored as follows.

```
<fx:Script>
<![CDATA[

    private var currentAudio:Sound;
    private var currentChannel:SoundChannel;

    private function init():void {

        var req:URLRequest = new URLRequest("audio.mp3");
        var s:Sound = new Sound();
        s.addEventListener(Event.COMPLETE, onAudioLoaded);
        s.addEventListener(ProgressEvent.PROGRESS,
                            onProgress);
        s.addEventListener(IOErrorEvent.IO_ERROR,
                            onError);
        s.load(req);
    }

    private function onProgress(e:ProgressEvent):void {
        trace("loaded "+ Math.round(100 * (e.bytesLoaded /
            e.bytesTotal)) + "%");
```

```
    }
    private function onError(event:IOErrorEvent):void {
      trace("error in loading");
    }
    private function onAudioLoaded(event:Event):void {
      currentAudio = event.target as Sound;
      currentChannel = currentAudio.play();
    }
  ]]>
</fx:Script>
```

The `SoundChannel` class is great to manage the current position of the playback. For example, we can detect when the playback is completed. This is done in a pretty known way, by means of an event, as follows.

```
private function onAudioLoaded(event:Event):void {
  currentAudio = event.target as Sound;
  currentChannel = currentAudio.play();

  currentChannel.addEventListener(Event.SOUND_COMPLETE
                                  , onAudioComplete);
}

private function onAudioComplete(event:Event):void {
    // audio complete code.
}
```

Managing Volume and Panning

When working with audio, one of the key features is to control audio. As mentioned above, volume manipulation is made by means of the `SoundTransform` class. The class can be instantiated by providing two parameters, `volume` and `pan`, as follows.

```
var audioProps:SoundTransform =
            new SoundTransform(0.2, 0);
```

The volume can range from 0 to 1 (minimum to maximum), whereas panning varies from –1 (all the way to the left) to 1 (all the way to the right), with 0 being balanced. Such an instance can be used as follows when the audio file is played.

```
currentChannel = currentAudio.play(0, 0, audioProps);
```

Now we have all the elements to build a basic MP3 player.

Building a Basic MP3 Player

In this example we focus on the functionalities rather than the design to get acquainted with the mechanisms underlying Flash player audio API.

We start with a very simple UI, which includes a button and two sliders (Figure 3.26). The button is used to play and pause the audio file, whereas the sliders are used to change volume and panning.

The first slider is the one for the volume. We customize it as in Figure 3.27. In fact, the volume will change from 0 to 1 by steps of 0.1. We also assign it an ID, because we will need to refer to such a component.

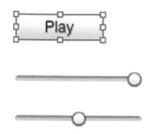

Figure 3.26 UI for a basic MP3 player.

The settings for the panning are slightly different, in that panning ranges from −1 to 1 (see Figure 3.28).

The play button will have just a label and an ID. Now we can reuse part of the code illustrated above, the `init` function, and events associated to the loading of the audio file. For brevity we will skip the `progress` event.

```
private function init():void {

    var req:URLRequest = new URLRequest("audio.mp3");
    var s:Sound = new Sound();
    s.addEventListener(Event.COMPLETE, onAudioLoaded);

    s.addEventListener(IOErrorEvent.IO_ERROR, onError);
    s.load(req);

}

private function onError(event:IOErrorEvent):void {

    trace("error in loading");

}
```

▼ Common	
ID:	volumeSlider
In states:	All States
Minimum:	0
Maximum:	1
Step size:	0.1
Value:	1

Figure 3.27 Settings for the volume slider.

▼ Common	
ID:	panSlider
In states:	All States
Minimum:	−1
Maximum:	1
Step size:	0.1
Value:	0

Figure 3.28 Settings for the panning slider.

```
private function onAudioLoaded(event:Event):void {

    currentAudio = event.target as Sound;

}
```

Now we need some accessory variables to store some data, according to the state of the application.

```
private var currentChannel:SoundChannel;
private var pos:int = 0;
private var audioProps:SoundTransform = new
                          SoundTransform(1, 0);
```

The `currentChannel` is used to refer to the current playback, `pos` is used to keep track of the position of the playback, whereas `audioProps` will store values about volume and panning. To update such values we need an event handler, which notifies whenever one of the sliders changes value. We create a function and we associate it to both the sliders.

```
protected function onPropChange(event:Event):void {

    currentChannel.soundTransform = new
              SoundTransform(volumeSlider.value,
                          panSlider.value);
}...
<s:HSlider
    value="1"
    id="volumeSlider"
    change="onPropChange(event)"
    minimum="0" maximum="1" stepSize="0.1"/>

<s:HSlider
    value="0"
    id="panSlider"
    change="onPropChange(event)"
    minimum="-1" maximum="1" stepSize="0.1"/>
```

Such a function updates the playback properties of the channel as the user drags the pin of the slider.

Finally, we are left with the function that plays and pauses the audio file. When the audio is playing the function saves the current position, stops the playback, and updates the label accordingly. In case the audio is paused it resumes from the saved position.

```
<s:Button
    id="playbackButton"
    label="Play"
    click="playPause()"
/>

private function playPause():void {

    if (currentChannel) { // when audio is playing
      pos = currentChannel.position;
```

```
                    currentChannel.stop();
                    playbackButton.label = "Play";
                    currentChannel = null;

                } else { // when audio is paused
                    playbackButton.label = "Pause";
                    currentChannel =
                        currentAudio.play(pos, 0, audioProps);

                }

            }
```

The following is the final code of the application.

```
<s:Application
    xmlns:fx="http://ns.adobe.com/mxml/2009"
    xmlns:s="library://ns.adobe.com/flex/spark"
    xmlns:mx="library://ns.adobe.com/flex/mx"
    minWidth="955" minHeight="600"
    creationComplete="init()">

<fx:Script>
<![CDATA[
        private var currentAudio:Sound;
        private var currentChannel:SoundChannel;
        private var pos:int = 0;
        private var audioProps:SoundTransform = new
                            SoundTransform(1, 0);

        private function init():void {
            var req:URLRequest = new URLRequest("audio.
mp3");

            var s:Sound = new Sound();
            s.addEventListener(Event.COMPLETE,
onAudioLoaded);

            s.addEventListener(ProgressEvent.PROGRESS,
                            onProgress);
            s.addEventListener(IOErrorEvent.IO_ERROR,
                            onError);

            s.load(req);

        }

        private function onProgress(e:ProgressEvent):
void {

            trace("loaded "+
                Math.round(100 * (e.bytesLoaded / e.
bytesTotal))
                + "%");

        }

        private function onError(event:IOErrorEvent):
void {
```

```
            trace("error in loading");

        }

        private function onAudioLoaded(event:Event):void {

            currentAudio = event.target as Sound;

        }

        private function playPause():void {

            if (currentChannel) { // playing

                pos = currentChannel.position;
                currentChannel.stop();
                playbackButton.label = "Play";
                currentChannel = null;

            } else { // stopped

                playbackButton.label = "Pause";
                currentChannel =
                     currentAudio.play(pos, 0, audioProps);

            }

        }

        protected function onPropChange(event:Event):void {

            currentChannel.soundTransform =
                new SoundTransform(volumeSlider.value,
                                    panSlider.value);

        }

]]>
</fx:Script>

<s:Button
    id="playbackButton"
    label="Play"
    click="playPause()" x="62" y="58"/>

<s:HSlider x="62" y="104"
    value="1"
    id="volumeSlider"
    change="onPropChange(event)"
    minimum="0" maximum="1" stepSize="0.1"/>

<s:HSlider x="62" y="135"
    value="0"
    id="panSlider"
    change="onPropChange(event)"
    minimum="-1" maximum="1" stepSize="0.1"/>

</s:Application>
```

Conclusion

In this section we explored two important tools for data-driven applications: charts and audio/video. For charts, we showed how to work with the main components of the chart library included in Flash Builder. For audio/video, we illustrated the multimedia capabilities of Flash Builder—that is, how to manipulate video and audio files.

PROJECT 3: YOUTUBE INSPECTOR

We will build an application that retrieves a list of videos from YouTube. The application allows watching and interacting with the video. Moreover, it will show a chart to display the proportion between the number of views, favorites, and comments. The development of this project will help us to get acquainted with the usage of web services (YouTube API), events managed in ActionScript, and Flex chart libraries.

Description of the Project

This project will load a list of the most viewed YouTube videos and display them, by title, in a list. When the user selects an item on the list, the corresponding video is loaded, with the default user interface provided by YouTube. On the side, a chart shows information related to the video, such as number of views, number of people that favored it, and number of comments. The user interface updates each time the user interacts with the list.

The elements included are:
- A web service to query the YouTube repository.
- A list to show videos.
- A video player to display the video.
- A chart component to show information about a single video.

Design of the User Interface

The user interface for this application is pretty straightforward. We need to place on the stage three visual elements: a List, a SWFLoader, and a ColumnChart. We will use the List to render the array of videos retrieved from the web service. The SWFLoader will be used to show the YouTube video. This component behaves in essence as the image component: you set a source and it handles loading and rendering. SWFLoader is a bit more complex because you also have access to its content. We will need this feature to pilot the video via ActionScript code. The

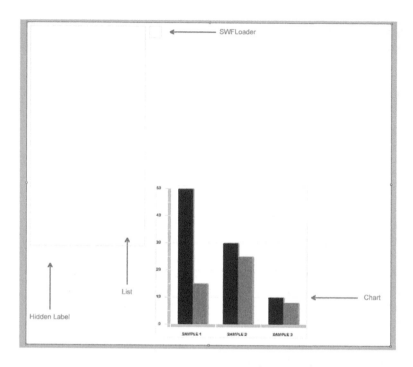

Figure 3.1 The UI design of our YouTube application.

third element is a ColumnChart, which includes three columns to show the number of views, favorites, and comments. We will also set up some states to provide correct feedback to users. We add a label to signal when data are loading or there is an error in the retrieval. Our design view should look like Figure 3.1.

The code should look like the following.

```
<s:Application ...
   currentState="Normal"
   width="960' height="850">

<s:states>
   <s:State name="Normal"/>
   <s:State name="Loading"/>
   <s:State name="Error"/>
</s:states>

<s:List id="videoList"
   width="300" height="580"
   x="10" y="10">

</s:List>

<mx:SWFLoader id="videoDisplay"
   x="320" y="10"/>

<mx:ColumnChart
   x="980" y="10">

   <mx:series>
       <mx:ColumnSeries />
```

```
                <mx:ColumnSeries />
                <mx:ColumnSeries />
            </mx:series>

        </mx:ColumnChart>

        <s:Label
            x="10" y="618"
            text="Loading ..."
            includeIn="Error,Loading"
            text.Error="Error in loading video list"
            color.Error="#FF0000"/>

    </s:Application>
```

Configuration of the Web Service

The documentation for the YouTube API is available at *http://code.google.com/apis/youtube/2.0/reference.html*. There is a detailed description of everything we need to retrieve information about videos and feeds. In particular, we are interested in standard feeds,[1] as highlighted in Figure 3.2.

This URL will retrieve the list of most viewed videos on YouTube. Data are formatted in Atom,[2] but tags are enhanced with elements from different schemas. Here is a skeleton of the result.

```
<feed>
  <id> ... </id>
  <updated> ... </updated>

  ...

  <entry>
    <id>...</id>
    <published>...</published>
    <updated>...</updated>

    ...
    <title type="text"> ... </title>
    ...
  <gd:comments>
      <gd:feedLink href="..." countHint="2059962"/>
  </gd:comments>

  ...

  <yt:statistics
      favoriteCount="46087"
      viewCount="344881911"/>
  </entry>

  ...

</feed>
```

---

[1] See *http://code.google.com/apis/youtube/2.0/reference.html#Standard_feeds*.
[2] See *http://en.wikipedia.org/wiki/Atom_(standard)*.

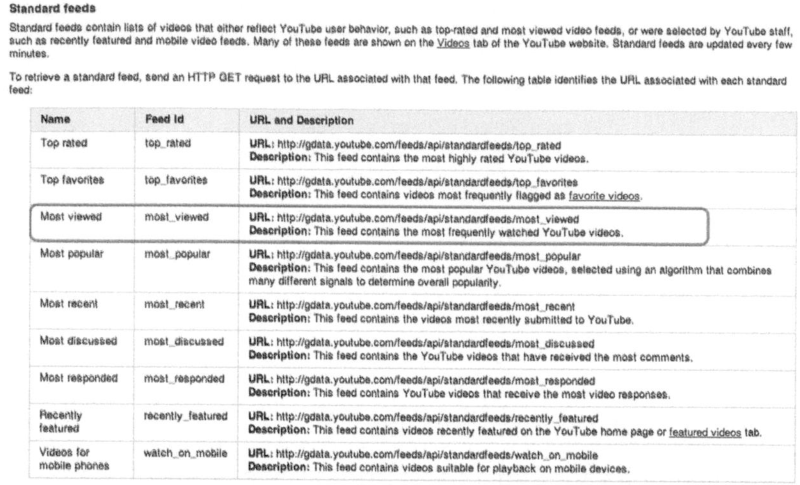

Standard feeds

Standard feeds contain lists of videos that either reflect YouTube user behavior, such as top-rated and most viewed video feeds, or were selected by YouTube staff, such as recently featured and mobile video feeds. Many of these feeds are shown on the Videos tab of the YouTube website. Standard feeds are updated every few minutes.

To retrieve a standard feed, send an HTTP GET request to the URL associated with that feed. The following table identifies the URL associated with each standard feed:

Name	Feed Id	URL and Description
Top rated	top_rated	**URL:** http://gdata.youtube.com/feeds/api/standardfeeds/top_rated **Description:** This feed contains the most highly rated YouTube videos.
Top favorites	top_favorites	**URL:** http://gdata.youtube.com/feeds/api/standardfeeds/top_favorites **Description:** This feed contains videos most frequently flagged as favorite videos.
Most viewed	most_viewed	**URL:** http://gdata.youtube.com/feeds/api/standardfeeds/most_viewed **Description:** This feed contains the most frequently watched YouTube videos.
Most popular	most_popular	**URL:** http://gdata.youtube.com/feeds/api/standardfeeds/most_popular **Description:** This feed contains the most popular YouTube videos, selected using an algorithm that combines many different signals to determine overall popularity.
Most recent	most_recent	**URL:** http://gdata.youtube.com/feeds/api/standardfeeds/most_recent **Description:** This feed contains the videos most recently submitted to YouTube.
Most discussed	most_discussed	**URL:** http://gdata.youtube.com/feeds/api/standardfeeds/most_discussed **Description:** This feed contains the YouTube videos that have received the most comments.
Most responded	most_responded	**URL:** http://gdata.youtube.com/feeds/api/standardfeeds/most_responded **Description:** This feed contains YouTube videos that receive the most video responses.
Recently featured	recently_featured	**URL:** http://gdata.youtube.com/feeds/api/standardfeeds/recently_featured **Description:** This feed contains videos recently featured on the YouTube home page or featured videos tab.
Videos for mobile phones	watch_on_mobile	**URL:** http://gdata.youtube.com/feeds/api/standardfeeds/watch_on_mobile **Description:** This feed contains videos suitable for playback on mobile devices.

Figure 3.2 Documentation for YouTube's standard feeds.

Here we see in action one of the great features of Flash Builder. We do not have to dig deeper into the documentation of the result format, because Flash Builder will build a data model for us. In our scenario we are particularly interested in the entry element, which represents an instance of video.

We should be fairly used to configuring web services: open the wizard, paste the URL, invoke the service, and instruct Flash Builder on how to match results (Figure 3.3).

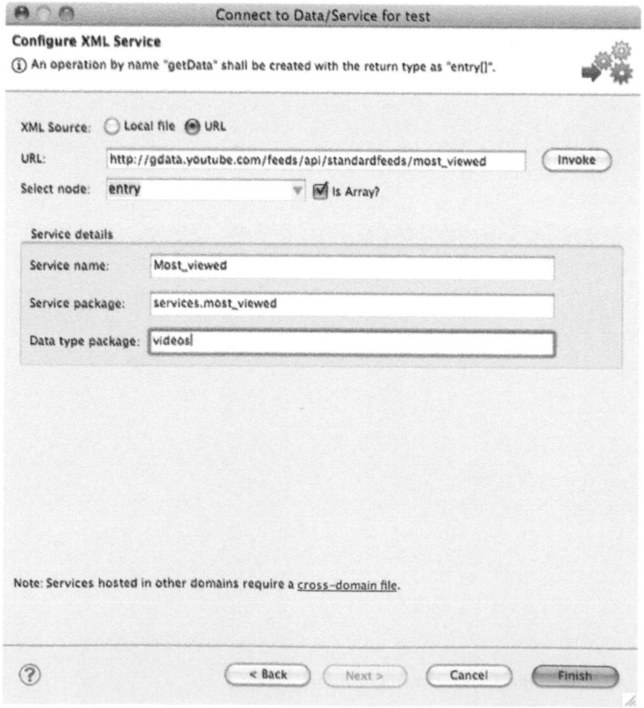

Figure 3.3 Configuration of YouTube's most viewed web service.

To be sure that the web service works correctly we can test it. We can also get a tree view of the structure of returned data (Figure 3.4).

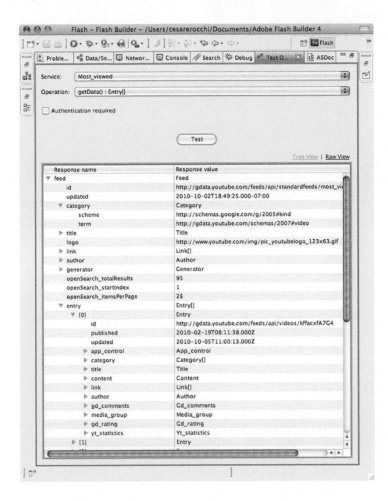

Figure 3.4 Tree view of the YouTube data in the Test Operation panel.

Showing Videos in the List

To connect the web service to the list we drag and drop the `getData` operation onto the instance of `List`, as we are used to. The mapping is defined as in Figure 3.5.

This is the portion of generated code.

```
<fx:Script>
 <![CDATA[

    import mx.controls.Alert;
     import mx.events.FlexEvent;

    protected function
         videoList_creationCompleteHandler(
                         event:FlexEvent):void {
```

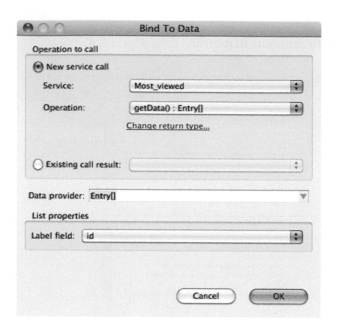

Figure 3.5 Mapping the YouTube service to the `List` component.

```
        getDataResult.token = most_viewed.getData();

  }

]]>

</fx:Script>

<fx:Declarations>
  <s:CallResponder id="getDataResult"/>
  <most_viewed:Most_viewed
    id="most_viewed" fault="..."
    showBusyCursor="true"/>
</fx:Declarations>

<s:List id="videoList"
  width="300" height="580"
  x="10" y="10"
  creationComplete="
    videoList_creationCompleteHandler(event)"
  labelField="id">

<s:dataProvider>
  <s:AsyncListView
    list="{getDataResult.lastResult}"/>
</s:dataProvider>

</s:List>
```

Like in the previous section, we make some modifications to the code to make it more suitable to our needs. First, we can delete the `creationComplete` on the `List` component and move the code in a `init()` function associated to the application. Second, we can get rid of the `labelField` property and create a custom function to show the title of the video in the list. Finally, we add state-switching code where appropriate. The refactored version of the code follows (with changes highlighted).

```
<s:Application ...
    creationComplete="init()"
    ...
    xmlns:most_viewed="services.most_viewed.*">

<fx:Script>
<![CDATA[

protected function init():void {

    getDataResult.token = most_viewed.getData();
    currentState = "Loading";

}

private function getLabelField(item:Object):String{

    return item.media_group.media_title.title;

}

]]>

</fx:Script>

<fx:Declarations>
    <s:CallResponder id="getDataResult"/>
    <most_viewed:Most_viewed
        id="most_viewed"
        fault="currentState = 'Error'"
        result="currentState = 'Normal'"
        showBusyCursor="true"/>
</fx:Declarations>

<s:List id="videoList"
    labelFunction="getLabelField"
    width="300" height="580"
    x="10" y="10">

  <s:dataProvider>
      <s:AsyncListView
          list="{getDataResult.lastResult}"/>
  </s:dataProvider>

</s:List>
```

Figure 3.6 List populated with most recent YouTube videos.

If we run the application at this point we should see that the web service is called at startup and the list is correctly populated (Figure 3.6).

Showing the Video

To show the video we will use YouTube's embedded player, which comes with common components like volume controls and playhead indicator. According to the documentation[3] the correct schema of URL to be loaded is *http://www.youtube.com/v/ VIDEO_ID?version=3*. This is the URL that we have to set as the source for our SWFLoader component. Unfortunately, there is not a quick way to extract the ID of a video from the feed returned by the web service. We will have to do some string processing, as in the following code, which is executed whenever a list item is clicked.

```
private function onItemClick():void {

  var googleID:String =
          videoList.selectedItem.id as String;
  var arr:Array = googleID.split('/');
  var videoID:String = arr[arr.length-1];
  var u:String =
     "http://www.youtube.com/v/"+videoID+"&version=3";
  videoDisplay.source = u;

}

<s:List
    id="videoList"
    click="onItemClick()"
    ... >
    ...
</s:List>
```

This is needed because the ID of a YouTube video has the form *http://gdata.youtube.com/feeds/api/videos/VIDEOID*, and we have to extract just its final part. Then we can build a URL as requested and set it as the source of our SWFLoader instance.

Stop Current Video

If you play with the example built so far you will notice a bug. When you start playing a video and then click on a different item on the list, the audio of the previous video keeps playing. This happens because we load a new video without stopping the previous one. Moreover, whenever we load a new video we loose the reference to the previous one, so things can get messy quickly.

To overcome this situation we need to stop the current video before loading a new one. There is a small code to add to our handler, as follows.

[3] See *http://code.google.com/apis/youtube/flash_api_reference.html#GettingStarted.*

```
private function onItemClick():void {

    var player:Object = videoDisplay.content as Object;

    if (player)
        player.stopVideo();

    var googleID:String =
                videoList.selectedItem.id as String;
    var arr:Array = googleID.split('/');

    var videoID:String = arr[arr.length-1];

    var u:String =
        "http://www.youtube.com/v/"+videoID+"&version=3";
    videoDisplay.source = u;

}
```

If the player variable has a value it means there is a selected video. We have to call its `stopVideo()` before loading a new one.

At this point we are left with the final step, showing statistics.

Displaying Data on the Chart

Unlike the examples shown during the explanation of charts, in this example we do not have an XML-based representation of a data chart and we have to build it on-the-fly. Instead of creating an XML string we directly create an ArrayCollection class, and we populate it with the data we want to show in the chart. First, we add an instance of it to the application and we make it bindable, so it notifies listeners whenever it changes.

```
<fx:Script>
<![CDATA[

    import mx.collections.ArrayCollection;

    [Bindable]
    private var statsArray:ArrayCollection =
                            new ArrayCollection();

    ...

</fx:Script>
```

Second, we create a function that builds the elements of the ArrayCollection class. The elements are of type `Object`. Elements are made key/value couples and carry the data related to the item currently selected in the list of videos.

```
private function buildChartData():void {

    statsArray.removeAll();

    var entry:Entry = videoList.selectedItem as Entry;

    var vCount:Object =
```

```
                                     {viewCount:entry.yt_statistics.viewCount,
                                         name:"Views"};

                            var fCount:Object =
                                     {favCount:entry.yt_statistics.favoriteCount,
                                         name:"Favorites"};

                            var cCount:Object =
                                     {commentCount:
                                         entry.gd_comments.gd_feedLink.countHint,
                                     name:"Comments"};

                            statsArray.addItem(vCount);
                            statsArray.addItem(fCount);
                            statsArray.addItem(cCount);

                     }
```

Then we can call this function at the end of the `onItemClick()` handler.

```
                    private function onItemClick():void {

                        var player:Object = videoDisplay.content as Object;

                        ...

                        buildChartData();

                    }
```

Finally, we modify the chart as follows.

```
            <mx:ColumnChart
                visible="{videoList.selectedItem != null}"
                dataProvider="{statsArray}"
                showDataTips="true"
                x="339" y="430">

                <mx:horizontalAxis>
                        <mx:CategoryAxis categoryField="name"/>
                </mx:horizontalAxis>

                <mx:series>
                        <mx:ColumnSeries yField="viewCount"/>
                        <mx:ColumnSeries yField="favCount"/>
                        <mx:ColumnSeries yField="commentCount"/>
                </mx:series>
            </mx:ColumnChart>
```

Notice that the fillers of the `yField` and `categoryField` properties have to match the property names used in the elements of the ArrayCollection class.

Figure 3.7 shows a screenshot of the final application working.

Not all the videos are viewable in our application. Some have been restricted to play only on the YouTube web site. To find out which one, you should explore the property `app_control.yt_state.state` of the Entry class.

Here is the final code of the main application.

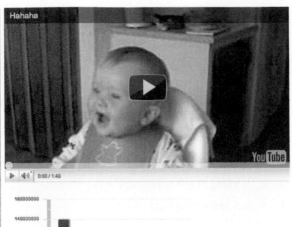

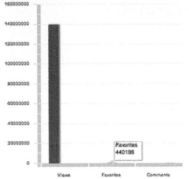

Figure 3.7 A screenshot of the YouTube application.

```
<s:Application ...
  creationComplete="init()"
  currentState="Normal"
  width="960" height="850"
  xmlns:most_viewed="services.most_viewed.*">

  <s:states>
    <s:State name="Normal"/>
    <s:State name="Loading"/>
    <s:State name="Error"/>
  </s:states>

  <fx:Script>

  <![CDATA[
    import mx.collections.ArrayCollection;

    [Bindable]
    private var statsArray:ArrayCollection =
                          new ArrayCollection();

    protected function init():void {

        getDataResult.token = most_viewed.getData();
        currentState = "Loading";

    }

    private function onItemClick():void {
```

```
        var player:Object =
                        videoDisplay.content as Object;

        if (player)
            player.stopVideo();

        var googleID:String =
                    videoList.selectedItem.id as String;
        var arr:Array = googleID.split('/');
         var videoID:String = arr[arr.length-1];
        var u:String =
        "http://www.youtube.com/v/"+videoID+"&version=3";

        videoDisplay.source = u;

    buildChartData();

}

private function buildChartData():void {

    statsArray.removeAll();
    var entry:Entry =
                    videoList.selectedItem as Entry;

    var vCount:Object =
        {viewCount:entry.yt_statistics.viewCount,
        name:"Views"};

    var fCount:Object =
        {favCount:entry.yt_statistics.favoriteCount,
        name:"Favorites"};

    var cCount:Object =
        {commentCount:
          entry.gd_comments.gd_feedLink.countHint,
        name:"Comments"};

    statsArray.addItem(vCount);
statsArray.addItem(fCount);
statsArray.addItem(cCount);

}

private function getLabelField(it:Object):String{

        return it.media_group.media_title.title;

}

]]>
</fx:Script>

<fx:Declarations>
    <s:CallResponder id="getDataResult"/>
    <most_viewed:Most_viewed
            id="most_viewed"
            fault="currentState = 'Error'"
            result="currentState = 'Normal'"
```

```
                    showBusyCursor="true"/>
    </fx:Declarations>

    <s:List id="videoList"
        click="onItemClick()"
        labelFunction="getLabelField"
        width="300" height="580"
        x="10" y="10">

    <s:dataProvider>
      <s:AsyncListView
          list="{getDataResult.lastResult}"/>
    </s:dataProvider>

    </s:List>

    <mx:SWFLoader
        id="videoDisplay"
        x="320" y="10"/>

    <mx:ColumnChart
        visible="{videoList.selectedItem != null}"
        dataProvider="{statsArray}"
        showDataTips="true"
        x="339" y="430">

            <mx:horizontalAxis>
                <mx:CategoryAxis categoryField="name"/>
            </mx:horizontalAxis>

            <mx:series>
                <mx:ColumnSeries yField="viewCount"/>
                <mx:ColumnSeries yField="favCount"/>
                <mx:ColumnSeries yField="commentCount"/>
            </mx:series>

    </mx:ColumnChart>

    <s:Label
        x="10" y="618"
        text="Loading..."
        includeIn="Error,Loading"
        text.Error="Error in loading video list"
        color.Error="#FF0000"/>

</s:Application>
```

Possible Improvements

This project can be refined by implementing the following features:

- Add a search web service.
- Add animation to the chart.
- Filter out videos that are not playable in the application.

BUILDING AIR APPLICATIONS

In this section we describe an Adobe AIR application and its differences with respect to Flex applications. We also describe how to set up an Adobe AIR project and explain the different ways to package an application for distribution. We highlight the capabilities of the Adobe AIR framework, such as reading and writing files, interacting with local databases, and detecting and manipulating storage devices connected to the computer.

AIR is an acronym for Adobe Integrated Runtime. Much like the Java runtime, it is an environment that allows executing desktop applications built with the Adobe AIR SDK (Software Development Kit). It enables developers to build desktop applications by using well-known web technologies like HTML, CSS (Cascading Style Sheets), JavaScript (JS), and ActionScript. The result is a client application that can exploit the additional features of the desktop, such as running in the background, saving data to a disk, interacting with native processes of the operative system, etc. Recently, Adobe AIR has been extended to support smart phones such as those running on the Android platform (see *http://www.android.com*).

An Adobe AIR application can be built by using two different technologies: with a combination of HTML, JS, and CSS, or with Flash. To create an AIR application you can use many different tools:

- Your preferred editor (to type code and build it with the compiler)
- Adobe Dreamweaver
- Adobe Fireworks
- Adobe Flash
- Flex Builder
- Flash Builder

In this section we illustrate how to build AIR applications with Flash Builder.

Architecture of an AIR Application

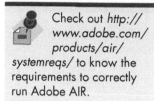

Check out *http://www.adobe.com/products/air/systemreqs/* to know the requirements to correctly run Adobe AIR.

As stated, there are two technologies to build an AIR application: with a combination of HTML, JavaScript, and CSS, or with Flash. In both cases, the runtime handles all the tasks of executing an application and bridging the gap with the desktop. As you can see in Figure 4.1, AIR supports all the three major operating systems: Mac OS X, Linux, and Windows.

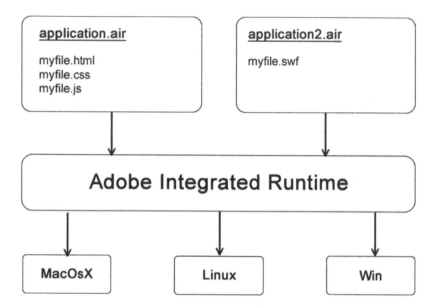

Figure 4.1 Architecture of an AIR application.

In essence, to run Flash content in the browser you need the Flash plug-in; to run an Adobe AIR application on your computer you need the AIR runtime, which comes for free and can be downloaded at *http://get.adobe.com/air/*.

A common way to distribute an Adobe AIR application is by means of an .air package, which in essence is a zip file containing all the files needed to run the application. With the introduction of Adobe AIR 2.0 you can also package your applications as native installers (e.g., .exe for Windows or .dmg for Mac OS X).

Differences between Web and Desktop Applications

Although we use the very same IDE to build an application there are conceptual differences that we should have in mind when we build an AIR application. So far we have been used to seeing `<s:Application>` as the main tag, which wraps every part of our application. When we develop an AIR application we will see a new tag: `<s:WindowedApplication>`. In this change, many things are hidden:

- The runtime is AIR and not the Flash player anymore.
- A different compiler is used (`AMXMLC`).
- A different debugger will be used (`ADL`).
- A whole lot of new libraries are available (e.g., the flash. desktop package).

All these new tools allow developers to build applications that can leverage all the capabilities of Flex. In addition, they can:

- Read and write data on disks.
- Access devices like USB keys.
- Access Internet resources.
- Appear like a native application, with native menus and icons.
- Save data on an embedded database.
- Have a different look and feel according to the operative system.
- Manipulate and record audio from the microphone.
- Interact with native processes.

Is this list stimulating your creativity? It should.

First Dummy Application

Now we will see how to set up a project for creating an Adobe AIR application. It is very similar to the process of creating a Flex application, but there are few key differences to highlight. As we have seen in Section 1 we start the new project wizard ("File > New > Flex Project"). We have to pay attention and select "Desktop" instead of "Web" (Figure 4.2). Just this choice will instruct the IDE to set up an Adobe AIR application, by selecting the appropriate compiler and preconfiguring the run and debug tasks.

At this point we are ready to build our application by exploiting all the knowledge of Flex that we have illustrated so far. In fact, we can use all the user interface (UI) components, containers, and ActionScript code that we have already developed in different projects and use them in this new one. Actually, since the Adobe AIR framework is an extension of the Flex framework, all the code can be reused.

 There are a few exceptions about code reuse. For example, the class spark. components.Application is available only when developing a Flex application. Its corresponding class in AIR is flash.desktop. NativeApplication.

Application Descriptor

If you check out the code generated by the new project wizard you might notice the file "FirstAirApplication-app.xml." This is something new with respect to Flex projects and we will have a look at it.

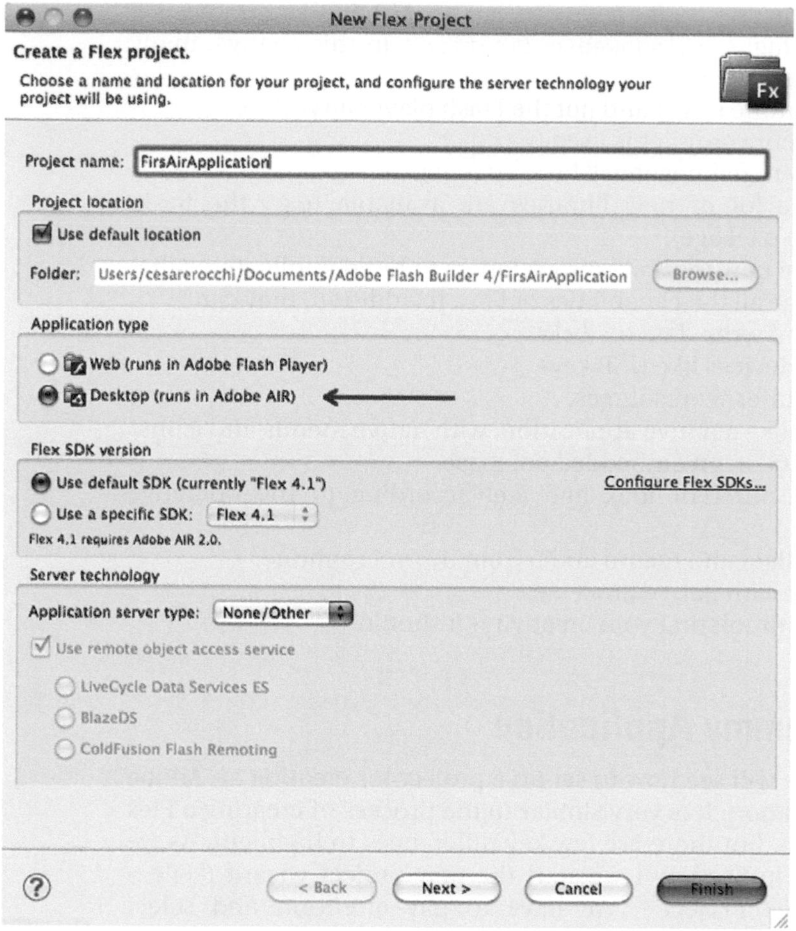

Figure 4.2 AIR project definition.

This file is an *application descriptor*, which contains information to identify, generate, install, and run the application. A desktop application needs some information to correctly appear and work on top of the operative system. Let's see some key properties that are suggested to specify.

id: It identifies your application worldwide. It is better to prefix it with a reversed domain name, like com.studiomagnolia. myapplication.

Filename: The name of the .air file generated by the compiler.

Name: The name of the application itself, shown in the installer.

Description: A snippet of text shown during the installation that is useful to provide information about the application.

Version: The version number of the application; it is useful to show it to the user and to check whether the currently running application needs an update.

initialWindow: Contains information about the first window, which is shown when the application is run; we could also call it the "main" window. We can specify which content to load, which title to show, whether the window is minimizable/resizable, and its geometric properties like position and size.

supportedProfiles: We can describe on which platform the application can run. The default value is "all."

Icon: We can provide a list of icons, with different sizes, to accommodate the rendering of the application's icon in different operative systems.

FileTypes: This allows defining a particular file format that opens the application when double-clicked in a folder.

Some of these fields are optional, but it is suggested to specify them in order to obtain an optimal integration with the hosting operative system.

A Word about Chrome

During the previous description we skipped, on purpose, the property systemChrome. This needs a more detailed description, because it affects the way an application appears on the screen. The chrome is the look and feel of the main window, which hosts the application. If we do not change anything we get a standard chrome, which is the basic look of a standard window according to the operating system (see Figures 4.3–4.5).

Notice that there is a set of handy features already implemented:

- We can move and resize the window.
- We can maximize and minimize by using the buttons at the top of the bar.

FirsAirApplication

Figure 4.3 Native window on Mac OS X.

Figure 4.4 Native window on Ubuntu.

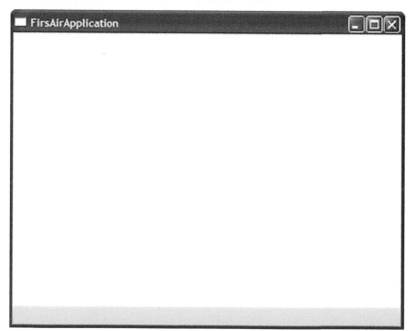

Figure 4.5 Native window on Windows XP.

- On Mac OS X we have the menu application already implemented with a set of default items (Figure 4.6).
- On Windows and Linux we already have a standard menu when you right-click on the bottom bar (Figure 4.7).

If we set the chrome property to "none," then we are left with just a borderless window, which features just the resize capability

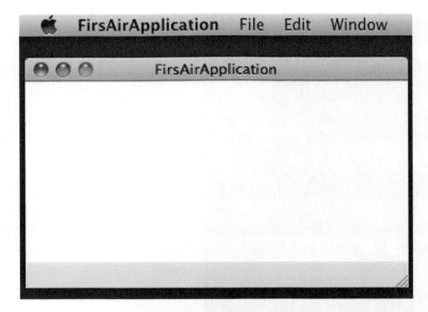

Figure 4.6 Native menu on Mac OS X.

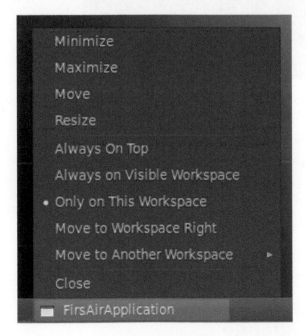

Figure 4.7 Native menu on Ubuntu 10.04.

if you grab the border. This is useful when we want to implement an application with a custom background, like in Figure 4.8. In this case we have to reimplement the features of dragging, minimize, and maximize.

A third option is to use the Flex chrome. This information is not contained in the descriptor file but it is specified as a skin in

Figure 4.8 Application with a custom background.

the `WindowedApplication` tag.[1] So we still set the `systemChrome` to "none" and modify the main MXML file as follows.

```
<Author text type >
<s:WindowedApplication ...>
  <fx:Style>
     @namespace "library://ns.adobe.com/flex/spark";
     WindowedApplication {
        skinClass:ClassReference(
"spark.skins.spark.SparkChromeWindowedApplicationSkin"
           );
        }
     </fx:Style>
</s:WindowedApplication>
```

This way we end up with the window chrome that comes with the Flex library (see Figures 4.9 and 4.10).

---

[1]Since we have not yet introduced the notion of *skin*, we just show how to set the Flex chrome without further explanation. Please refer to Section 5 to learn more about skins.

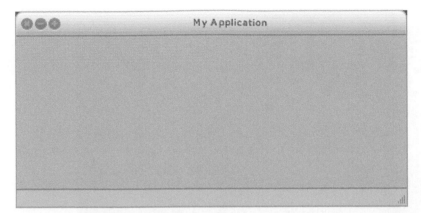

Figure 4.9 Application with the Flex chrome on Mac OS X.

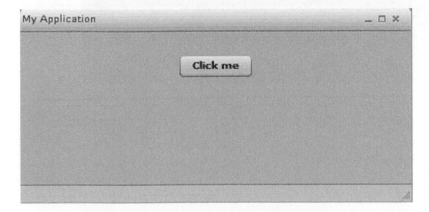

Figure 4.10 Application with the Flex chrome on Windows XP.

Installation and Uninstallation

Another handy feature integrated with Adobe AIR is the ability to act as a native application during installation and uninstallation. When you download or buy an AIR application packaged as an .air file you just need to double-click the file and, provided you have installed the runtime component, it will start a wizard that helps you to install the application. The first step is just a confirmation, which also shows the publisher identity (Figure 4.11). The second step asks the user where to install the application and whether to launch it after completion (Figure 4.12).

As for uninstallation, we can follow the very same procedure adopted to uninstall other binary applications. For example, on Windows XP, we can remove the application by means on the control panel (Figure 4.13).

As we will see at the end of this section it is also possible to package the application as a native installer.

Figure 4.11 First step of the installation wizard.

Figure 4.12 Second step of the installation wizard.

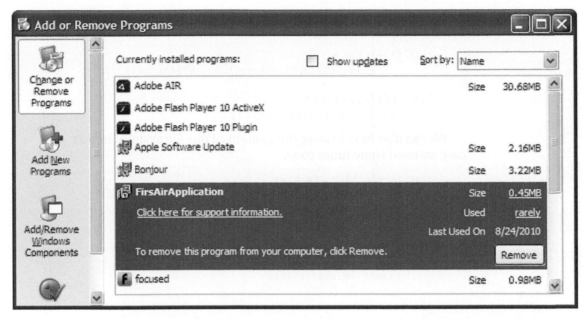

Figure 4.13 Uninstallation in Windows XP.

Read and Write Files

One of the biggest limitations of the Flash player, due to the nature of web browsers and plug-ins, is the inability to access local files. Finally, with Adobe AIR, we have a framework that enables developers to access both local and remote resources. The package `flash.filesystem.*` contains the classes that allow manipulation of local files and directories. The approach is very similar to the one adopted when loading remote URLs: There are classes to represent local files and there are events that notify when the resources are available. Let's start by first illustrating some static properties of the File class.

`File.applicationStorageDirectory` is an application-specific folder, useful, for example, to store temporary data. It has a different path according to the operative system, but in the code we use the very same property to refer to that location.

`File.applicationDirectory` is the folder where the AIR application is installed, for example, /Applications/APPNAME on Mac OS X. Other self-explaining properties are: `File.desktopDirectory`, `File.documentsDirectory`, and `File.userDirectory`.

Let's see a quick example:

```
var file:File =
        File.desktopDirectory.resolvePath("test");
```

This piece of code creates a reference to a folder named Test on the desktop. We said "reference" on purpose because we are not sure whether it exists. In case it does not, we can easily create it, by means of the following instruction.

```
var file:File =
        File.desktopDirectory.resolvePath("test");

if (!file.exists)
    file.createDirectory();
```

We can also fully browse the content of our file system. In this case we need some more code.

```
var file:File = new File();
file.addEventListener(Event.SELECT, onFileSelected);
file.browseForDirectory("Select a directory");

...

private function onFileSelected(e:Event):void {

    trace(file.nativePath);

}
```

As you can see, in this case we need a reference to a void file instance to which we attach an event listener. The event is fired when the file is selected. In that case we can trace the path of the file. We can also read and write the content of files. Since some concepts are better understood when in action, we will build a basic text editor.

Building a Basic Text Editor

Our text editor will implement the following features:
- Open a file.
- Save a file.
- Save a new file if not editing an existing file.

The content of the files manipulated will be simple text. We will put three UI components on the stage: two buttons (to fire Open and Save actions) and a text area, to edit the content. So the visual part of our application is the following.

```
<s:WindowedApplication ...>

    <s:Button label="Open"/>
    <s:Button label="Save"/>
    <s:TextArea id="textArea"/>

</s:WindowedApplication>
```

Let's start with the Open functionality. First, we define a variable to reference the currently opened file and a `FileFilter` object that we'll need to constrain the selection only to .txt files.

```
<s:WindowedApplication ... >

    ...

    private var currentFile:File;

    private var filter:FileFilter =
            new FileFilter("Text Files (txt)","*.txt;");

    ...

    <s:Button label="Open"/>
    <s:Button label="Save" />
    <s:TextArea id="textArea"/>

</s:WindowedApplication>
```

Then we add the open() function as follows.

```
<s:WindowedApplication ... >

 ...

    private var currentFile:File;

    private var filter:FileFilter =
            new FileFilter("Text Files (txt)","*.txt;");

    private function open():void {

       var f:File = new File();
       f.addEventListener(Event.SELECT,
                          onFileSelectedForOpen);
       f.browseForOpen("Select a directory", [filter]);

    }
       <s:Button label="Open" click="open()" />
       <s:Button label="Save" />
       <s:TextArea id="textArea" />

    </s:WindowedApplication>
```

Here we create a reference to a file instance, we attach an event listener, and we call browseForOpen(). This function will open a native menu to browse for files. We constrain the selection by passing the filter created above in an array. At this point we can even run our application. When clicking on the Open button we will see a native dialog to browse our file system (Figure 4.14).

We did not write much code and we are already there! Let's now handle the event when the user selects a .txt file.

```
<s:WindowedApplication ... >
  private var currentFile:File;
  private var filter:FileFilter =
          new FileFilter("Text Files (txt)","*.txt;");
```

Figure 4.14 Native dialog on Mac OS X.

```
private function open():void {

  var f:File = new File();
  f.addEventListener(Event.SELECT,
                     onFileSelectedForOpen);
  f.browseForOpen("Select a directory", [filter]);
}

private function onFileSelectedForOpen
                        (e:Event):void {

  currentFile = new File(e.target.nativePath);
  var inStream:FileStream = new FileStream();

  inStream.open(currentFile, FileMode.READ);
  textArea.text =
        inStream.readUTFBytes(inStream.bytesAvailable);

}

...

<s:Button label="Open" click="open()" />
<s:Button label="Save" />
<s:TextArea id="textArea" />

</s:WindowedApplication>
```

Here, we save the reference to the `currentFile`, so we are ready in case we need to save it. To read data from the file we use an instance of `FileStream`. This class allows manipulating data to be written to or read from a file instance. You might also notice that, when we call its `open()` method, we pass a `FileMode` constant besides the reference to the current file. In this case we passed only Read mode, because we are just copying the data in the file to the `textArea` component. We will use the same class later when we write new content to the file. At this stage we can again run our application and see the result: The text in the file will be displayed in the `textArea` component of our application.

We are now left with the Save part. Let's start with the following function.

```
...

private function save():void {

    var outStream:FileStream = new FileStream();
    outStream.open(currentFile, FileMode.WRITE);

    outStream.writeUTFBytes(textArea.text);
    outStream.close();

}

...
```

We again use a `FileStream` class but this time we need to open in the Write mode. We are then ready to dump the text into the file and close the stream. There is just one scenario left out. What if the user opens the application and starts typing? This is allowed. However, what happens when he or she clicks "Save"? The application crashes because the reference to `currentFile` is undefined, given that it is instantiated in the Open method. In this case we need to modify our Save functionality as follows.

```
private function save():void {

    if (!currentFile) {
        saveAs();
        return;
    }

    var outStream:FileStream = new FileStream();
    outStream.open(currentFile, FileMode.WRITE);

    outStream.writeUTFBytes(textArea.text);
    outStream.close();

}
```

When the variable is not instantiated we call another function and skip the rest of the code. The `saveAs` method uses another feature of the `File` class, `browseForSave`.

```
private function saveAs():void {

    var f:File = File.documentsDirectory;
    f.browseForSave("Save As");
    f.addEventListener(Event.SELECT,
                       onFileSelectedForSave);

}
```

This opens the same native dialog with a box to specify the name of the file to be saved (Figure 4.15).

The last step is the definition of the event when the user has defined the name of the file to be saved, and this is pretty similar to the Save method just defined.

```
private function onFileSelectedForSave
                       (event:Event):void {
    var file:File = File(event.target);
    var outStream:FileStream = new FileStream();
    outStream.open(file,FileMode.WRITE);
    outStream.writeUTFBytes(textArea.text);
    outStream.close();

}
```

Now our application is complete and we can play with it by opening, modifying, and saving text files on our disks. Here is the complete listing.

```
<s:WindowedApplication .. >

<fx:Script>
<![CDATA[

    private var currentFile:File;
    private var filter:FileFilter =
        new FileFilter("Text Files (txt)","*.txt;");

    private function open():void {

        var f:File = new File();
        f.addEventListener(Event.SELECT,
                           onFileSelectedForOpen
                           );
```

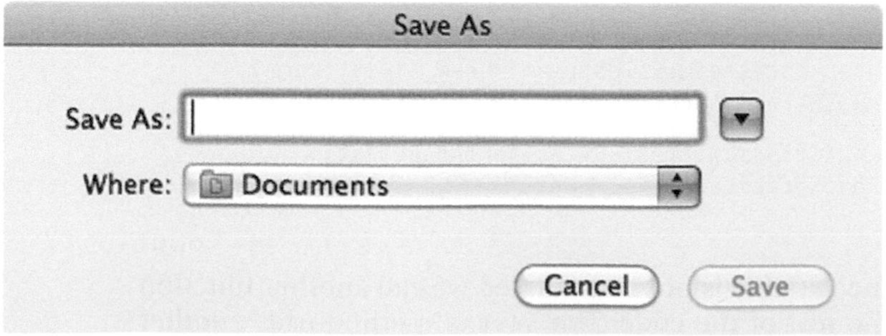

Save As

Save As: |

Where: [📁] Documents

Cancel   Save

Figure 4.15 Native dialog in Save mode on Mac OS X.

```
    f.browseForOpen("Select a directory", [filter]);

}

private function onFileSelectedForOpen
                    (e:Event):void {

    currentFile = new File(e.target.nativePath);
    var inStream:FileStream = new FileStream();
    inStream.open(currentFile, FileMode.READ);
    textArea.text =
        inStream.readUTFBytes(inStream.bytesAvailable);

}

private function save():void {

    if (!currentFile) {
      saveAs();
      return;

}

    var outStream:FileStream = new FileStream();
    outStream.open(currentFile, FileMode.WRITE);
    outStream.writeUTFBytes(textArea.text);
    outStream.close();

}

private function saveAs():void {

    var f:File = File.documentsDirectory;
    f.browseForSave("Save As");
    f.addEventListener(Event.SELECT,
                    onFileSelectedForSave);

}

private function onFileSelectedForSave
                       (event:Event):void {

    var file:File = File(event.target);
    var outStream:FileStream = new FileStream();
    outStream.open(file,FileMode.WRITE);
    outStream.writeUTFBytes(textArea.text);
    outStream.close();

}

]]>
</fx:Script>

<s:Button label="Open" click="open()"/>
<s:Button label="Save" click="save()"/>
<s:TextArea id="textArea" width="492" height="280"/>

</s:WindowedApplication>
```

Detect Storage Devices

Since we just illustrated how to browse data on local disks, let's have a look at a complimentary aspect: how to manipulate data on USB-connected storage devices. This is a new feature introduced in Adobe AIR 2.0, so it will not work on previous versions.

A new class `StorageVolumeInfo` has been introduced. It is a singleton class, much like Application class, which notifies us when a storage volume has been connected to a computer.

Its usage is pretty simple and, with respect to a file, we save one line of code because we do not need to create an instance, but we simply attach an event listener as follows.

```
StorageVolumeInfo.storageVolumeInfo.addEventListener(
    StorageVolumeChangeEvent.STORAGE_VOLUME_MOUNT,
    onVolumeMounted);
```

> A *Singleton* class is a class that can be instantiated only once. It is pretty useful when you need one object (and just one) to coordinate information across an application.

From now on we will be notified when a storage volume has been successfully mounted and the corresponding callback will be executed. Let's now extend the previous example with a new feature, Save to Key. Besides Open and Save we will add a third button that gets enabled when a storage volume is connected. When the user presses the button the file will be backed up to the USB key. When the application starts up we set up event listeners.

```
<s:WindowedApplication
    creationComplete="init()">

<fx:Script>
<![CDATA[

  private function init():void {

    StorageVolumeInfo.storageVolumeInfo.addEventListener(
        StorageVolumeChangeEvent.STORAGE_VOLUME_MOUNT,
        onVolumeMounted);

    StorageVolumeInfo.storageVolumeInfo.addEventListener(
        StorageVolumeChangeEvent.STORAGE_VOLUME_UNMOUNT,
        onVolumeUnmounted);

  }
</fx:Script>

</s:WindowedApplication>
```

Then we need a variable to refer to the storage volume. We make it bindable, so we will use it to enable/disable the Save to Key button.

```
<s:WindowedApplication
    creationComplete="init()">
```

```
<fx:Script>
<![CDATA[

  [Bindable]
  private var volume:StorageVolume;

    private function init():void {

      ...

    }

  </fx:Script>

  ...

  <s:Button

    enabled="{volume != null}"

    label="Save to key"

    click="saveToKey()"/>

</s:WindowedApplication>
```

The final step is to define a method to copy the file on the volume storage.

```
private function saveToKey():void {

    if (currentFile && volume.isWritable) {

      var f:File = this.volume.rootDirectory;
      currentFile.copyTo(f.resolvePath(currentFile.name),
                          true);

    }

}
```

In this case we have to check if the currentFile is set and if the volume is writable. Then we can transfer the file to the key by appending the filename to the path of the storage volume. Here is the complete code with highlighted changes with respect to the previous version.

```
<s:WindowedApplication
    creationComplete="init()">

  <fx:Script>
  <![CDATA[
  private var currentFile:File;
  private var filter:FileFilter =
              new FileFilter("Text Files (txt)","*.
  txt;");

  [Bindable]
  private var volume:StorageVolume;
```

```
        private function init():void {

              StorageVolumeInfo.storageVolumeInfo.
        addEventListener(
                    StorageVolumeChangeEvent.STORAGE_
        VOLUME_MOUNT,
                    onVolumeMounted);

              StorageVolumeInfo.storageVolumeInfo.
        addEventListener(
                    StorageVolumeChangeEvent.STORAGE_
        VOLUME_UNMOUNT,
                    onVolumeUnmounted);

        }

        private function
              onVolumeMounted(e:StorageVolumeChange
        Event):void {
              volume = e.storageVolume;

        }

        private function
              onVolumeUnmounted(e:StorageVolumeChange
        Event):void {
              volume = null;

        }

        private function open():void {

              var f:File = new File();
              f.addEventListener(Event.SELECT,
                             onFileSelectedForOpen);
              f.browseForOpen("Select a directory", [filter]);

        }

        private function onFileSelectedForOpen (e:Event):void {
              currentFile = new File(e.target.nativePath);
              var inStream:FileStream = new FileStream();
              inStream.open(currentFile, FileMode.READ);
              textArea.text =
                    inStream.readUTFBytes(inStream.
        bytesAvailable);

        }

        private function save():void {
              if (!currentFile) {
                 saveAs();
                 return;
              }

              var outStream:FileStream = new FileStream();
              outStream.open(currentFile, FileMode.WRITE);
              outStream.writeUTFBytes(textArea.text);
```

```
        outStream.close();
    }

    private function saveAs():void {
        var f:File = File.documentsDirectory;
        f.browseForSave("Save As");
        f.addEventListener(Event.SELECT,
                        onFileSelectedForSave);

    }

    private function onFileSelectedForSave
            (event:Event):void {
        var file:File = File(event.target);
        var outStream:FileStream = new FileStream();
        outStream.open(file,FileMode.WRITE);
        outStream.writeUTFBytes(textArea.text);
        outStream.close();

    }

    private function saveToKey():void {
        if (currentFile && volume.isWritable) {
         var f:File = this.volume.rootDirectory;
         currentFile.copyTo(f.resolvePath
(currentFile.name),
                        true);

        }
    }
    ]]>
    </fx:Script>

    <s:Button label="Open" click="open()"/>
    <s:Button label="Save" click="save()"/>
    <s:Button
        enabled="{volume != null}"
        label="Save to key"
        click="saveToKey()" />
    <s:TextArea id="textArea"
        width="492" height="280"/>
</s:WindowedApplication>
```

Interacting with the Database

The Adobe AIR runtime also includes a full SQL database engine, which runs locally, and uses the SQLite database system. This opens up endless possibilities like caching data or storing preferences and documents or any kind of data that, for example, you want to be available when the computer is offline. Technically, for each database, the AIR runtime creates a file where data are stored. Databases can also be encrypted in case we want them to be accessed only by the application or a particular user who has been provided with credentials to access it.

There are a few classes that we should know in order to work with local databases:

- flash.data.SQLConnection—to create/open/interact with the database
- flash.data.SQLStatement—to represent an SQL query/command and parameters
- flash.data.SQLResult—to represent the output of a command
- flash.event.SQLEvent—to carry data about an SQL operation (in asynchronous mode)

There are two ways to interact with local databases: synchronous and asynchronous. In the first case the operation is executed in the same sequence of the action code. For example, let's look at the following code.

```
obj.method1();

// synchronous database operation

obj.method2();
```

In this case method2() is called when the operation on the database is finished. It is not wrong or right, it just depends on the scenario. If the code in method2() can be performed without waiting for the result of the database, then it is better to adopt an asynchronous approach to a database operation, which is in general a more flexible approach, but requires a bit more code to be written—for example, to set up event listeners and callback handling.

Create a Database

To create a database we follow a process very similar to the creation of a file. We create an instance of SQLConnection. We can optionally pass a file and open the connection, as in the following code.

```
var connection:SQLConnection = new SQLConnection();
var f:File =
       File.applicationStorageDirectory.resolvePath(
          "DBSample.db" );

connection.openAsync(f); //asynchronous
connection.open(f); //synchronous
```

If we do not provide a file, the database is created in the memory of the computer. Let's assume we follow the asynchronous way. We need to set up some callback to handle events. This has to be done before calling the openAsynch() method.

```
var connection:SQLConnection = new SQLConnection();
var f:File =
        File.applicationStorageDirectory.resolvePath(
            "DBSample.db" );

c.addEventListener(SQLEvent.OPEN, onSQLOpen);
c.addEventListener(SQLErrorEvent.ERROR, onSQLError);
connection.openAsync(f);
```

We can handle events by means of methods as we are used to.

```
private function onSQLOpen(e:SQLEvent) {
        trace("database open");
}

private function onSQLError(e:SQLErrorEvent) {
        trace("error in opening database");
}
```

If this database is new, it is empty. It does not even have a schema—that is, a description of the data to be stored. In SQLite, data are described in the form of tables, so let's create one.[2] The following is the corresponding SQL statement.

```
CREATE TABLE IF NOT EXISTS people

(id INTEGER PRIMARY KEY AUTOINCREMENT,
 firstName TEXT,
 lastName TEXT
);
```

This code instructs the database to create a new table named `people`. Each row in the table (read each instance of object described in the table) has three fields: an ID, and two textual fields, first name and last name. Now that we know how to interact with the database let's put this instruction into ActionScript code. We will exploit the SQLStatement class, which is devised exactly to interact with databases. We have to create an instance, set its connection property to the connection opened previously, and attach the SQL instruction as a string. After setting up the listeners, finally we call execute.

```
var st:SQLStatement = new SQLStatement();
st.sqlConnection = conn;
var sql:String =
   "CREATE TABLE IF NOT EXISTS people (" +
     " id INTEGER PRIMARY KEY AUTOINCREMENT, " +
     " firstName TEXT, " +
     " lastName TEXT)";
```

[2] We will use very basic SQL code, which should be intuitive. If you are not familiar with SQL statements you can check the documentation at *http://www.sqlite.org/lang.html*.

```
st.addEventListener(SQLEvent.RESULT,
                    onStatementSuccess);
st.addEventListener(SQLErrorEvent.ERROR,
                    onStatementError);

st.text = sql;
st.execute();
```

This is one way to interact with the database, but it is not considered a good way. For example, we need to pass parameters when we want to insert an item in the table, like in this SQL statement.

```
"INSERT INTO people (firstName, lastName)
        VALUES ("Cesare", "Rocchi")";
```

Porting this into ActionScript we get to a pretty messy code, where it is easy to get lost or mistype a comma or quote.

```
var name:String = "Cesare";
var surname:String = "Rocchi";
var s:String =
    "INSERT INTO people (firstName, lastName) "+
        "VALUES ("+name+", "+ surname + ")";
```

A much better way is to exploit parameters, which lead to a much cleaner code and a better performance, since the statement string is created just once. Let's see how it works. We create an SQL string of the following form.

```
var sql:String =
    "INSERT INTO people (name, surname)" +
        "VALUES (:name, :surname)";
```

As you can see there are two "placeholders" in the string, `:name` and `:surname`. At this point we can keep this string for all the statements related to the insertion of an item and change the values of the placeholders, by means of the following syntax.

```
sql.parameters[":name"] = "Cesare";
sql.parameters[":surname"] = "Rocchi";
```

Then we proceed as usual, set up event listeners, and call execute. Let's see all this in action with a simple example, an address book.

Building a Simple Address Book

Our application will have simple visuals since we want to focus on database features. There will be a form to insert data, and a data grid to render the items in the database, like in Figure 4.16.

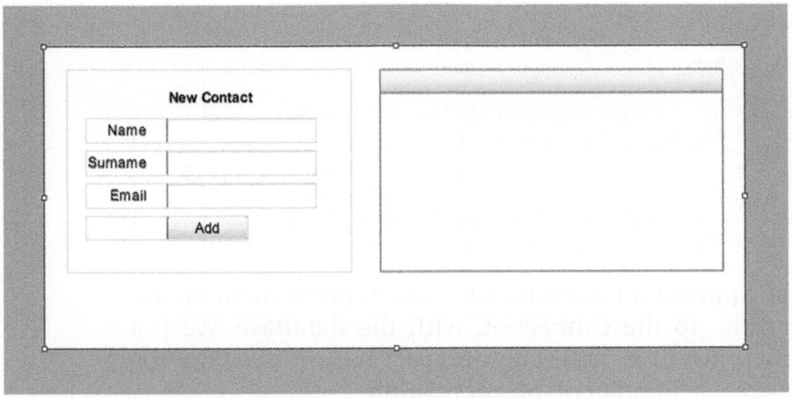

Figure 4.16 Skeleton of our Address Book application.

The code will look like the following.

```
<s:WindowedApplication>
    <mx:Form x="20" y="20" width="244" height="175">
      <mx:FormHeading label="New Contact"/>

      <mx:FormItem label="Name">
         <s:TextInput id="inputName"/>
      </mx:FormItem>

      <mx:FormItem label="Surname">
         <s:TextInput id="inputSurname"/>
      </mx:FormItem>

      <mx:FormItem label="Email">
         <s:TextInput id="inputEmail"/>
      </mx:FormItem>

      <mx:FormItem>
         <s:Button label="Add" click="insert()"/>
      </mx:FormItem>
    </mx:Form>

    <mx:DataGrid
         id="resultsGrid"
         x="288" y="21" width="297" height="174"/>
</s:WindowedApplication>
```

Now we need some variables that will help us manage the database connection and interaction. We will add an SQLConnection instance to be used whenever we have to execute a statement. To query the database we will adopt the parameters approach described above, so we prepare a set of SQL strings to create the table, insert items, and retrieve all the contacts.

```
private var conn:SQLConnection = new SQLConnection();

private var createStatementString:String =
        "CREATE TABLE IF NOT EXISTS people (" +
        " id INTEGER PRIMARY KEY AUTOINCREMENT, " +
        " firstName TEXT, " +
```

```
                        " lastName TEXT, " +
                        " email TEXT " +
                        ")";

        private var insertStatementString:String =
                "INSERT INTO people (firstName, lastName, email)
                                VALUES (:name, :surname, :email)";

        private var allContactsStatementString:String =
                "SELECT * FROM people";
```

When the application starts up we want to perform an operation like setting up the connection with the database. We put these instructions in a method that will be attached to the `creationComplete` handler of the application.

```
        private function init():void {

          var dbFile:File =
            File.desktopDirectory.resolvePath("addressBook.db");
            conn.addEventListener(SQLEvent.OPEN, onOpenSuccess);
            conn.addEventListener(SQLErrorEvent.ERROR,
                                onOpenError);
          conn.openAsync(dbFile);

        }
```

Here we point to two event handlers, which are defined as follows.

```
        private function onOpenSuccess(e:SQLEvent):void {

            trace("connection successfull");
            createTable();
            loadData();
        }

        private function onOpenError(e:SQLErrorEvent):void {

            trace("error in connecting to db");

        }
```

In case of a successful connection we exploit the opportunity to create the table, if it does not exist, and load the items stored in the database. The first time we run the application the schema will be created but the data grid will be empty. On subsequent starts, the application will display people's data in the grid.

```
        private function createTable():void {
            var createStatement:SQLStatement =
                    new SQLStatement();
        createStatement.sqlConnection = conn;
        createStatement.text = createStatementString;
        // might want to setup listeners
        createStatement.execute();

        }
```

```
private function loadData():void {

    allContactsStatement = new SQLStatement();
    allContactsStatement.sqlConnection = conn;
    allContactsStatement.text =
                allContactsStatementString;

    allContactsStatement.addEventListener(
            SQLEvent.RESULT,
            onContactsReceived);

    allContactsStatement.execute();

}
```

Both methods follow the same schema of code:
- Set up an instance of a statement.
- Specify a connection to the database.
- Assign an SQL string.
- Set up listeners.
- Call execute.

When the query to load data is successful we get the results and show them into the grid as follows.

```
private function onContactsReceived(e:SQLEvent):void {

    var result:SQLResult =
            allContactsStatement.getResult();
    resultsGrid.dataProvider = result.data;

}
```

Now we are left with the implementation on data insertion. The method, attached to the click event of the button, is defined as follows.

```
private function insert():void {

    insertStatement = new SQLStatement();
    insertStatement.sqlConnection = conn;
    insertStatement.text = insertStatementString;
    insertStatement.parameters[":name"] =
                        inputName.text;

    insertStatement.parameters[":surname"] =
                        inputSurname.text;

    insertStatement.parameters[":email"] =
                        inputEmail.text;

    insertStatement.addEventListener(SQLEvent.RESULT,
                    onInsertSuccess);

    insertStatement.addEventListener(SQLErrorEvent.ERROR,
                    onInsertError);

    insertStatement.execute();

}
```

With respect to previous statements, which have no parameters, we have to set up the parameter for the insert query. Such parameters are the values typed by the user in the form. If the insertion is successful we reload data from the database to show updates in the grid and we clean up the form.

```
private function onInsertSuccess(e:SQLEvent):void {

    loadData();
    inputName.text = "";
    inputSurname.text = "";
    inputEmail.text = "";

}
```

We are done! Here is the complete code for the example. For sake of clarity, we have omitted a few event handlers, substituted by some comment.

```
<s:WindowedApplication ...
  creationComplete="init()"
  width="604" height="260">

  <fx:Script>
  <![CDATA[

  private var conn:SQLConnection = new SQLConnection();
  private var createStatementString:String =
          "CREATE TABLE IF NOT EXISTS people (" +
            "id INTEGER PRIMARY KEY AUTOINCREMENT, " +
            "firstName TEXT, " +
            "lastName TEXT, " +
            "email TEXT " +
          ")";

  private var insertStatementString:String =
        "INSERT INTO people (firstName, lastName, email)
                    VALUES (:name, :surname, :email)";

  private var allContactsStatementString:String =
                  "SELECT * FROM people";

  private var insertStatement:SQLStatement;
  private var allContactsStatement:SQLStatement

  private function init():void {

    var dbFile:File =
        File.desktopDirectory.resolvePath(
                              "addressBook.db");

        conn.addEventListener(SQLEvent.OPEN,
                              onOpenSuccess);
        conn.addEventListener(SQLErrorEvent.ERROR,
                              onOpenError);
        conn.openAsync(dbFile);

    }
```

```
private function createTable():void {

    var createStatement:SQLStatement =
        new SQLStatement();

    createStatement.sqlConnection = conn;

    createStatement.text = createStatementString;

    // setup handlers

    createStatement.execute();

}

private function onOpenSuccess(e:SQLEvent):void {

    trace("connection successfull");
    createTable();
    loadData();

}

private function onOpenError(e:SQLErrorEvent):void {

  trace("error in connecting to db");

}

private function insert():void {

  insertStatement = new SQLStatement();
  insertStatement.sqlConnection = conn;
  insertStatement.text = insertStatementString;
  insertStatement.parameters[":name"] =
                    inputName.text;
  insertStatement.parameters[":surname"] =
                    inputSurname.text;
  insertStatement.parameters[":email"] =
                    inputEmail.text;

  insertStatement.addEventListener(SQLEvent.RESULT,
                                onInsertSuccess);

  insertStatement.addEventListener(
                SQLErrorEvent.ERROR, onInsertError);

  insertStatement.execute();

}

private function onInsertSuccess(e:SQLEvent):void {

  loadData();

}

private function
            onInsertError(e:SQLErrorEvent):void {
  trace("error in inserting");

}
```

```
private function loadData():void {

  allContactsStatement = new SQLStatement();
  allContactsStatement.sqlConnection = conn;
  allContactsStatement.text =
              allContactsStatementString;
  allContactsStatement.addEventListener(
              SQLEvent.RESULT, onContactsReceived);
  allContactsStatement.execute();

}

private function
        onContactsReceived(e:SQLEvent):void {

  var result:SQLResult =
            allContactsStatement.getResult();
  resultsGrid.dataProvider = result.data;

}
]]>
</fx:Script>

<mx:Form x="20" y="20" width="244" height="175">

    <mx:FormHeading label="New Contact"/>

    <mx:FormItem label="Name">
        <s:TextInput id="inputName"/>
    </mx:FormItem>

    <mx:FormItem label="Surname">
        <s:TextInput id="inputSurname"/>
    </mx:FormItem>

    <mx:FormItem label="Email">
        <s:TextInput id="inputEmail"/>
    </mx:FormItem>

    <mx:FormItem>
        <s:Button label="Add" click="insert()"/>
    </mx:FormItem>
</mx:Form>

<mx:DataGrid
    id="resultsGrid"
    x="288" y="21"
    width="297" height="174"/>
</s:WindowedApplication>
```

Figure 4.17 is a screenshot of the application running.

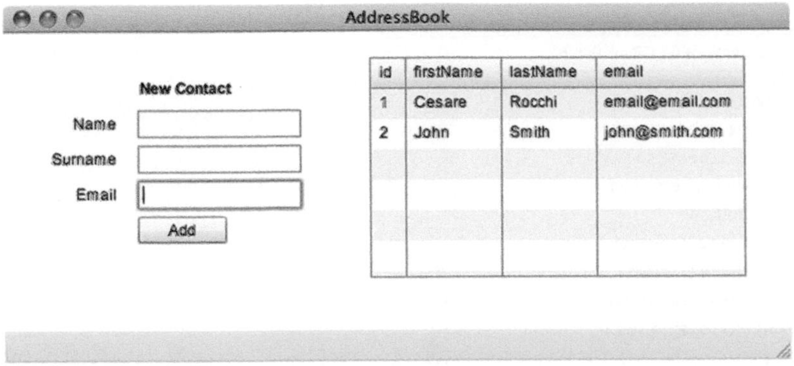

Figure 4.17 Our Address Book application running.

Deploy an AIR Application

So far we have been executing applications in Run or Debug mode. Unlike Flex applications, which are delivered in the form of SWF files, AIR applications need to be packaged in a desktop application form. The are two ways to distribute an AIR application: as a .air package or as a native installer.

The .air package is the classic way to distribute an application since version 1.0 of Adobe AIR. A .air package is a zipped file that contains all the resources needed to install and run the application. If you take an already packaged application and you unzip it, you will see something like Figure 4.18.

The uncompressed folder contains assets, file descriptors, and an SWF file. All this is needed to correctly run the application on the desktop computers. The native installer creates a different file according to the operative system: .exe for Windows, .dmg for Macintosh, and .deb or .rpm for Linux. Let's try to package our last application, the Address Book.

We right-click the project and select "Export" (Figure 4.19). This opens a wizard, which helps us step by step. We select "Release Build" from the options (Figure 4.20). Then we need to select which format to generate. In this case we choose "AIR" (Figure 4.21).

Next is a very important step: the signature of the application. Each AIR application needs to be signed with a certificate, so that the final users will trust the downloaded package to install it. If you do not have a valid certificate you can generate one on-the-fly by clicking "Create" (Figure 4.22). This opens another dialog that allows the creation of a certificate (Figure 4.23).

Once we have it we can go back to the previous dialog, browse for the certificate, and type its password. We can click "Finish" and check out our new packaged application. If we install this file we will see something like in Figure 4.24.

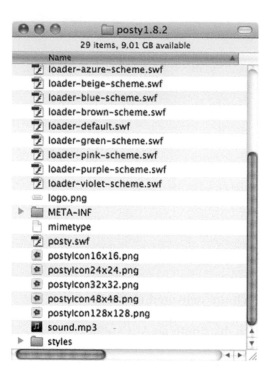

Figure 4.18 Contents of an AIR package.

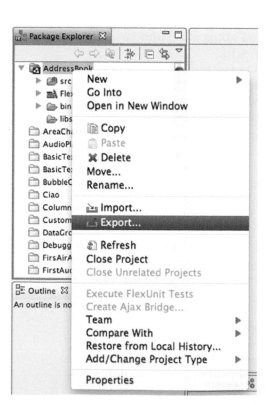

Figure 4.19 To start the export procedure.

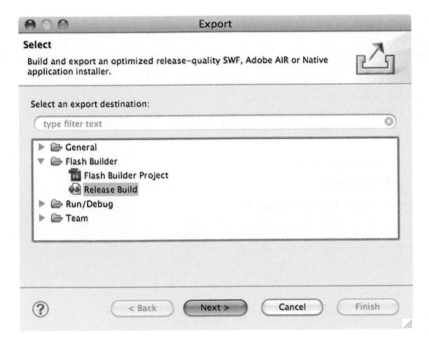

Figure 4.20 Selection of the type of export.

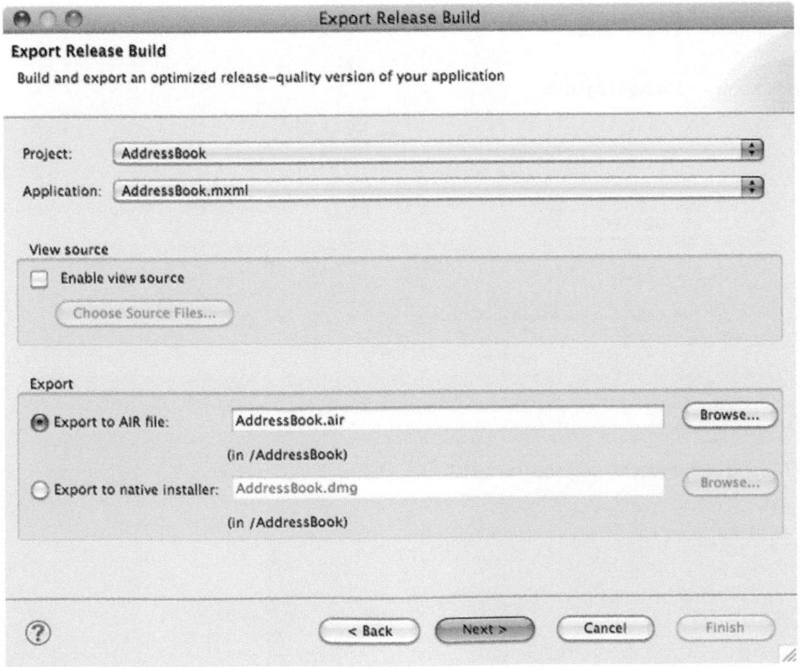

Figure 4.21 Selection of the type of installer.

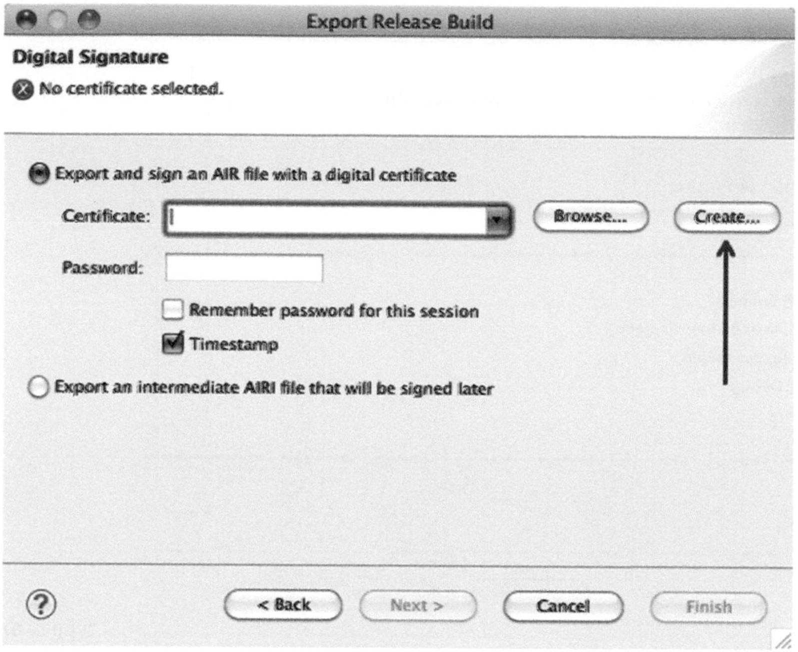

Figure 4.22 To create a self-signed certificate, click "Create."

Figure 4.23 The wizard to create a self-signed certificate.

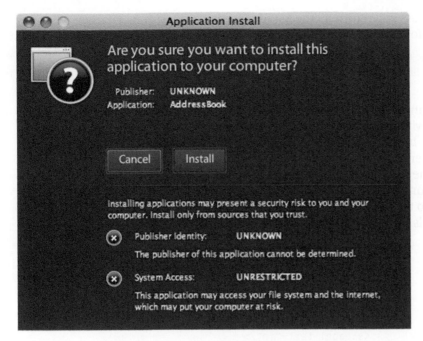

Figure 4.24 Installation of the
packaged application.

This happens because the certificate used to sign the application is self-generated—that is, no authority recognizes it. To obtain a valid certificate, which identifies you or your company worldwide, you have to contact an authority like Thawte (*http:// www.thawte.com/code-signing/index.html*). They will release to you a certificate that identifies you worldwide as a publisher who signs AIR applications.

Interacting with Native Processes

One of the greatest things introduced with Adobe AIR 2.0 is the ability to interact with native processes of the operative system.

Let's suppose you want to look for a file on the local disk. Although you can freely browse the file system, as we have seen previously, you can also exploit features already built (and probably well optimized) in the operative system. For example, on Mac OS X (and Linux) there is a shell command that allows finding files, and it is called Find.[3] Let's suppose we want to look for our certificate, which we lost. We just remember the name: cert.p12. We can open the terminal and type the following command:

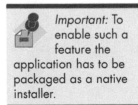

Important: To enable such a feature the application has to be packaged as a native installer.

```
~> find . -name cert.p12
```

[3]To get acquainted with Unix commands you can check out *http://mally.stanford. edu/~sr/computing/basic-unix.html*. The same command can be available on Windows if you install the Cygwin environment; see *http://www.cygwin.com/*.

The process will return all the list of files available with its relative path, as follows:

```
~> find . -name cert.p12
./Desktop/cert.p12
~>
```

We can let Adobe AIR "talk to" this process—for example, running it with parameters and then read returned data. Let's see how. We have to set up a UI to accommodate the input of two parameters: the name of the file to be searched and the path from which the search started (Figure 4.25). We will let the user chose the option to type the path or browse for it. Finally, we need a button to trigger the process and a text area to show the results.

Here is the corresponding code so far.

```
<s:WindowedApplication ...>

    <s:HGroup width="369"
            x="26" y="24" verticalAlign="middle">

            <s:Label text="Find:"/>
            <s:TextInput id="fileToFind"/>
            <s:Label text="in"/>
            <s:TextInput text="{path}"/>
    </s:HGroup>
    <s:Button label="Select Path" />
    <s:Button label="Find" />

    <s:TextArea
            id="output"
```

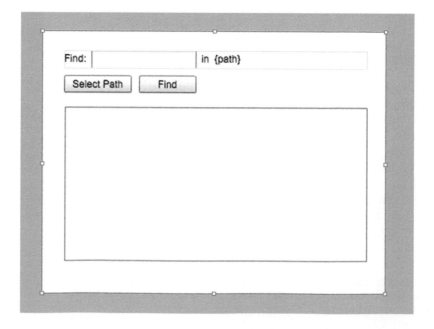

Figure 4.25 UI for the native process Find application.

```
       x="27" y="92"
       width="368" height="188"/>

</s:WindowedApplication>
```

Now we start working on the logic. First, we set up two variables to store the process object and the path from which the search is started. The path will be bindable, so that we disable the button if it is not specified. A search with no path does not make sense. As an alternative we could have put a default parameter like the Home directory. We also set up an initializer to check whether the native process is supported in the environment.

```
<s:WindowedApplication ...
   applicationComplete="init()" >

<fx:Script>
<![CDATA[

   private var process:NativeProcess;
   [Bindable]
   private var path:String;

   public function init():void {
   if (!NativeProcess.isSupported) {
      output.text += "NativeProcess is not supported";
   }
 }

]]>
</fx:Script>

<s:Button
   label="Find"
   click="findFile()"
   enabled="{path != null}" />

...

</s:WindowedApplication>
```

Now we add a method that allows selecting a path on disk, instead of typing it (the user might mistype and this is a handy feature).

```
<s:WindowedApplication ...
   applicationComplete="init()" >

<fx:Script>
<![CDATA[

 private function selectPath():void {
   var file:File = new File();
   file.addEventListener(Event.SELECT,
        function onFolderSelected(e:Event):void {
           path = file.nativePath;

      });
```

```
  file.browseForDirectory("Select a directory");
}

]]>
```

```
</fx:Script>

<s:Button label="Select Path" click="selectPath()"/>

...

</s:WindowedApplication>
```

This is exactly the way to browse for a directory that we have seen before. You might notice that instead of creating a method we pass a function definition directly. This is called a *closure*, which is a definition of an anonymous function. Of course, we could have provided a name for a function, and its separate definition as a method, like we have seen many times in this book.

Now we are left with the core of the application, the Find function. Let's see the conceptual schema to build it:

- Create a file that refers to the command.
- Create an information object to set up details about the process.
- Set up an array of arguments for the command.
- Assign the arguments to the information object.
- Assign event listeners.
- Start the process.
- Handle results in the handlers.

Here it is as code.

```
private function findFile():void {

  var file:File = new File();

  try {

    if (Capabilities.os.toLowerCase().indexOf("win") > -1) {

    //set up for windows

    } else {

      file = new File("/usr/bin/find");

    }

    var processInfo:NativeProcessStartupInfo =
        new NativeProcessStartupInfo();
    processInfo.executable = file;
    var args:Vector.<String> = new Vector.<String>;
    args.push(path);
    args.push('-name');
    args.push(fileToFind.text);
```

```
        processInfo.arguments = args;
        process = new NativeProcess();

        process.addEventListener(
                    ProgressEvent.STANDARD_OUTPUT_DATA,
                    onProcessOutput);

        process.addEventListener(
                    ProgressEvent.STANDARD_ERROR_DATA,
                    onProcessError);

        process.start(processInfo);

    }

  catch (e:Error) {

      output.text += "Error: " +e.message;

  }

}

// Handlers

private function
        onProcessOutput(event:ProgressEvent):void {
    var data:String =
        process.standardOutput.readUTFBytes(
                process.standardOutput.bytesAvailable);
    output.text += data;

}

private function
        onProcessError(event:ProgressEvent):void {
    var data:String =
        process.standardError.readUTFBytes(
                process.standardError.bytesAvailable);
    output.text += data;

}
```

We wrap the creation of the file into a try/catch block, so if something goes wrong we have a notification of possible errors. We should remember to set the path according to the operative system. Unfortunately, different systems have different paths. The delicate part is the definition of parameters, which are not directly assigned to the process, but are stored into an instance of NativeProcessStartupInfo. Parameters are in the form of an array of strings, which are to be in exactly the same order requested by the command.

Finally, we set up listeners and we start the process of passing the information object. The two handlers just print the text area of the result returned by the process. Here is the complete code for the application.

Try/catch is used when some code may fail and we want to intercept the error. In our case, the path to a file might exist, and the creation of the corresponding object might fail, throw an error, and possibly crash the application. If we use a try/catch block we can capture the error and notify the user accordingly.

```
<s:WindowedApplication ...
   title="NativeProcess Find"
   applicationComplete="init()"
   width="418" height="320">

<fx:Script>
<![CDATA[

  private var process:NativeProcess;
  [Bindable]
  private var path:String;

  public function init():void {
     if (!NativeProcess.isSupported) {
       output.text += "NativeProcess is not supported";
     }

  }

   private function findFile():void {

     var file:File = new File();

     try {
       if (Capabilities.os.toLowerCase().indexOf("win")
           > -1) {
       //set up for windows

       }

       else {

         file = new File("/usr/bin/find");

       }

       var processInfo:NativeProcessStartupInfo =
             new NativeProcessStartupInfo();
       processInfo.executable = file;
       var args:Vector.<String> = new Vector.<String>;
       args.push(path);
       args.push('-name');
       args.push(fileToFind.text);
       processInfo.arguments = args;
       process = new NativeProcess();

       process.addEventListener(
             ProgressEvent.STANDARD_OUTPUT_DATA,
             onProcessOutput);

       process.addEventListener(
             ProgressEvent.STANDARD_ERROR_DATA,
             onProcessError);

       process.start(processInfo);

     }

     catch (e:Error) {
```

```
      output.text += "Error: " +e.message;

    }

  }

  private function
          onProcessOutput(event:ProgressEvent):void {

    var data:String =
          process.standardOutput.readUTFBytes(
              process.standardOutput.bytesAvailable);
    output.text += data;

  }

  private function
          onProcessError(event:ProgressEvent):void {

    var data:String =
          process.standardError.readUTFBytes(
              process.standardError.bytesAvailable);
    output.text += data;

  }

  private function selectPath():void {

    var file:File = new File();

    file.addEventListener(Event.SELECT,
          function onFolderSelected (e:Event):void {
              path = file.nativePath;
          });

    file.browseForDirectory("Select a directory");

  }
]]>
</fx:Script>
  <s:HGroup
      width="369"
      x="26" y="24"
      verticalAlign="middle">
        <s:Label text="Find:"/>
        <s:TextInput id="fileToFind"/>
        <s:Label text="in"/>
        <s:TextInput text="{path}"/>
  </s:HGroup>

  <s:Button
      label="Select Path"
      click="selectPath()"
      x="26" y="54"/>

  <s:Button
      label="Find"
```

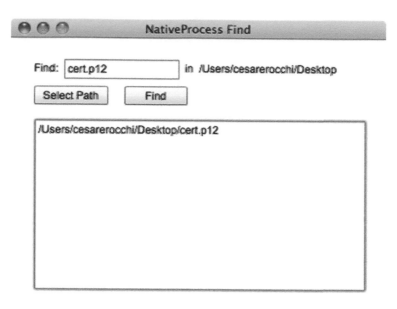

Figure 4.26 A screenshot of the application in action.

```
          click="findFile()"
          enabled="{path != null}"
          x="117" y="54"/>

   <s:TextArea
       id="output"
       x="27" y="92"
       width="368" height="188"/>
</s:WindowedApplication>
```

We should remember that to test all the functionalities of the application we cannot just use the Debug menu. Applications run this way are temporary Adobe AIR–packaged applications, so the interaction with the native process will throw an error. To run it correctly, we have to export it as a native application installer. Figure 4.26 is a screenshot of the application in action.

Conclusion

In this section we have described the architecture of the Adobe AIR framework and the key differences with respect to Flex. In essence, we can consider AIR as an *extension* to the Flex library to handle interaction with the operative system. We have provided different examples of AIR applications, and we have shown how to package them for distribution. Finally, we have highlighted the capabilities of the framework, such as reading and writing files, interacting with local databases, and detecting and manipulating storage devices connected to the computer.

PROJECT 4: FLICKR WITH CACHE

We will build an application that retrieves a set of pictures from Flickr. The application exploits Adobe AIR capability of caching data to access the data when you are offline. The development of this project will help us to get acquainted with the usage of item renderers, ActionScript-managed web services, file system functionalities, and caching.

Description of the Project

This project allows searching for pictures on the popular Flickr service. Pictures will be displayed in a grid, together with their title. The application caches every image loaded and saves it on the file system. Each cached image will be associated to the keyword that the user has searched. If there is no Internet connection the application will show cached versions of images.

Design of the User Interface

The UI of this application is pretty simple. There are input components (a TextInput and a Button), a Label to provide some feedback, and a List. The application has two states: Normal and Loading. Figure 4.1 shows a screenshot of the design view.

We assign an ID to input components, we set a grid layout for the List, the Button is disabled when the text input is empty, and the Label is shown only in the Loading state. The corresponding code is the following.

```
<s:WindowedApplication
   ...
   currentState="Normal">

<s:List
    x="19" y="39"
    width="780" height="400" >
```

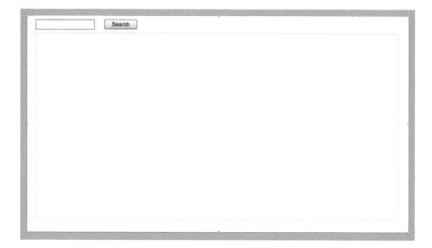

Figure 4.1 The UI design of our Flickr application.

```
<s:layout>
  <s:TileLayout/>
</s:layout>

</s:List>

<s:Button
    x="168" y="10"
    label="Search"
    enabled="{inputKey.text != ''}"/>

<s:TextInput
    id="inputKey"
    x="19" y="10"/>

<s:Label
    x="249" y="15"
    text="Loading"
    fontSize="16"
    includeIn="Loading"/>

</s:WindowedApplication>
```

Set Up the Web Service

Unlike previous projects we set up the web service without using the Data/Services wizard, to get acquainted with what happens behind the scenes of interaction with remote resources. To keep things simple we will use Flickr's public feeds, so there is no need to set up an authentication procedure. The documentation for the feeds is available at *http://www.flickr.com/services/feeds/*. In particular, we will use the public photos feed documented as in Figure 4.2, which allows queries by tag.

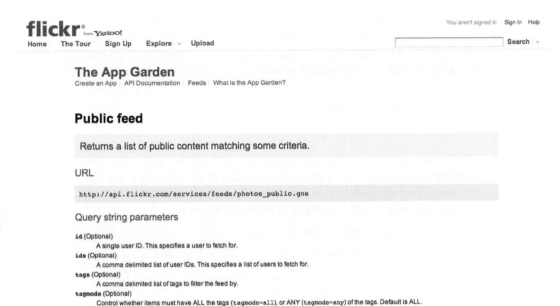

Figure 4.2 Documentation of the public photos feed.

In the declaration section of our application we add an instance of the HTTPService class defined as follows.

```
<fx:Declarations>

    <s:HTTPService
        id="flickrSearchService
        url=
"http://api.flickr.com/services/feeds/photos_public.gne"
        result="onResult(event)"
        fault="onError(event)"/>

</fx:Declarations>
```

Then we add a bindable ArrayCollection class to store the result and we define the handlers as follows.

```
[Bindable]
private var res:ArrayCollection =
                                new ArrayCollection();

private function onResult(event:ResultEvent):void {

  currentState = "Normal";
  res =
    event.result.rss.channel.item as ArrayCollection;

}

private function onError(e:FaultEvent):void {
    trace("error in loading");

}
```

In case of error we just trace a message. If the retrieval is successful we filter all the <item> elements of the result and we store them in the ArrayCollection class we set up as a bindable variable. Finally, we can set the collection as a dataProvider of our list.

```
<s:List
    dataProvider="{res}"
    x="19" y="39"
    width="780" height="400" >
```

To see some results we need a method to call the web service—the search() function associated to the click on the button. The function builds an object that carries parameters and passes it to the send() method of our web service.

```
private function search():void {

  res.removeAll();

  var params:Object = new Object();
  params.format = 'rss_200';
  params.tags = inputKey.text;
  flickrSearchService.send(params);

}

...

<s:Button
    x="168" y="10"
    label="Search"
    click="search()"
    enabled="{inputKey.text != ''}"/>
```

At this point, if we run the application we should see something like in Figure 4.3.

As you can see, everything works as expected, but the application does not know how to render the result, so it just prints out its default string representation. To modify this behavior we need to create an item renderer.

Figure 4.3 First run of our Flickr application.

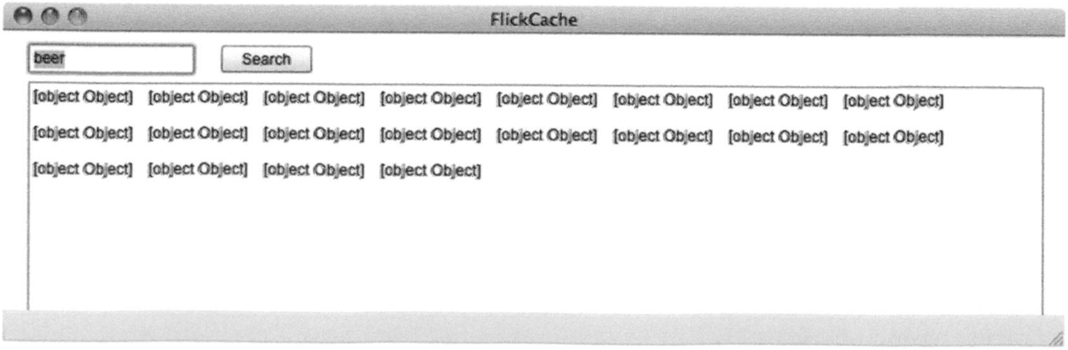

FlickCache

beer   Search

[object Object] [object Object] [object Object] [object Object] [object Object] [object Object] [object Object] [object Object]

[object Object] [object Object] [object Object] [object Object] [object Object] [object Object] [object Object] [object Object]

[object Object] [object Object] [object Object] [object Object]

Creation of the Item Renderer

An item renderer is the component in charge to render data in list-based containers like List, Tree, DataGrid, and so on. It can be composed of subcomponents. For example, in this case, we want to show a thumbnail of the picture and its title, so we create a renderer made of an image and a label. We start the wizard to create a new one (Figure 4.4).

We then specify a width, a layout, and the two components as follows.

```
<s:ItemRenderer ...
  autoDrawBackground="true"
  width="150" >

  <s:layout>
      <s:VerticalLayout horizontalAlign="center"/>
  </s:layout>

  <mx:Image id="thumb"
      width="75" height="75"
      source="{data.thumbnail.url}"/>

  <s:Label text="{data.title}"
      width="100%"
      textAlign="center"
      height="12"/>

</s:ItemRenderer>
```

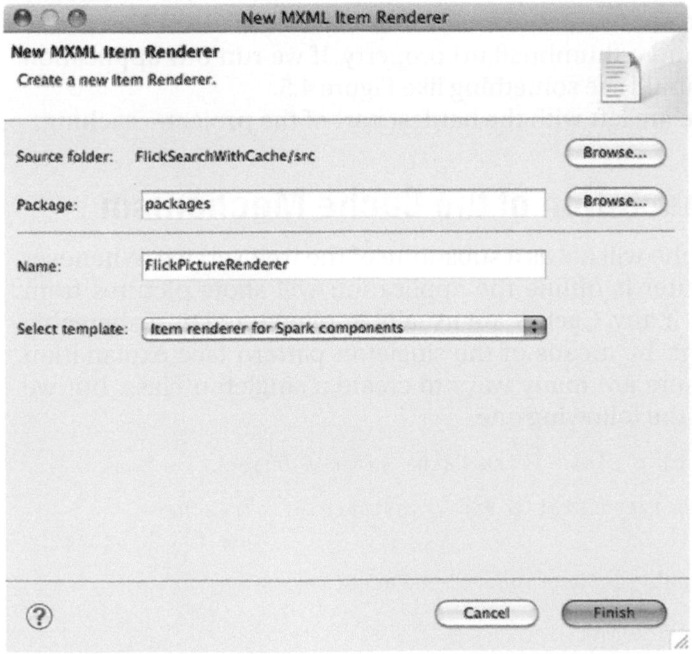

Figure 4.4 Creation of a custom renderer.

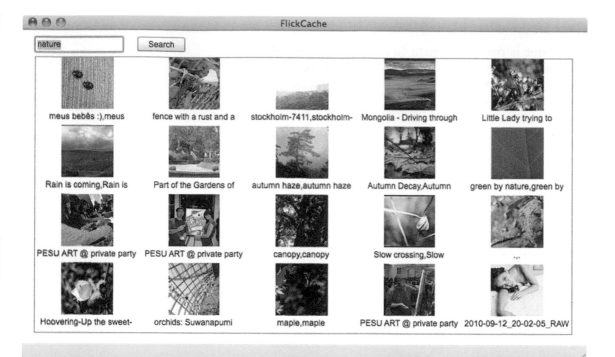

Figure 4.5 Application rendering Flickr pictures in the list.

It is important to notice the data keyword. That is the way to refer to the object currently rendered (one of those stored in the result array that is the dataProvider of the list). Here we already know that an <entry> element from the Flickr feed has a title property and a thumbnail.url property. If we run our application now we should see something like Figure 4.5.

Now we are left with the hardest part of the project—caching.

Implementation of the Cache Mechanism

The cache will act as a substitute of the web service. Whenever the computer is offline the application will show pictures from the cache, if any. Caches are usually implemented as a shareable component, by means of the singleton pattern (see explanation above). There are many ways to create a singleton class, but we will adopt the following one.

```
public class FlickrCache extends Object {
    private static var __instance:FlickrCache =
                                    new FlickrCache();
    public function FlickrCache() {
        super();
    }
}
```

```
public static function get instance():FlickrCache {

  return __instance;

  }
}
```

This code ensures that we don't need to create further instances of the FlickrCache class and that the `instance()` function returns always the same instance of cache. The role of the cache is to store a set of elements and classify them by keyword (the one typed by the user in the application). To do this we create an instance of `Dictionary`, which allows storing data in a key/value fashion. Values will be objects containing information about the `<entry>` elements returned by Flickr (see the next section regarding cache items). We also need a variable to store the current key searched by the user. Finally, we need two methods, one to add items to the cache and one to retrieve them.

The final implementation of the cache is the following.

```
public class FlickrCache extends Object {

  private static var __instance:FlickrCache =
                               new FlickrCache();
  private var _cache:Dictionary = new Dictionary();
  public var currentKey:String;

  public function FlickrCache() {
    super();

  }

  public static function instance():FlickrCache {
    return __instance;
  }

  public function addToCache(item:CacheItem):void {

    if (currentKey) {

      var arr:Array = _cache[currentKey] as Array;

      if (!arr) {
        arr = new Array();
      }

      arr.push(item);
        _cache[currentKey] = arr;

      } else {
        throw new Error("no key set");

      }
    }

    public function getItems(key:String):Array {
      return _cache[key] as Array;
    }

}
```

The getItems() returns an array of elements (might be empty). The addToCache() method inserts elements to be cached in the corresponding array. Let's see how elements of the cache are built.

Creation on the CacheItem

The CacheItem class carries all the data to represent an <entry> element returned by the Flickr web service. In our case we need to store the following properties: title and the image. The CacheItem is also responsible to store the image on the disk, so we also need to have the original Flickr URL (to extract the filename), plus a thumbnail object to maintain the same structure used by the renderer. Here is our class.

```
public class CacheItem extends Object {
  public var title:String;
  public var image:Image;
  public var thumbnail:Object = new Object();
  public var flickrUrl:String;

  public function CacheItem() {

    super();

  }

}
```

At this point we need to add the method that stores images on the disk, as in the following code.

```
public class CacheItem extends Object {

  public var title:String;
  public var image:Image;
  public var thumbnail:Object = new Object();
  public var flickrUrl:String;

  public function CacheItem() {
    super();
  }

  public function doCache():void {

    var imageData:BitmapData =
            new BitmapData(image.width, image.height);
    imageData.draw(image);
    var jpgEncoder:JPEGEncoder = new JPEGEncoder(60);
    var byteArray:ByteArray =
                          jpgEncoder.encode(imageData);

    var arr:Array = flickrUrl.split('/');
    var name:String = arr[arr.length-1];

    var file:File =
        File.desktopDirectory.resolvePath
                        ("flickrCache/"+ name );
```

```
var wr:File = new File( file.nativePath );
var stream:FileStream = new FileStream();
stream.open( wr, FileMode.WRITE);

stream.writeBytes (byteArray, 0,
                   byteArray.length );

stream.close();

thumbnail.url ="file:///"+file.nativePath;
}

}
```

To transfer information contained in an image we have to use the `JPEGEncoder`, which expects a `BitmapData` object, which we create by means of a `draw()` method. The result of the encoding is an array of bytes that we will dump in a file by means of the methods illustrated in this chapter. The files will be stored in a directory, FlickrCache, which we put on the desktop for simplicity. Now we are ready to cache elements.

Usage of the CacheItem

An element is ready to be stored in the cache when its corresponding image has been completely loaded. To enable this we need to modify our renderer to fire the caching mechanism when the image loading has been completed. We create a function, `doCache()`, which is associated to the `complete()` event of the `image` component.

```
<s:ItemRenderer ... >

   ...
<fx:Script>
<![CDATA[

  import cache.*;

  private function doCache():void {

    var item:CacheItem = new CacheItem();
    item.title = data.title;
    item.image = thumb;
    item.flickrUrl = data.thumbnail.url;
    item.doCache();
    FlickrCache.instance().addToCache(item);

  }
]]>
</fx:Script>

<mx:Image id="thumb"
    width="75" height="75"
    complete="doCache()"
```

```
        source="{data.thumbnail.url}"/>

    ...

    </s:ItemRenderer>
```

When the image is loaded the function will create an instance of CacheItem, set its properties, call its `doCache()` method, and add the item to the cache.

If we run the application and we perform a successful search we should see on our desktop a new folder, named FlickrCache, which contains a set of 20 images. They are the thumbs cached by our application (Figure 4.6).

Now we need to use them when there is no Internet connection.

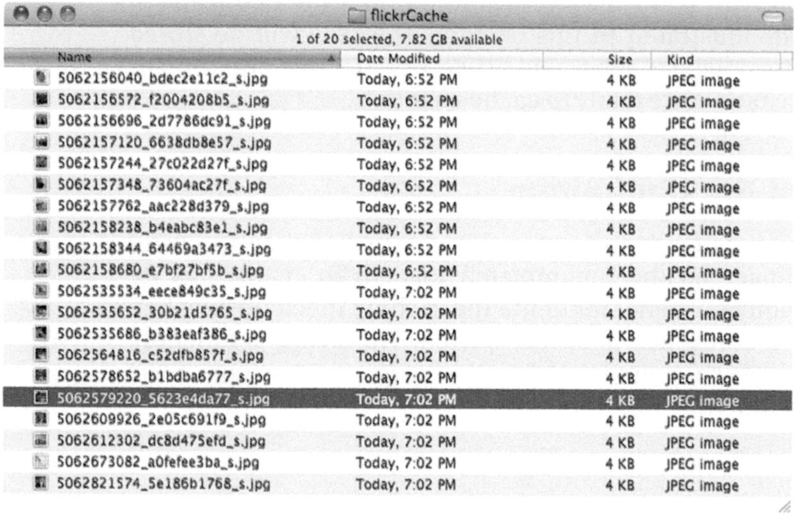

Name	Date Modified	Size	Kind
5062156040_bdec2e11c2_s.jpg	Today, 6:52 PM	4 KB	JPEG image
5062156572_f2004208b5_s.jpg	Today, 6:52 PM	4 KB	JPEG image
5062156696_2d7786dc91_s.jpg	Today, 6:52 PM	4 KB	JPEG image
5062157120_6638db8e57_s.jpg	Today, 6:52 PM	4 KB	JPEG image
5062157244_27c022d27f_s.jpg	Today, 6:52 PM	4 KB	JPEG image
5062157348_73604ac27f_s.jpg	Today, 6:52 PM	4 KB	JPEG image
5062157762_aac228d379_s.jpg	Today, 6:52 PM	4 KB	JPEG image
5062158238_b4eabc83e1_s.jpg	Today, 6:52 PM	4 KB	JPEG image
5062158344_64469a3473_s.jpg	Today, 6:52 PM	4 KB	JPEG image
5062158680_e7bf27bf5b_s.jpg	Today, 6:52 PM	4 KB	JPEG image
5062535534_eece849c35_s.jpg	Today, 7:02 PM	4 KB	JPEG image
5062535652_30b21d5765_s.jpg	Today, 7:02 PM	4 KB	JPEG image
5062535686_b383eaf386_s.jpg	Today, 7:02 PM	4 KB	JPEG image
5062564816_c52dfb857f_s.jpg	Today, 7:02 PM	4 KB	JPEG image
5062578652_b1bdba6777_s.jpg	Today, 7:02 PM	4 KB	JPEG image
5062579220_5623e4da77_s.jpg	Today, 7:02 PM	4 KB	JPEG image
5062609926_2e05c691f9_s.jpg	Today, 7:02 PM	4 KB	JPEG image
5062612302_dc8d475efd_s.jpg	Today, 7:02 PM	4 KB	JPEG image
5062673082_a0fefee3ba_s.jpg	Today, 7:02 PM	4 KB	JPEG image
5062821574_5e186b1768_s.jpg	Today, 7:02 PM	4 KB	JPEG image

Figure 4.6 Images cached by the application.

Usage of the FlickrCache When Offline

To detect whether the application is offline or not we will use a URLMonitor, of which the task is to periodically detect whether the Internet connection is available. We modify our main application as follows.

```
<s:WindowedApplication ...
    creationComplete="init()"
    currentState="Normal">

    <fx:Script>
    <![CDATA[

        import air.net.URLMonitor;
        import mx.collections.ArrayCollection;
        import mx.rpc.events.*;
```

```
    [Bindable]
    private var res:ArrayCollection =
                            new ArrayCollection();

    private var monitor:URLMonitor;

    private function init():void {

        monitor = new URLMonitor(
                new URLRequest("http://www.adobe.com"));
        monitor.start();

    }
    ]]>
    </fx:Script>
```

Finally, we can modify our search function to act according to the availability of the connection.

```
private function search():void {

  res.removeAll();

  if (monitor.available) {

    currentState = "Loading";
    var params:Object = new Object();
    params.format = 'rss_200';
    params.tags = inputKey.text;

     flickrSearchService.send(params);
    FlickrCache.instance().currentKey = inputKey.text;

  } else {

    res = new ArrayCollection(
      FlickrCache.instance().getItems(inputKey.text));
    currentState = "Normal";

  }

}
```

Now we can test the complete application. We start it and run two search operations (e.g., "nature" and "beer"). Then we can switch off the Internet connection and run again the "nature" search: previous results will show up. Here is the completed code of the main application.

```
<s:WindowedApplication
    creationComplete="init()"
    currentState="Normal">

  <fx:Script>
  <![CDATA[

    import air.net.URLMonitor;
    import cache.FlickrCache;
```

```
import mx.collections.ArrayCollection;
import mx.rpc.events.*;

[Bindable]

private var res:ArrayCollection =
                      new ArrayCollection();

private var monitor:URLMonitor;

private function init():void {
  monitor = new URLMonitor(
          new URLRequest("http://www.adobe.com"));
  monitor.start();

}

private function search():void {

  res.removeAll();

  if (monitor.available) {

    currentState = "Loading";
    var params:Object = new Object();
    params.format = 'rss_200';
    params.tags = inputKey.text;

    flickrSearchService.send(params);
    FlickrCache.instance().currentKey =
                            inputKey.text;

  } else {

    res = new ArrayCollection(
          FlickrCache.instance().getItems(
                          inputKey.text));

    currentState = "Normal";

  }

}

private function
          onResult(event:ResultEvent):void {

  currentState = "Normal";
  res = event.result.rss.channel.item
                        as ArrayCollection;

}

private function onError(e:FaultEvent):void {

  trace("error in loading");

}
]]>
</fx:Script>
```

```
<s:states>
    <s:State name="Normal"/>
    <s:State name="Loading"/>
</s:states>

<fx:Declarations>

    <s:HTTPService id="flickrSearchService
        url="
http://api.flickr.com/services/feeds/photos_public.gne"
        result="onResult(event)"
        fault="onError(event)"/>

</fx:Declarations>

<s:List
    itemRenderer="renderers.FlickrPictureRenderer"
    dataProvider="{res}"
    x="19" y="39"
    width="780" height="400" >

    <s:layout>
        <s:TileLayout/>
    </s:layout>

</s:List>

<s:Button
    x="168" y="10"
    label="Search"
    click="search()"
    enabled="{inputKey.text != ''}"/>

<s:TextInput
    id="inputKey"
    x="19" y="10"
    enter="search()" />

<s:Label
    x="249" y="15"
    text="Loading"
    fontSize="16"
    includeIn="Loading"/>

</s:WindowedApplication>
```

Possible Improvements

This application can be refined by implementing the following features:

- Add animation when images are loaded.
- Add an error state.
- Save the cache when closing the application.

CUSTOMIZING THE USER INTERFACE

In this section we describe how to modify the appearance of our Flex applications. First, we need some theoretical knowledge to get acquainted with terms like *theme*, *skin*, and *style*. We describe the difference between families of components (from the Flex 3 and Flex 4 libraries) and the ways of changing instances or classes of elements. Then we will dig deeper into the process of skinning by using Flash Builder and other tools of the Adobe suite like Illustrator and Catalyst.

We briefly describe how to skin components of the Flex 3 library, and then we conclude by illustrating transitions and the application of skins at runtime.

mx **and Spark Components**

When you want to customize the user interface of a Flex application you have to put hands on its visual components. The first thing to know when approaching this task is that there are two "families" of components. The first family of components is mx (sometimes referred to as *halo*). These are the components included in the Flex 3 framework, which are still available in the Flex 4 library. The second family of components is *spark*, which is a whole new set of components that enhance the possibilities of developing and customizing Flex applications. If you remember from Section 1, when you create a new project you are asked to specify many parameters to configure the application. On the last step of the project wizard you are asked to declare which components are used in your Flex application, as shown in Figure 5.1.

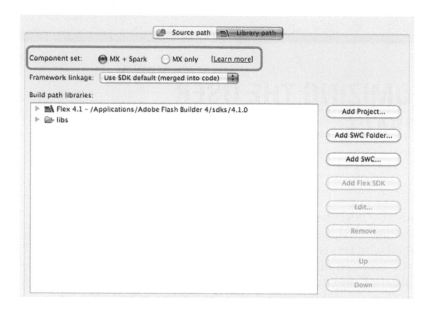

Figure 5.1 Selection of components for a Flex application.

To get to this step you have to click "Next" instead of clicking "Finish" on the first screen of the project wizard.

Let's see what the differences are in terms of code. If you choose "mx only" you end up with the following code.

```
<mx:WindowedApplication
    xmlns:fx="http://ns.adobe.com/mxml/2009""
    xmlns:mx="library://ns.adobe.com/flex/mx"
    layout="absolute">

</mx:WindowedApplication>
```

This is a Flex application that features only mx components. The main tag belongs to this family, and the defined namespace refers only to components included in the Flex 3 library.

```
<s:WindowedApplication
    xmlns:fx="http://ns.adobe.com/mxml/2009"
    xmlns:s="library://ns.adobe.com/flex/spark"
    xmlns:mx="library://ns.adobe.com/flex/mx">

</s:WindowedApplication>
```

Don't get confused by the name, WindowedApplication. It is the same as above but the package is different (s and not mx). This means we are in the "realm" of spark, where we can use both spark and mx components.

Why do they coexist? Not all the components of the mx family have been ported to the new spark library. For example, all form-related classes (Form, FormItem, etc.) are still mx and there is no spark counterpart. The same goes for charts and DataGrid.

Keep in mind the "don't get confused" mantra if you are developing an application that uses both families of components. The code completion utility prompts a list of items that include components from both packages. For example, let's start typing "but" to insert a button. As you can see in Figure 5.2 the list features both s:Button (from the spark package) and mx:Button (from the mx package).

If you highlight an mx component that has a spark counterpart, Flash Builder kindly suggests using the new component (Figure 5.3).

```
1  <?xml version="1.0" encoding="utf-8"?>
2  <s:WindowedApplication xmlns:fx="http://ns.adobe.com/mxml/2009"
3                         xmlns:s="library://ns.adobe.com/flex/spark"
4                         xmlns:mx="library://ns.adobe.com/flex/mx">
5      <fx:Declarations>
6          <!-- Place non-visual elements (e.g., services, value objects) here -->
7      </fx:Declarations>
8
9
       <but|
   </s:W
```

The Button component is a commonly used rectangular button. The Button component looks like it can be pressed. The default skin has a text label. Define a custom skin class to add an image to the control.

Buttons typically use event listeners to perform an action when the user selects the control. When a user clicks the mouse on a Button control, and the Button

```
< >  s:Button – spark.components
< >  mx:Button – use s:Button instead
< >  s:ButtonBar – spark.components
< >  mx:ButtonBar – use s:ButtonBar instead
< >  s:ButtonBarButton – spark.components
< >  s:ButtonBase – spark.components.supportClasses
< >  s:ButtonBarHorizontalLayout – spark.components
 o   s:buttonMode : Boolean – Sprite
```

All – Press '^ ' to show All Properties   Press 'Tab' or click for focus

Figure 5.2 Components from both families.

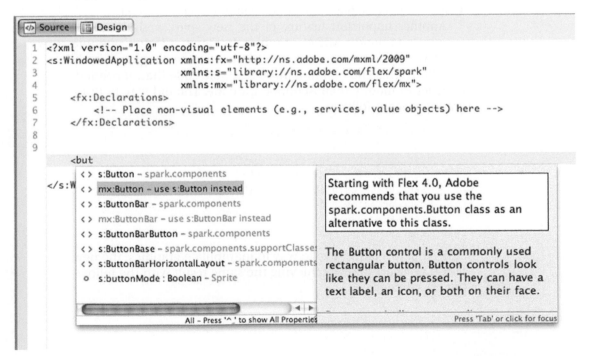

```
Source    Design

1  <?xml version="1.0" encoding="utf-8"?>
2  <s:WindowedApplication xmlns:fx="http://ns.adobe.com/mxml/2009"
3                         xmlns:s="library://ns.adobe.com/flex/spark"
4                         xmlns:mx="library://ns.adobe.com/flex/mx">
5      <fx:Declarations>
6          <!-- Place non-visual elements (e.g., services, value objects) here -->
7      </fx:Declarations>
8
9
       <but
   </s:W
```

```
< >  s:Button – spark.components
< >  mx:Button – use s:Button instead
< >  s:ButtonBar – spark.components
< >  mx:ButtonBar – use s:ButtonBar instead
< >  s:ButtonBarButton – spark.components
< >  s:ButtonBase – spark.components.supportClasses
< >  s:ButtonBarHorizontalLayout – spark.components
 o   s:buttonMode : Boolean – Sprite
```

Starting with Flex 4.0, Adobe recommends that you use the spark.components.Button class as an alternative to this class.

The Button control is a commonly used rectangular button. Button controls look like they can be pressed. They can have a text label, an icon, or both on their face.

All – Press '^ ' to show All Properties   Press 'Tab' or click for focus

Figure 5.3 Suggestion to use a component from the new family.

We stress this difference in this chapter because components of the `spark` family have different capabilities and a complete new architecture, which is tightly related to visual customization and skinning in particular. Although `mx` and spark components can coexist and be included with each other, the way they can be customized is pretty different. You will particularly notice the improvement if you work in a team. The old `mx` architecture does not allow a clear-cut separation of visuals and logic. If you have worked in a Flex team as a developer or designer, here is a common scenario you might have been part of:

- The designer creates a mockup using the design view of Flex.
- The code is pretty clear and readable but the developer has to modify it to fit the logic and introduce some improvement.
- The client changes his or her mind and proposes a redesign.
- The designer updates the project according to the new request.
- The developer has to readapt the code to accommodate the new modifications. Sometimes he or she also has to rewrite some of the code created previously.

As you can see, this workflow is not very scaleable. Wouldn't it be better if the logic and the visuals are clearly decoupled so that the developer and the designer can work independently and "synchronize" code and UI whenever needed? Yes—and the new spark architecture has been conceived to match this need.

Another important feature of the new spark architecture is the ability to handle MXML graphics. In Flex 4, it is now possible to draw geometric elements like circles and rectangles directly in MXML. This ends up in a more readable code that, if needed, is easier to modify than ActionScript code. The old way to draw graphics was as follows.

```
var rect:Sprite = new Sprite();
addChild(rect);
rect.graphics.lineStyle(1,0x00ff00);
rect.graphics.beginFill(0xFFFFFF);
rect.graphics.drawRect(0,0,100,100);
rect.graphics.endFill();
rect.x = 10;
rect.y = 10;
```

Even if this is still a valid way to manipulate graphics, the new Flex framework allows achieving the same result with the following MXML code.

```
<s:Rect
    width="100" height="100"
    x="10" y="10">

    <s:fill>
        <s:SolidColor color="#ffffff"/>
```

```
    </s:fill>
    <s:stroke>
        <s:SolidColorStroke color="#00ff00"/>
    </s:stroke>
</s:Rect>
```

Isn't that simpler, more readable, and more maintainable? Figure 5.4 shows that the graphical result is identical.

Moreover—and this is great news for designers—MXML graphics code can be generated by other applications of the Adobe suite like Illustrator and Catalyst. For example, in Adobe Illustrator it is possible to export the graphics directly in FXG format (Figure 5.5).

During the export process we can specify options for the conversion. In general, if it is a mockup or we want the graphics to be modifiable afterward in Flex, we should select the option "Convert to FXG" (Figure 5.6).

We can also preview the code for graphics that will be generated by the exportation process (Figure 5.7). You will see a portion of code that is exactly the one described previously.

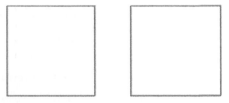

AS3 Generated   Flex4 Generated

Figure 5.4 Same graphical result for ActionScript 3– and Flex 3–generated rectangle.

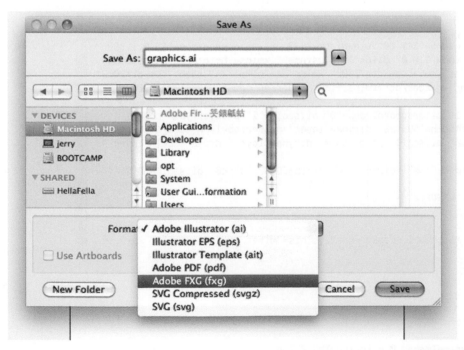

Figure 5.5 Exporting graphics ready for Flex from Adobe Illustrator.

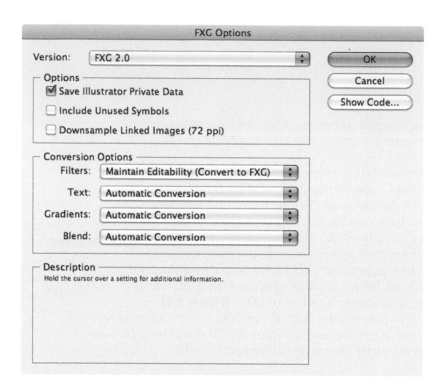

Figure 5.6 Options to export graphics for Flex from Adobe Illustrator.

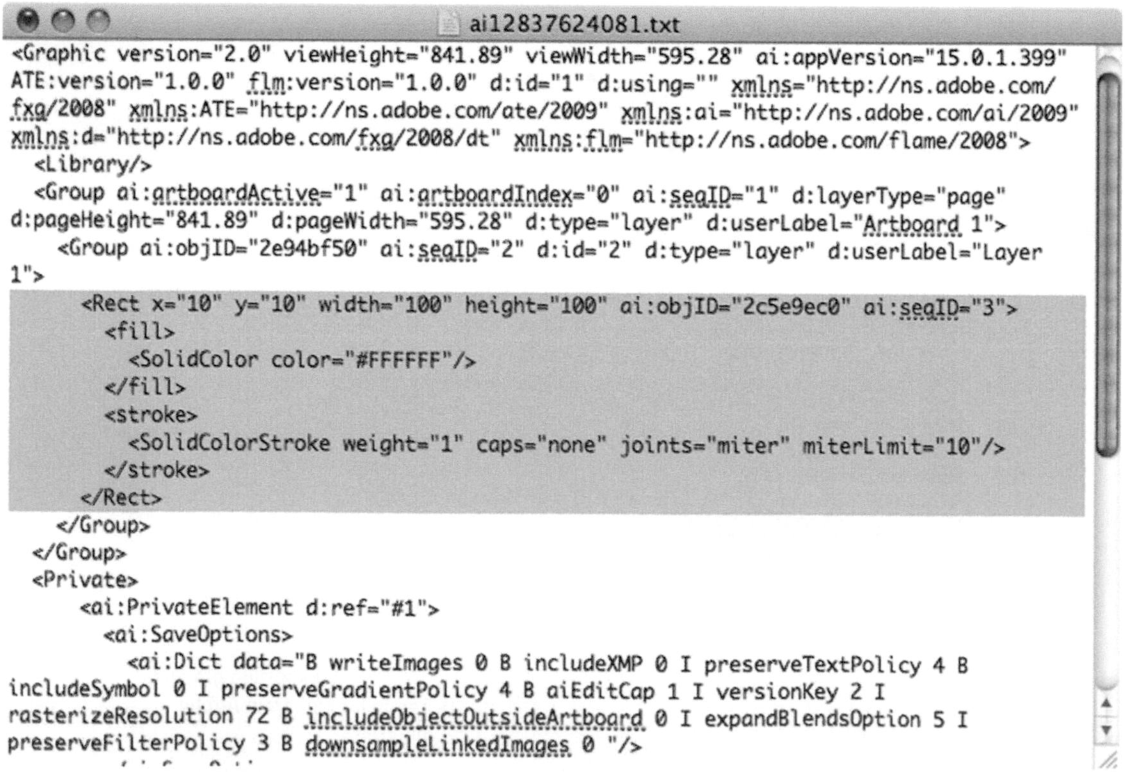

```
ai12837624081.txt
<Graphic version="2.0" viewHeight="841.89" viewWidth="595.28" ai:appVersion="15.0.1.399"
ATE:version="1.0.0" flm:version="1.0.0" d:id="1" d:using="" xmlns="http://ns.adobe.com/
fxg/2008" xmlns:ATE="http://ns.adobe.com/ate/2009" xmlns:ai="http://ns.adobe.com/ai/2009"
xmlns:d="http://ns.adobe.com/fxg/2008/dt" xmlns:flm="http://ns.adobe.com/flame/2008">
  <Library/>
  <Group ai:artboardActive="1" ai:artboardIndex="0" ai:seqID="1" d:layerType="page"
d:pageHeight="841.89" d:pageWidth="595.28" d:type="layer" d:userLabel="Artboard 1">
    <Group ai:objID="2e94bf50" ai:seqID="2" d:id="2" d:type="layer" d:userLabel="Layer
1">
      <Rect x="10" y="10" width="100" height="100" ai:objID="2c5e9ec0" ai:seqID="3">
        <fill>
          <SolidColor color="#FFFFFF"/>
        </fill>
        <stroke>
          <SolidColorStroke weight="1" caps="none" joints="miter" miterLimit="10"/>
        </stroke>
      </Rect>
    </Group>
  </Group>
  <Private>
      <ai:PrivateElement d:ref="#1">
        <ai:SaveOptions>
          <ai:Dict data="B writeImages 0 B includeXMP 0 I preserveTextPolicy 4 B
includeSymbol 0 I preserveGradientPolicy 4 B aiEditCap 1 I versionKey 2 I
rasterizeResolution 72 B includeObjectOutsideArtboard 0 I expandBlendsOption 5 I
preserveFilterPolicy 3 B downsampleLinkedImages 0 "/>
```

Figure 5.7 FXG code preview.

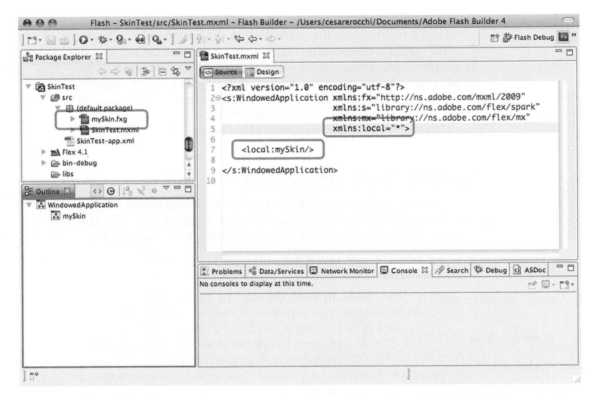

Figure 5.8 Skin in use in a Flex project.

Once we have exported our .fxg file we can drag and drop it into our Flex project. Then we are ready to use the new skin in our project, as highlighted in Figure 5.8.

This way, pure designers who do not feel comfortable with the design view of Flash Builder can use their preferred tool to contribute graphics for a Flex project.

So far we have seen only a simple way to customize the appearance of a Flex application. Let's dig deeper into customization, but first we have to clarify some terminology.

Illustrator and Fireworks have commands to generate flex skins. They are for Flex 3 skins (mx namespace) and will not work with the new spark architecture.

Themes, Skins, and Styles

It is likely that while learning how to visually customize Flex applications, you will read often these three words: theme, skin, and style. Let's clarify their meaning.

A *theme* is a combination of skins and styles. A *skin* defines the graphical appearance of a component. For example, if we look at the default skin of some components, they are made of many parts (Figure 5.9).

For example, the button has a gray background that changes according to over, down, and disabled states. The font is Arial. A radio button has the skin of a circle and a label for the test, and it

Figure 5.9 Skins of basic spark components.

is very similar to the checkbox. The horizontal slider is made of a "rail," which constrains the movement to the horizontal axis, and a "head," which slides over the rail. We can change the default font of a button or its chrome. In this case we are styling the button. If we want more—for example, a triangular button—with different gradients we need to create a new skin—that is, a new set of graphical components that substitute the original ones.

Now that terminology should be clear, we can start with styling.

Styling Single Components

There are many ways of creating a style for components. We will see them all. We can change the style of a single button. This can be done by changing the fontFamily style property. (Figure 5.10)

```
<s:Button label="Button" />
<s:Button label="Button" fontFamily="Times"/>
```

Button   Button with default font

Button   Button with Times font

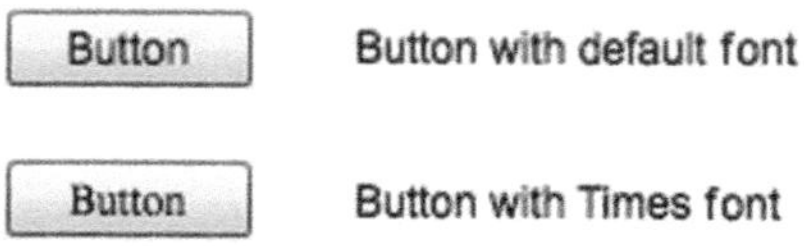

Figure 5.10 Styling the font of a single button.

If we want to style the font of all the buttons in our application we can exploit CSS styling. This way of styling is pretty popular, and if you have a background in HTML and CSS, it will sound very familiar. The essence is the same for CSS styling of web pages: For each selector you can provide a definition of its style. A selector is a way to select a visual element. It can be general (e.g., all the buttons) or specific (e.g., all the buttons contained in a panel).

Since we can style both mx and spark components we need to prefix selectors with the appropriate namespace. For example, let's suppose we want to change the font of all the buttons. We can do it with the following code.

```
<fx:Style>
    @namespace s "library://ns.adobe.com/flex/spark";
    @namespace mx "library://ns.adobe.com/flex/mx";

    s|Button {

      fontFamily: Times;

    }

</fx:Style>
```

This way all the spark buttons will have a Times font.

We want more. Let's say we want all the buttons within a panel with a particular color combination. Let's first create the visuals: a panel with two buttons within and one outside.

```
<s:Panel x="26" y="30" title="Panel">

    <s:Button label="Button"
        x="10" y="10"/>
    <s:Button label="Button"
        x="10" y="39"/>
```

```
</s:Panel>
<s:Button label="Button Outside"
    x="26" y="182"/>
```

Now we need to define two selectors: the first for the font (as before) and the second to style buttons within a panel.

```
<fx:Style>
    @namespace s "library://ns.adobe.com/flex/spark";
    @namespace mx "library://ns.adobe.com/flex/mx";

    s|Button {

     fontFamily: Times;

    }

    s|Panel s|Button {

        chrome-color: black;

        color: gray;

    }

</fx:Style>
```

In this case we end up with an interface like the one in Figure 5.11.

This is due to the definition of the second CSS selector (highlighted), which can be read as: "All the buttons that have a panel as ancestor." It is important to notice that we have written "ancestor" and not simply "parent." In fact, this definition applies to all the buttons that are contained in a spark panel, regardless of direct or indirect relationship. For example, in the following code, the button within the form will have the same style of the button outside.

```
<s:Panel
    x="26" y="30"
    title="Panel"
    width="253" height="238">

 <s:Button label="Outside the form"
    x="10" y="10"/>

    <mx:Form width="119" height="84"
      x="36" y="68">

        <s:Button label="Inside the form"/>

    </mx:Form>

</s:Panel>
```

The same definition can be applied to different classes. For example, in the previous example, the panel still has the default font. If we want to change it we do not need to add a new definition like this (though it will work):

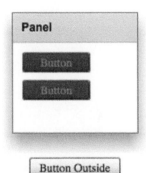

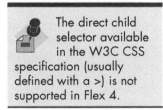

Figure 5.11 Styling buttons within a panel.

The direct child selector available in the W3C CSS specification (usually defined with a >) is not supported in Flex 4.

```
s|Panel {

  fontFamily: Times;

}
```

However, we can group it with the style definition of the button class, like this:

```
s|Button, s|Panel {

  fontFamily: Times;

}
```

This selector can be read as: "All the spark buttons *and* all the spark panels."

We should notice that more specific styles *override* these class definitions. For example, we can have a button with a red color within a panel.

```
<fx:Style>
    @namespace s "library://ns.adobe.com/flex/spark";
    @namespace mx "library://ns.adobe.com/flex/mx";

    s|Panel s|Button {

      chrome-color: black;
      color: gray;

    }

</fx:Style>
  <s:Panel x="26" y="30"
      title="Panel"
      width="98" height="124">

  <s:Button label="Button1"
      x="10" y="10"/>
  <s:Button label="Button2"
      x="9" y="47"
      color="red"/>

</s:Panel>
```

This happens because the style definition provided inline is considered more specific of the class definition in the CSS, so every style property defined in the instance of the component overrides both default and CSS-defined properties.

Defining a Custom Class Style

So far we have seen a pretty powerful technique of styling a class of components—for example, all the buttons or all the panels. There is more we can do. For example, we can define our custom style and apply it to different components.

To define a custom style we use the class syntax of CSS, which requires a dot as the first character. Then we can use any arbitrary name, as in the following example.

```
<fx:Style>
    @namespace s "library://ns.adobe.com/flex/spark";
    @namespace mx "library://ns.adobe.com/flex/mx";

    .darkStyle {

        chrome-color: black;
        color: gray;
    }

</fx:Style>
```

Here we have defined something that has two different colors for the chrome and the text. To apply it to an instance of component we use the `styleName` property as before.

```
<s:Panel title="Panel"
    styleName="darkStyle">

    ...

</s:Panel>

<s:Button label="Button2"
    styleName="darkStyle" />

<s:Button label="Button1"
    x="165" y="47" />
```

This way, only the components that have the style attached are rendered accordingly, while `Button1` has the default style (Figure 5.12)

Defining a Custom Style by ID

We already know that each instance of a Flex component can have an ID, which can be used as a reference. The very same ID can also be used to define the style. In this case the CSS selector starts with a # character, as in the standard CSS specification. The following example shows two panels, but only the first, which has the ID `myPanel`, is customized (see Figure 5.13).

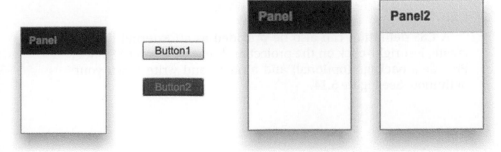

Figure 5.12 Definition of a custom style.   **Figure 5.13** Definition of a custom style by ID.

```
<fx:Style>
    @namespace s "library://ns.adobe.com/flex/spark";
    @namespace mx "library://ns.adobe.com/flex/mx";

    #myPanel {

      chrome-color: black;
      color: gray;

    }

</fx:Style>
  <s:Panel x="26" y="30"
      title="Panel"
      width="98" height="124"
      id="myPanel">

  </s:Panel>

  <s:Panel x="150" y="30"
      title="Panel2"
      width="98" height="124">

</s:Panel>
```

Defining a Custom Style for a State

In the style definition we also have access to the states of components. For example, we can define the color of a button when it is clicked. In this case the corresponding state is down and we access it with a : character.

```
s|Button:down {

  chrome-color: black;
  color: gray;

}
```

When providing this type of definition, we should carefully read the documentation. The compiler does not detect if you mistype a name, and, therefore, at runtime you will not get the expected result.

External CSS

A CSS definition can also be provided as an external file. To create, just right-click on the project and select "New > CSS File." Provide a package (optional) and a name and write down your definition. See Figure 5.14.

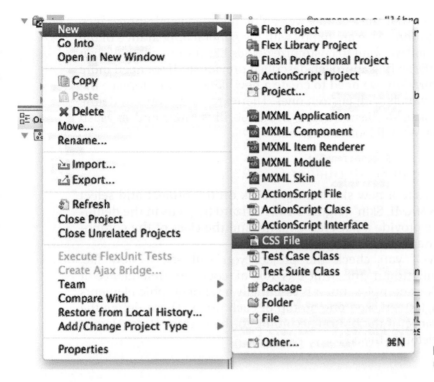

Figure 5.14 Creating an external CSS file.

To use CSS definitions in a component, just specify the source file, as follows:

```
<fx:Style source="myStyle.css"/>
```

Skinning

Skinning is the process of changing the visual of a component by modifying or replacing its visual elements. Such elements can be images, .swf files, or a custom definition of a skin defined in MXML or ActionScript. As we mentioned before, it is also possible to define the entire appearance of a component or just a part. For example, it is possible to change just the head of a slider and keep the default appearance of the rail.

The notion of skin is tightly coupled with the notion of state, which we have already introduced in Section 2. A *state* is a particular configuration of visuals according to the current interaction of the user. For example, a button has four relevant states:

- `over` (when the user moves the mouse over the button).
- `up` (normal state, mouse is not over the button).
- `down` (when the user clicks on the button).
- `disabled` (when the button is disabled).

For each of these states we can define the visual appearance of the button. If we are happy with the general appearance of the button and we want to customize details like font or color, we can follow the styling approach described previously. If we need more customization, we need to create a new skin—that is, replace the default visuals with custom ones. There are many ways to define a new skin: in Flash Builder, in Adobe Illustrator, and in Flash Catalyst. We will look at them all.

Skinning in Flash Builder

To create a new skin we right-click on the project and select "New > MXML Skin" (Figure 5.15). A wizard helps us in the definition. We provide a package, a name, and the class of the component we are customizing (Figure 5.16).

Now if you check the project you will see a new file, CustomButton.mxml, which is full of code. At first glance it might look complex, but it is essentially a set of graphic elements (rectangles), stacked one on top of each other. These define the appearance of the button according to the current state. Here is the skeleton of the code.

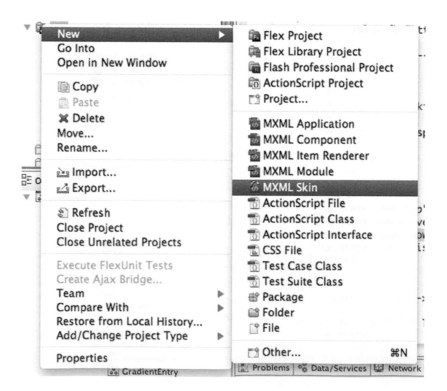

Figure 5.15 Creating a new skin in Flash Builder.

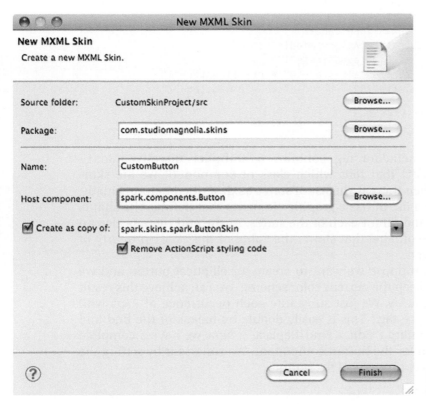

Figure 5.16 Specifying options of the new skin.

```
<s:SparkSkin ...>

   <fx:Metadata>
    <![CDATA[
        HostComponent("spark.components.Button")]
    ]]>
   </fx:Metadata>

  <s:states>
   <s:State name="up" />
   <s:State name="over" />
   <s:State name="down" />
   <s:State name="disabled" />
  </s:states>

  <s:Rect ... >

  </s:Rect>

  <s:Rect ... >

  </s:Rect>

  <s:Rect ... >

  </s:Rect>
```

```
<s:Label id="labelDisplay"
    textAlign="center"
    verticalAlign="middle"
    maxDisplayedLines="1"
    horizontalCenter="0" verticalCenter="1"
    left="10" right="10" top="2" bottom="2">

</s:Label>

</s:SparkSkin>
```

The metadata tag contains a compiler directive (Host-Component) that tells which class of component we are skinning. Then there is the list of states as described before. Finally, there is a list of basic graphic elements that defines the shape, stroke, and fill for each of the states. At the end there is also an instance of label that shows the value of the label property of the button.

Let's suppose we want to create an elliptical button and we want to keep the current color scheme. We can achieve this result pretty quickly. We just substitute each occurrence of Rect with an Ellipse tag.[1] This is easily doable by means of the find and replace utility ("Edit > Find/Replace"). Now we have a complete new skin for the button component. We can use it by setting the skinClass property of the button.

```
<s:Application>

    <fx:Script>
     <![CDATA[
        import com.studiomagnolia.skins.CustomButton;
        ]]>
     </fx:Script>

    <s:Button
      label="Button"
      skinClass="com.studiomagnolia.skins.
CustomButton"
        />

   </s:Application>
```

Figure 5.17 An elliptical custom button.

We end up with the result in Figure 5.17, an elliptical button with the same behavior and color scheme of the default spark component.

Since the code generated by the wizard is well commented it should be easy for you to play and customize the color scheme according to the different states. An alternative way to assign a skin is via a style sheet, as follows.

---

[1]We also have to remove each statement of radiusX="2", because that is not a property of the Ellipse tag.

```
<fx:Style>
    @namespace s "library://ns.adobe.com/flex/spark";
    @namespace mx "library://ns.adobe.com/flex/mx";

    s|Button {

      skinClass: ClassReference(
            "com.studiomagnolia.skins.CustomButton");
    }

</fx:Style>

<s:Button
    label="Button"
    x="34" y="29"/>
```

The result is exactly the same.

Let's have a look at a slightly more complex component, the HSlider. To create a new skin we follow the procedure described before to have the code from which to start the customization. We should now have a file, CustomSlider.mxml, which contains the skin definition of a slider component. At the bottom you might notice two buttons, the "track" (previously referred to as "rail") and the thumb.

```
<s:Button id="track"
    left="0" right="0" top="0" bottom="0"
      minWidth="33" width="100"
        skinClass="spark.skins.spark.HSliderTrackSkin" />

<s:Button id="thumb"
    top="0" bottom="0" width="11" height="11"
      skinClass="spark.skins.spark.HSliderThumbSkin" />
```

Wondering why the track is a button. Because you can click it to change the position of the thumb. Try!

To find this information you can also consult the Flex documentation.[2] Each Flex 4 component has a "Skin Parts" section that describes its skinning architecture, as in Figure 5.18.

Now that we have seen the internal structure of the HSlider, we should realize that for a simple customization we don't even need a new skin. For example, if we want to change the color of the thumb we can use the following CSS.

```
<fx:Style>
    @namespace s "library://ns.adobe.com/flex/spark";
    @namespace mx "library://ns.adobe.com/flex/mx";

    s|HSlider s|Button#thumb {

      chrome-color: gray;
    }
```

---

[2]Documentation for HSlider can be found at *http://help.adobe.com/en_US/ FlashPlatform/reference/actionscript/3/spark/components/HSlider.html.*

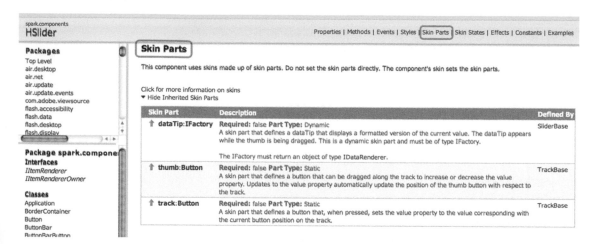

Figure 5.18 Documentation for the "Skin Parts" of the `HSlider` component.

```
s|HSlider s|Button#thumb:down {

    chrome-color: black;

    }

</fx:Style>

<s:HSlider x="10" y="116"/>
```

The first CSS definition selects a button with ID "thumb" contained in an `HSlider`. The second CSS definition describes the appearance when the thumb is clicked. This example has been provided to show that for simple modifications, it is not needed to create a new skin.

Let's suppose we want to create a slider that has a thumb with the elliptical skin that we created previously. In this case a few modifications are needed. We change the skin class and we raise the width a bit.

```
<s:Button id="thumb"
    top="0" bottom="0" width="30" height="11"
    skinClass="com.studiomagnolia.skins.CustomButton" />
```

Then, in the main MXML file, we assign the new custom slider skin to the component.

```
<s:HSlider
    skinClass="com.studiomagnolia.skins.CustomSlider" />
```

Figure 5.19 A slider with a custom thumb.

Figure 5.19 shows the final result.

From this example we should have learned that:

- Simple modifications do not imply creating a new skin.
- Complex components are made of parts (basic components). For example, the slider is made of two buttons and a data tip.
- In the skin of complex components you can also define the skin of its parts.

Skinning in Adobe Illustrator

An alternative way to generate skins for Flex 4 components is to use Adobe Illustrator. As we have already seen in the previous section a skin can be thought of as a stack of graphical elements, which appear/disappear according to the current state. Instead of writing MXML code to generate geometric shapes we can design UI elements in Illustrator and export them in FXG format. Let's see how. We will create a triangular button that will substitute the default thumb of the slider.

Drawing Graphics and Exporting

For this task we need three triangles with different colors to highlight according to the states of the thumb's slider. Open Illustrator and set up an artwork to draw elements. Designers probably know that the quickest way to draw a rectangle is to use the star tool. You can select it from the toolbar on the left (Figure 5.20).

Draw a star and then click on the stage to bring up the customization panel. Set the number of points to 3 (Figure 5.21).

Now let's create three copies of the triangle and change their color: the white will be the normal state, the gray represents the over state, and the black is shown when the thumb is clicked (Figure 5.22).

To customize the fill color of a triangle, select it and use the appearance panel on the right of the stage (Figure 5.23).

Once we are done we can stack the triangles on the same position so that the white is at the top, the gray is in the middle, and the black is on the bottom. This operation is important because all the graphic elements have to have the same dimension and position. Now we are ready to export the skin in FXG format, via the "Save As" command (Figure 5.24). We can keep the default settings for exportation (Figure 5.25).

Figure 5.20 Selecting the star tool.

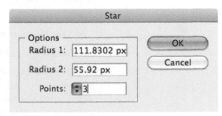

Figure 5.21 Customizing the star as a triangle.

Figure 5.22 Three triangles for the thumb state.

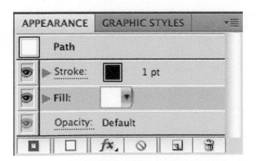

Figure 5.23 Panel to customize fill and stroke.

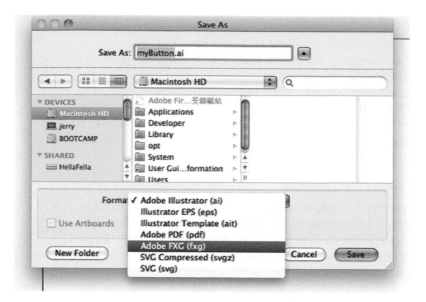

Figure 5.24 Exporting FXG graphics.

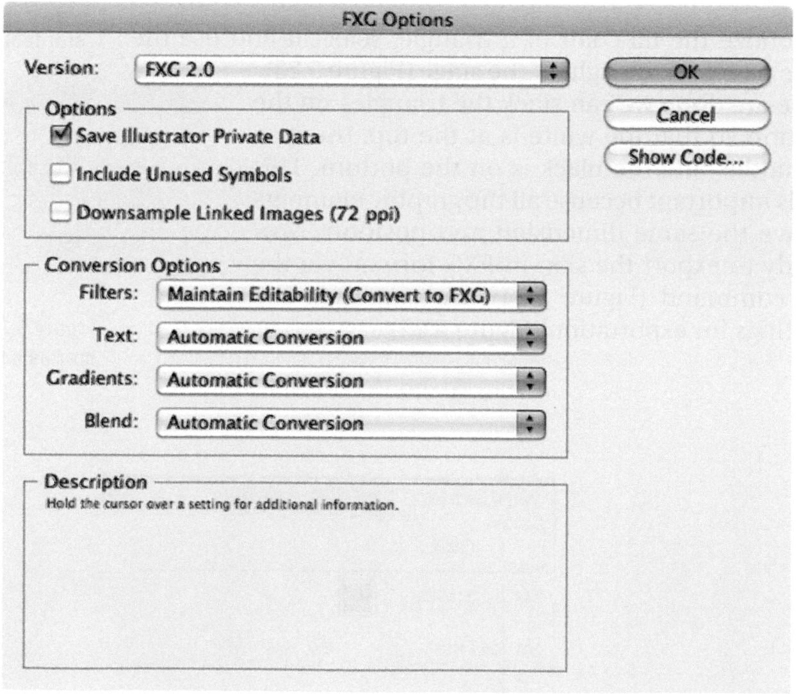

Figure 5.25 Settings for FXG exportation.

Now we have a .fxg file that includes the description of all the elements that we have created. The file as a structure looks like the following.

```
<Graphic ...>
  <Group ...>
    <Path ... data="...">
      <fill>
        ...
      </fill>
      <stroke>
        ...
      </stroke>
    </Path>
    <Path ... data="...">
      ...
    </Path>
    ...
  </Group>
</Graphic>
```

We are interested in the Path elements, which are exactly the triangles that we have drawn previously. You can notice that they contain different strokes and the code has the same order in which we stacked the triangles in Illustrator: the first tag is the white, the second is the gray, and the third is the black.

Now let's create a new skin, TriangularThumb, following the procedure described before. We end up with a clone of a button skin. We can delete all the occurrences of the Rectangle class, and also the label at the end. The final result should be the following code.

```
<s:SparkSkin ... >
  <fx:Metadata>
    <![CDATA[
    [HostComponent("spark.components.Button")]
    ]]>
  </fx:Metadata>
  <s:states>
      <s:State name="up" />
      <s:State name="over" />
      <s:State name="down" />
      <s:State name="disabled" />
```

```
        </s:states>


            ...


        </s:SparkSkin>
```

Now we will paste the three new instances of `Path` generated by Illustrator, in place of the previous dots. If we try to compile, we will find an inconvenience: Unfortunately, tags are not preceded by the `s` namespace, so the compiler will complain. Each occurrence has to be replaced as follows:

- `<Path>` → `<s:Path>`
- `<fill>` → `<s:fill>`
- `<stroke>` → `<s:stroke>`

and so on. To achieve this you could use the replace utility in the "Edit > Find/Replace" menu.

Another part we can get rid of is any occurrence of properties included in the `ai:` package, which are not needed. The third modification is related to the positions. You might have noticed that Adobe Illustrator generates elements with absolute references, as in the following (highlighted).

```
<Path
    x="26.4409" y="22.8042" ...
        data="..." >
</Path>
```

These are not needed and, indeed, might generate problems in the rendering of the skin. We can delete them. Now we should have the following code for our new skin.

```
<s:SparkSkin ... >

    <fx:Metadata>
        <![CDATA[
        [HostComponent("spark.components.Button")]
        ]]>
    </fx:Metadata>

    <!-- states -->

    <s:states>
        <s:State name="up" />
        <s:State name="over" />
        <s:State name="down" />
        <s:State name="disabled" />
    </s:states>

    <!-- White Triangle: Up state -->
    <s:Path
        data="M0 0.0546875 6.14502 0.027832 12.2896 0
                9.24121 5.33545 6.19238 10.6709 3.09619
                5.36279 0 0.0546875Z">
```

```
    <s:fill>
      <s:SolidColor color="#FFFFFF"/>
    </s:fill>

    <s:stroke>
      <s:SolidColorStroke
        weight="1" caps="none"
        joints="miter" miterLimit="9"/>
    </s:stroke>

  </s:Path>

  <!-- Gray Triangle: Over state -->
  <s:Path includeIn="over"
      winding="nonZero"
      data="M0 0.0551758 6.14502 0.027832 12.2896 0
            9.24121 5.33545 6.19238 10.6709 3.09619
            5.36279 0 0.0551758Z">

    <s:fill>
      <s:SolidColor color="#808285"/>
    </s:fill>

    <s:stroke>
      <s:SolidColorStroke weight="1" caps="none"
        joints="miter" miterLimit="9"/>
    </s:stroke>
  </s:Path>

  <!-- Black Triangle: Down state -->
  <s:Path includeIn="down" winding="nonZero"
      data="M0 0.0551758 6.14502 0.027832 12.2896 0
      9.24121 5.33545 6.19238 10.6709 3.09619
      5.36279 0 0.0551758Z">

    <s:fill>
      <s:SolidColor color="#000000"/>
    </s:fill>

    <s:stroke>
      <s:SolidColorStroke weight="1" caps="none"
        joints="miter" miterLimit="9"/>
    </s:stroke>
  </s:Path>

</s:SparkSkin>
```

The last step is to assign this new skin to the custom slider created previously. We open its definition and change the skin's class as follows.

```
<s:Button id="thumb"
    top="-2" bottom="-2" width="15" height="11"
    skinClass="
        com.studiomagnolia.skins.TriangularThumb" />
```

Figure 5.26 A horizontal slider with a custom thumb.

Figure 5.26 shows the final result.

Skinning in Flash Catalyst

A third way to create skins and themes is provided by Flash Catalyst. Flash Catalyst is an interaction design tool that allows us to build interactive projects with no need to write code. It is ideal for designers to build interactive mockups that behave nearly as the final application. Flash Catalyst shows its power when you have a static prototype of a web site or application and you want to make it interactive. One of the key features of Catalyst is the possibility to select graphics and transform them into interactive components like buttons, text forms, and so on. This is why it is extremely helpful when we need to create skins for Flex applications.

Let's go back for a moment to our scenario. We have built the graphics for a new triangular thumb with Illustrator. Instead of exporting the FXG graphics we open Flash Catalyst and import the Illustrator file (Figure 5.27).

This process analyzes the structure of the file, recognizes elements and layers, and prepares the file to be edited in Flash Catalyst. After importation, you should notice we have the stage populated with three layered triangles, as defined in Illustrator (Figure 5.28).

If we select the triangles a dynamic menu is activated. This is a key step: You can convert a set of graphical elements into a component. In this case we want a button (Figure 5.29).

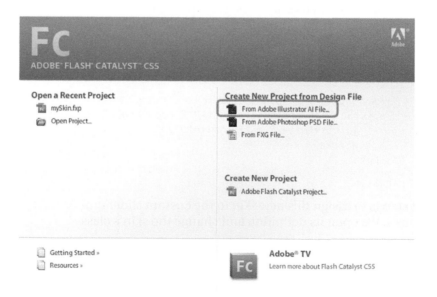

Figure 5.27 Importing an Illustrator file into Flash Catalyst.

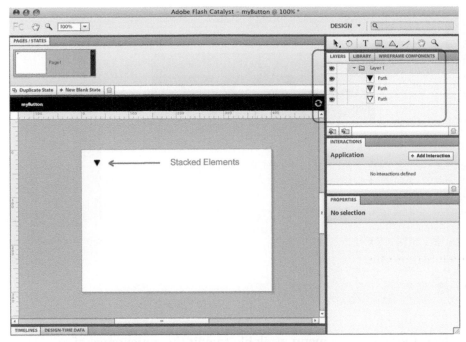

Figure 5.28 The Illustrator file imported in Catalyst.

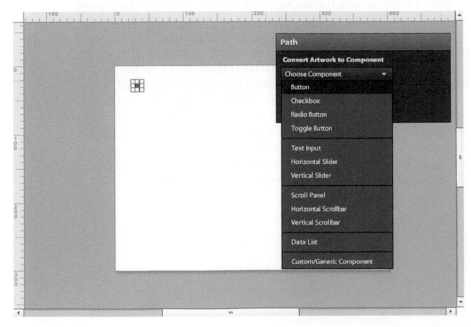

Figure 5.29 Conversion of the triangles into a button.

Figure 5.30 Menu to edit button appearance and states.

If you like you can check the code generated by this configuration. Just switch to the Flash Catalyst code view by means of the top right button.

Now there is a new menu available to edit the appearance of the button (Figure 5.30). Does it look familiar? Those are exactly the states that we have seen previously, declared in Flex components and skins. Let's click on a state.

Now we are editing the appearance of the button. At the top we see the list of states: up, over, down, and disabled. Each contains the three instances of triangles created previously. We just need to delete unnecessary elements. For example, in the up state we delete the black and the gray buttons (Figure 5.31). At the end of this process the states bar should look like that in Figure 5.32.

Now we can save the edited file, which will have an .fxp extension. Such a file type is a Flex project that can be imported right in Flash Builder. If we open the project we can check the generated code. There is a main application, some other package, and the skin of the button as edited in Flash Catalyst (Figure 5.33).

The code of the skin should look like the following.

```
<s:Skin …>

  <fx:Metadata>
      [HostComponent("spark.components.Button")]
  </fx:Metadata>

  <s:states>
    <s:State name="up"/>
    <s:State name="over"/>
    <s:State name="down"/>
    <s:State name="disabled"/>
  </s:states>
```

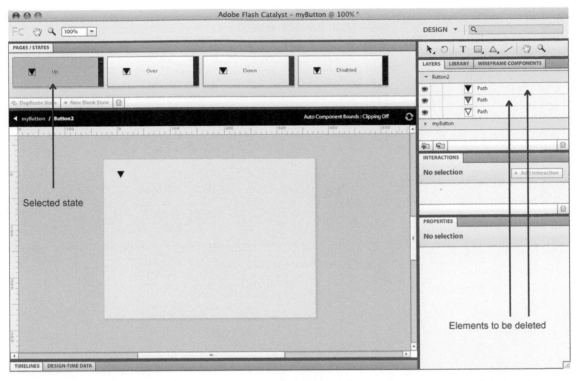

Selected state

Elements to be deleted

Figure 5.31 Deleting elements according to the state.

Figure 5.32 Final configuration of states for our custom button.

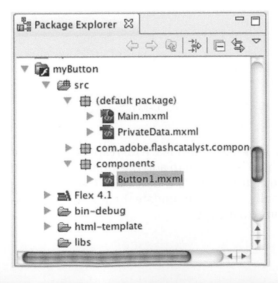

Figure 5.33 The skin file generated by Flash Catalyst.

```
<s:Path
  data="M 0.5 0.559 L 6.645 0.532 L
        12.79 0.504 L 9.741 5.839 L 6.692
        11.175 L 3.596 5.867 L 0.5 0.559 Z"
  winding="nonZero" x="-0.059" y="0.3"
  includeIn="disabled,up">

  <s:fill>
      <s:SolidColor color="#FFFFFF"/>
  </s:fill>

  <s:stroke>
      <s:SolidColorStroke caps="none"
      joints="miter" miterLimit="9" weight="1"/>
  </s:stroke>

</s:Path>
  <s:Path
    data="..." winding="nonZero"
    x="-0.059" y="0.3"
    includeIn="disabled,over">

    <s:fill>
        <s:SolidColor color="#6D6F71"/>
    </s:fill>

    <s:stroke>
        <s:SolidColorStroke caps="none"
        joints="miter" miterLimit="9" weight="1"/>
    </s:stroke>
  </s:Path>

    <s:Path data="..."
      winding="nonZero" x="-0.059" y="0.3"
      includeIn="disabled,down">

  <s:fill>
    <s:SolidColor/>
  </s:fill>

  <s:stroke>
    <s:SolidColorStroke caps="none"
      joints="miter" miterLimit="9" weight="1"/>
  </s:stroke>
</s:Path>

  <fx:Private></fx:Private>

</s:Skin>
```

Does it look like a skin? Yes! With respect to Illustrator (previous section) there is no need to add the s namespace to the tags. Now we can copy this code to a new skin, CatalystTriangularThumb. mxml. Finally, we have to update the reference to this new skin in the CustomSlider class.

```
<s:Button id="thumb"
  top="-2" bottom="-2" width="15" height="11"
  skinClass="
    com.studiomagnolia.skins.CatalystTriangularThumb"
/>
```

Figure 5.34 Our new slider with a custom thumb.

Figure 5.34 shows the final result, which is identical to Figure 5.26.

Skins of `mx` Components

As we have mentioned earlier in this chapter not all the components of the Flex 3 library have been imported to the Flex 4 framework. For example, `form` and `form`-related elements are still included in the `mx` package. For the sake of completeness we have to know also how to create skins for `mx` components.

Let's suppose we want to add some gradient to the background of a form, like in Figure 5.35. The first thing we can do is to create an image that fits exactly the dimensions of the form and apply it as a skin. Assuming the form is 100×100 pixels we create an image with such dimensions and save it as a .png file. Then we import it in the project and we assign it to the form as follows.

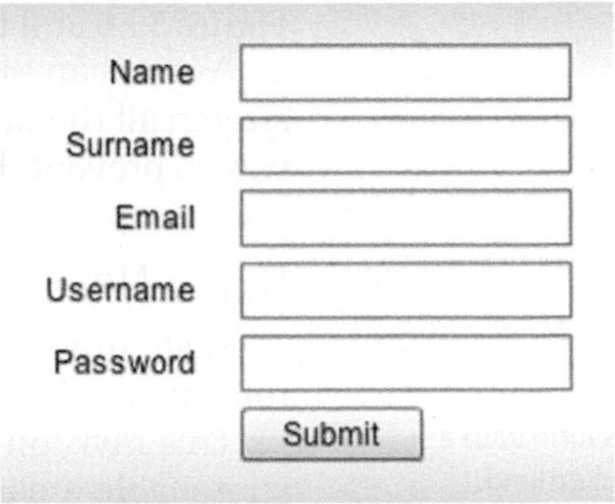

Figure 5.35 A form with a custom background.

```
<fx:Style>

    @namespace mx "library://ns.adobe.com/flex/mx";

    mx|Form {

      borderSkin: Embed(source="skins/formBG.png");

    }

</fx:Style>

<mx:Form >

    <mx:FormItem label="Name">
        <s:TextInput/>
    </mx:FormItem>

    <mx:FormItem label="Surname">
        <s:TextInput/>
    </mx:FormItem>

    <mx:FormItem label="Email">
        <s:TextInput/>
    </mx:FormItem>

    <mx:FormItem label="Username">
        <s:TextInput/>
    </mx:FormItem>
```

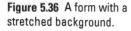

```
                              <mx:FormItem label="Password">
                                    <s:TextInput/>
                              </mx:FormItem>

                              <mx:FormItem>
                                    <s:Button label="Submit"/>
                              </mx:FormItem>

                        </mx:Form>
```

This works as we expect so we could say "mission accomplished." But what if the form gets bigger? The result is shown in Figure 5.36 and this is probably not expected.

As you can see the default behavior of the Flex framework is to stretch all the images to fit the dimensions of the form. There is a way to prevent this, called *scale nine*.

Figure 5.36 A form with a stretched background.

Scale Nine

Scale nine is an approach to formatting that allows defining nine areas of an image, as in Figure 5.37.

This division allows us to instruct the rendering of fixed and stretchable areas, like the central one. The syntax to define these areas is the following.

```
mx|Form {

   borderSkin: Embed(source="skins/formBG.png",
   scaleGridTop="31",scaleGridLeft="1",
   scaleGridRight="99",scaleGridBottom="69");

}
```

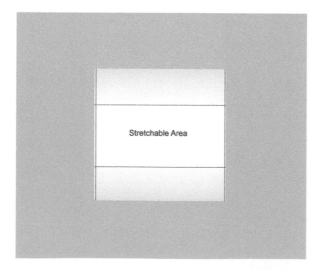

Figure 5.37 Scale nine format of the form custom background.

In practice, we provide the coordinates of four points of which the lines, when crossed, define the areas. By means of this definition the content of the corners is fixed, top and bottom are scaled horizontally (when needed), and left and right are scaled vertically. This way the custom skin is adaptable to all the dimensions of the form, as in Figure 5.38.

Transitions

To enhance the experience of a user interface a good tool is the use of the transition effect. For example, you might notice that the standard button goes from the up to the over state immediately and the graphics associated are sort of swapped as quick as possible. It is possible to animate this state change and the definition can be embedded right in the skin.

Let's go back to the skin we have built with Flash Catalyst. As illustrated, it has three elements with different color. To enable transitions we need to refer to those elements with an ID, so we create one for each as highlighted in the following code.

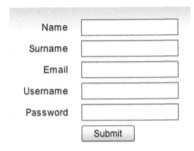

Figure 5.38 Correct skinning of a larger form.

```
<s:Skin ...>

    <fx:Metadata>
        [HostComponent("spark.components.Button")]
    </fx:Metadata>

    <s:states>
        <s:State name="up"/>
        <s:State name="over"/>
        <s:State name="down"/>
        <s:State name="disabled"/>
    </s:states>

    <s:Path id="upTriangle" data="..." >

        ...

    </s:Path>

    <s:Path id="overTriangle" ...>

        ...

    </s:Path>
    <s:Path id="downTriangle" ...>

        ...

    </s:Path>

</s:Skin>
```

Now we add a new element, transitions, which defines a set of animations. The first element includes a Fade effect.

```
<s:transitions>

<s:Transition toState="over">
  <s:Fade
    targets="{[upTriangle, overTriangle]}"/>
</s:Transition>

</s:transitions>
```

Notice that we did not provide any value other than an array of identifiers. The framework does the rest: fades out visible elements and fades in invisible elements. If you run the application you can already experience the transition when you move the mouse over the thumb.

You can also tune the duration of the transition by specifying a duration in milliseconds.

```
<s:Transition toState="over">

  <s:Fade
    targets="{[upTriangle, overTriangle]}"
    duration="500"/>
</s:Transition>
```

In running the application you might have noticed that when you roll the mouse out of the thumb there is no effect and the change is as quick as in the default state. This is correct because we did not define a transition when we move to the up state, so the default behavior occurs. To add the animation to the roll out we need to add another element, as follows.

```
<s:transitions>

<s:Transition toState="up">
  <s:Fade targets="{[upTriangle, overTriangle]}" />
</s:Transition>

<s:Transition toState="over">
  <s:Fade targets="{[upTriangle, overTriangle]}" />
</s:Transition>

</s:transitions>
```

Now our task is completed and the elements fade both when we go from the up to the over state and vice versa.

Changing Skins at Runtime

Skins can be applied to components at runtime. Let's resume our custom slider example. If you remember in the main MXML we had the following code.

```
<s:Application...>
  <s:HSlider
      skinClass="com.studiomagnolia.skins.CustomSlider"
      x="10" y="116" width="214"/>

</s:Application>
```

This statically applies a skin when the application runs. If we want to add it at runtime we should get rid of the skinClass setting, assign an ID to the slider, and add a checkbox to turn on/off the new skin.

```
<s:HSlider id="mySlider"
    x="10" y="116" width="214"/>

  <s:CheckBox
      id="skinCheckBox"
      click="toggleSkin(event)"
      label="Toggle custom skin"/>
```

Now we change the skin according to the selection of the checkbox.

```
<fx:Script>
  <![CDATA[

  import com.studiomagnolia.skins.CustomSlider;
  import spark.skins.spark.HSliderSkin;

  private function toggleSkin(event:MouseEvent):void{

    if (skinCheckBox.selected) {

    mySlider.setStyle("skinClass",
                      Class(CustomSlider));

  }

   else {

     mySlider.setStyle("skinClass",
                       Class(HSliderSkin));
   }

  }

]]>

</fx:Script>
```

It is important to notice that a skin is a class, so we have to use the Class() directive when we set the style of the component. The final result is shown in Figure 5.39.

☐ Toggle custom skin   ☑ Toggle custom skin

Figure 5.39 Switching skins at runtime via a checkbox.

Conclusion

In this section we described how to modify the appearance of Flex applications. We introduced the concepts of theme, skin, and style. We illustrated the mx (halo) and the spark (s) families of components (respectively, from the Flex 3 and Flex 4 libraries). Finally, we described in depth the process of skinning by means of Flash Builder, Adobe Illustrator, and Flash Catalyst.

PROJECT 5: CUSTOMIZING PROJECTS

In this project we will customize the user interface components used in the previous projects. We will group all the applications built so far in an Adobe AIR application and we apply a custom style to all its components.

Description of the Project

This project will include all the projects built in previous sections. Each application will become a component and a tab bar will allow switching between them. We will describe the porting process and then build custom skins for the components that will populate our application. We will skin the following elements:

- Application
- Close button
- Text input
- Combo box
- List

Design of the User Interface

This project will be an Adobe AIR application that will include the caching functionalities that we implemented in Project 4. The skeleton of the application is pretty simple, for it is made of a top bar, which holds the tab bar and the close button. The rest is reserved to the view stack to visualize our applications (Figure 5.1).

The corresponding code is the following.

```
<s:WindowedApplication ...>

  <s:Group
      id="topBar"
      width="100%"
      horizontalAlign="center"
      top="7">

    <s:TabBar
        dataProvider="{applicationStack}"/>
```

Figure 5.1 The skeleton of our application.

```
    </s:Group>

    <s:Button
        right="5" top="5" />

        <mx:ViewStack id="applicationStack"
            width="100%" height="100%"
            y="30">

            <!-- Application components here -->

        </mx:ViewStack>

    </s:WindowedApplication>
```

The view stack will contain our applications that we will transform into Flex components.

Grouping Projects Together

We create a new package to include our new custom components. The process to import applications will be the following:

- Create a new empty component.
- Copy and paste the code of the application.
- Import classes and packages needed by the application.
- Make some adjustments.

It is important to notice that a component included in a view stack has to extend `NavigatorContent`, so this is the tag that will wrap the code of our previous applications. Figure 5.2 shows how to specify this in the wizard.

The procedure will create the following code.

```
    <s:NavigatorContent
        xmlns:fx="http://ns.adobe.com/mxml/2009"
        xmlns:s="library://ns.adobe.com/flex/spark"
        xmlns:mx="library://ns.adobe.com/flex/mx" >

    </s:NavigatorContent>
```

Now we can fill it with all the code that we developed in the main application of Project 1. We should also remember to update the root tag with all the properties that we specified at that time, as follows.

```
    <s:NavigatorContent
        xmlns:fx="http://ns.adobe.com/mxml/2009"
        xmlns:s="library://ns.adobe.com/flex/spark"
        xmlns:mx="library://ns.adobe.com/flex/mx"
        currentState="startup"
        xmlns:getsongsservice="services.getsongsservice.*">
```

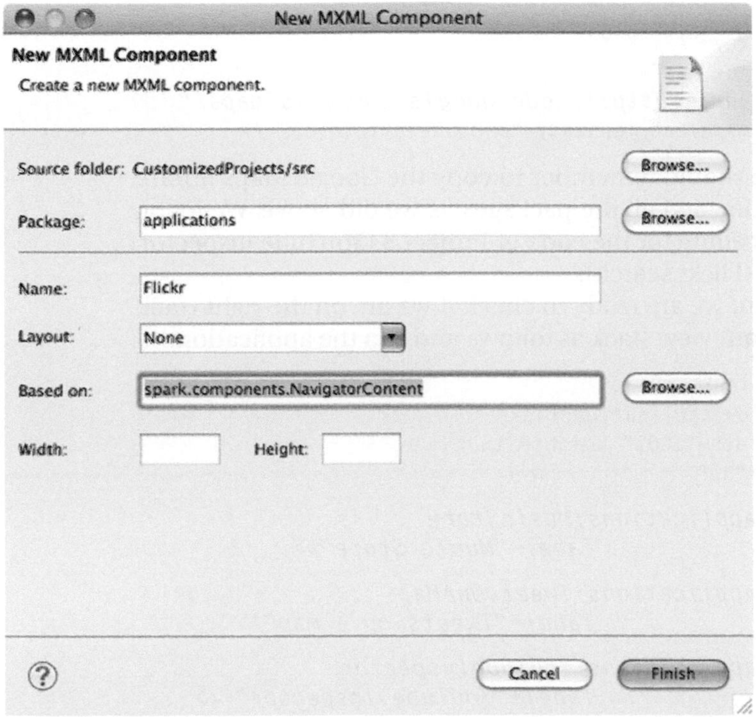

Figure 5.2 Extending the `NavigatorContent` component.

We also have to import the packages that were created for Project 1, in this case `itunesObjects` and `services`. We can just use the copy and paste functionality of the Package Explorer.

If you remember we created some classes and packages by means of the Data/Services wizard. Under the hood, this procedure includes references to Flex libraries that are needed to compile and run the project. So we need to update the project settings to include the following libraries:

- fds.swc
- fds_rb.swc
- serializers.swc
- serializers_rb.swc
- fiber.swc
- fiber_rb.swc
- playerfds.swc

We can just copy by right-clicking the references from the old project and replicate them in the current one.

The importation of Project 2, tweets on a map, is pretty similar. In this case we need to generate a new API key, because the previous one was meant for a web application and now we are building a desktop application. Moreover, the documentation[1] requires us to change the URL property of the map as follows.

[1]See *http://code.google.com/apis/maps/documentation/flash/tutorial-flexbuilder .html#AIRDevelopment.*

```
<maps:Map
      key="API_KEY"
      id="map"
      url="http://code.google.com/apis/maps/"
      mapevent_mapready="onMapReady(event)" />
```

Finally, we should remember to copy the Google Maps library, the assets folder, and all the packages as we did above. We follow the same procedure for the code of Project 3 (YouTube inspector) and Project 4 (Flickr search).

At this point we are ready to check if we are on the right track. We populate our view stack as follows and run the application.

```
<mx:ViewStack
    id="applicationStack"
    width="100%" height="100%"
    y="30">

    <applications:MusicStore
                label="Music Store"/>

    <applications:TweetsOnAMap
                label="Tweets on a map"/>

    <applications:YouTubeInspector
                label="YouTube Inspector" />

    <applications:FlickrSearchWithCache
                label="Flick with Cache"/>

</mx:ViewStack>
```

We should see something like in Figure 5.3.

You might need to make some modifications to accommodate the layout of the application and make it homogeneous throughout the tabs. We will leave this to your initiative. In this chapter we will focus on skinning and styling.

Figure 5.3 First run of the application.

Creating the Application Skin

We want to customize our application to look a bit more "personal." First, we get rid of the standard chrome and we set a transparent background. So we edit our XML descriptor file to include the following declarations.

```
. . .

<systemChrome>none</systemChrome>
<transparent>true</transparent>

. . .
```

At this point we have a chromeless window, which we can skin as we like. We start the new skin wizard and select the Application component. We will use a gray, rounded rectangle as the background with a bit of a border as follows.

```
<s:Skin ...>

    <fx:Metadata>
     <![CDATA[
       [HostComponent("spark.components.Application")]
     ]]>
    </fx:Metadata>

    <s:states>
        <s:State name="normal" />
        <s:State name="disabled" />
        <s:State name="normalAndInactive" />
    </s:states>

    <s:Rect id="backgroundRect"
        left="0" right="0" top="0" bottom="0"
        radiusX="20">

        <s:fill>
         <s:SolidColor
           id="bgRectFill"
           color="#e9e9e9"/>
        </s:fill>

        <s:stroke>
         <s:SolidColorStroke
           color="#999999"
           weight="2"/>
        </s:stroke>
    </s:Rect>

    <s:Group id="contentGroup"
        width="100%" height="100%"
        minWidth="0" minHeight="0" />

</s:Skin>
```

In this phase it is important to not touch the states declaration and the last group element, contentGroup, needed to host all the content of our application. For the rest we can customize it as we like, by changing colors, adding gradients, etc.

Once done, we assign the skin to our application as follows.

```
<s:WindowedApplication ...
    skinClass="skins.CustomApplicationSkin">
```

Then, we run it. We should see something like in Figure 5.4.

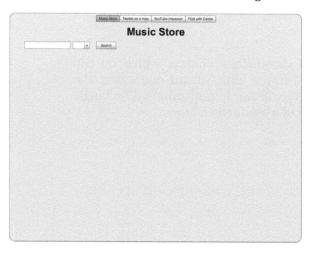

Figure 5.4 Our application with a custom background.

It is important to notice that since we have chosen a custom background we have lost some property of the standard chrome, like the possibility to drag the window and a button to close it. Let's add it.

Making the Application Draggable

To make the window draggable we need a visual component that listens for mouse clicks and triggers the drag functionality. We will use a group that is filled with a rectangle and shows the tab bar on top of it.

```
<s:Group
    id="topBar"
    width="100%">

  <s:TabBar dataProvider="{applicationStack}"
      top="7" horizontalCenter="0"/>
</s:Group>
```

This group has an ID that we need to set an event listener as follows.

```
private function init():void {

  topBar.addEventListener(MouseEvent.MOUSE_DOWN,
                        mouseDrag);

}
```

At this point we define the handler as follows.

```
private function mouseDrag(event:MouseEvent):void {
    stage.nativeWindow.startMove();
}
```

Now if we run the application the window is draggable if we grab it at the top.

Creating the Close Button

Another missing functionality is a close button. We will create it by means of Flash Catalyst. For sake of simplicity we will build a basic button but you are invited to experiment with shapes and color at your initiative. The button will be framed in a 14 × 14 rectangle, which has the same background color of the application. Then we draw a cross to symbolize the close action and we slightly vary the color according to the state, as in Figure 5.5.

Figure 5.5 The creation of a close button.

Now we switch to the code view of Flash Catalyst to copy the code for the button to be pasted in the custom skins in Flash Builder. Once done, we can update the close button as follows.

```
<s:Button
    skinClass="skins.CloseButton"
    right="12" top="9"
    click="close()"/>
```

Figure 5.6 shows our button.

Figure 5.6 The close button in place.

Customizing the Text Input

Now we want to change the appearance of all the TextInput components included in our application. We start the wizard as we are used to and we tweak the color as we like. In our case we have changed the background and the border as highlighted below.

```
<s:SparkSkin ...>

    <fx:Metadata>
        <![CDATA[
          [HostComponent("spark.components.TextInput")]
        ]]>
    </fx:Metadata>

    <s:states>
        <s:State name="normal"/>
        <s:State name="disabled"/>
    </s:states>

    <s:Rect
        left="0" right="0"
        top="0" bottom="0"
        id="border">

        <s:stroke>
            <s:SolidColorStroke id="borderStroke"
                weight="1" color="#999999" />
        </s:stroke>
    </s:Rect>

    <s:Rect id="background"
        left="1" right="1" top="1" bottom="1">

        <s:fill>
            <s:SolidColor id="bgFill"
                color="#e9e9e9"/>
        </s:fill>

    </s:Rect>

    <s:Rect left="1" top="1" right="1" height="1"
        id="shadow">

        <s:fill>
            <s:SolidColor color="0x000000"
                alpha="0.12" />
        </s:fill>
    </s:Rect>

    <s:RichEditableText
        id="textDisplay"
        verticalAlign="middle"
        widthInChars="10"
        left="1" right="1" top="1" bottom="1" />

</s:SparkSkin>
```

We then assign the new skin in the Style tag and we also tweak the color when it is selected.

```
<fx:Style>
    @namespace s "library://ns.adobe.com/flex/spark";
    @namespace mx "library://ns.adobe.com/flex/mx";
```

```
s|TextInput{
    skinClass: ClassReference("skins.InputTextSkin");
}
s|TextInput{
    focusColor: #333333;
}
</fx:Style>
```

Customizing the Combo Box

To customize the combo box we exploit skin parts. When you create a new skin for a combo box you will notice that it is made of parts. At the bottom there is an instance of TextInput. That is the only thing we need to update, as follows.

```
<s:SparkSkin>
    ...
    <s:TextInput I
        d="textInput"
        left="0" right="18" top="0" bottom="0"
        skinClass="skins.InputTextSkin"/>

</s:SparkSkin>
```

Now we assign the skin and we also tweak the combo box.

```
s|ComboBox {

    skinClass:
            ClassReference("skins.CustomComboBoxSkin");

}
s|TextInput,s|ComboBox {

    focusColor: #333333;

}
```

Figure 5.7 shows the customized appearance of the input components.

Finally, we change the background color of the List component to match the chosen color scheme.

Figure 5.7 Custom TextInput and ComboBox.

```
s|ComboBox, s|List {

    contentBackgroundColor: #e9e9e9;

}
```

If we run the application we should see it rendered as in the screenshots in Figures 5.8 through 5.11.

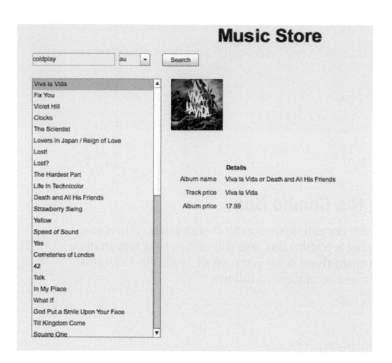

Figure 5.8 The Music Store tab.

Figure 5.9 The tweets on a map application.

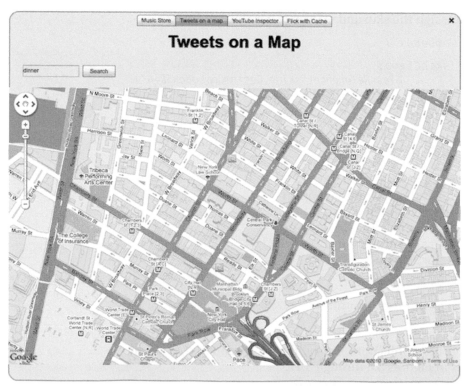

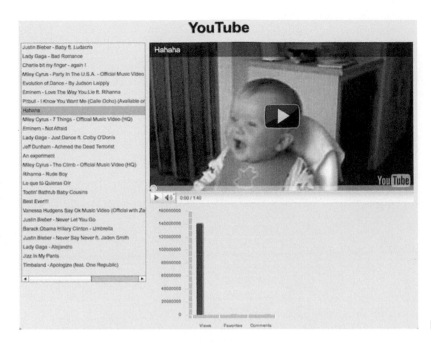

Figure 5.10 The YouTube tab.

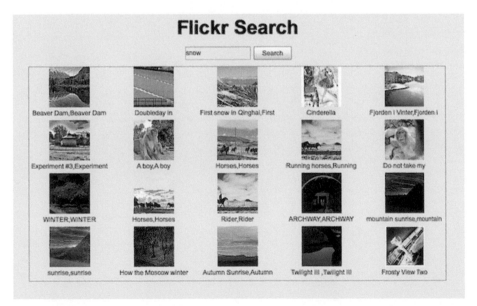

Figure 5.11 The Flickr search application.

Possible Improvements

This application can be refined by implementing the following features:

- Customize the tab bar (hint: it is made of buttons).
- Implement resizing of the window.
- Customize the selection color of the list.

YouTube

INDEX

Note: Page numbers followed by *b* indicate box *f* indicate figures, and *t* indicate tables.